THE PROFESSOR'S COMPANION TO TEST PREP

# THE ESSENTIAL GUIDE TO
# SAT® READING

TEST PREP FOR COLLEGE-BOUND STUDENTS

Thomas Charles, PhD

2020 Edition

Copyright 2019 by The Professors Companion, LLC.

All rights reserved. This book or any portion thereof may not be reproduced or used in any manner whatsoever without the express written permission of the publisher except for the use of brief quotations in a book review. For permission requests, please email tom@professorscompanion.com.

SAT® is a registered trademark of The College Board, which does not sponsor or endorse this product.

The graduation cap icon is licensed from ic8.link/1538

For information regarding bulk order purchases and discounts for classrooms, please contact me at tom@professorscompanion.com

ISBN-13: 978-1090995438

LCCN: 2019917637

First Printing

www.professorscompanion.com

# WELCOME TO *THE ESSENTIAL GUIDE TO SAT READING* .......... 5
- How to Use This Book .......... 6
- Getting the Official Practice Tests .......... 8
- Online Bonus Content .......... 9
- Doing Your Best .......... 10

# LESSON 1: UNDERSTANDING THE TEST .......... 11
- The Passages .......... 11
- The Questions .......... 12
- The Answers .......... 13
- The Clock .......... 13
- The Scoring .......... 14
- What about the PSAT? .......... 15
- Practice Test: Official Test 1 .......... 16
- Bonus Tip! Register early .......... 18

# LESSON 2: UNDERSTANDING THE PASSAGES .......... 19
- Relearning to Read: Underline, Annotate, and Identify .......... 20
- Practice Passage: Social Studies .......... 22
- Practice Passage: Literature .......... 27
- The Best Way to Improve is to Engage .......... 31
- Practice Test: Official Test 5 .......... 31

# LESSON 3: UNDERSTANDING THE QUESTIONS AND ANSWERS .... 33
- Restate, Recall, and Resolve .......... 33
- Practice Passage: History .......... 38
- Practice Test Review: Restate, Recall, and Resolve for Tests 1 and 5 .......... 42
- Bonus Tip! Find a Study-Buddy .......... 46

# LESSON 4: MASTERING THE QUESTIONS .......... 47
- Recognizing Question Types .......... 47
- Practice Passage: Science (with Data) .......... 49
- Practice Passage: History (Paired, antiquated English) .......... 69
- Practice Test: Official Test 6 .......... 71

# LESSON 5: MASTERING THE ANSWERS .......... 73
- When Your Recalled Answer Is In The Answer Bank .......... 73
- When Your Recalled Answer Isn't In The Answer Bank .......... 73
- When Should You Switch Your Answer? .......... 76
- What Should You Do If You Get Streaks of the Same Letter? .......... 77
- Get the Points You Have Earned .......... 78
- Practice Passage: Social Studies (with Data) .......... 79
- Practice Passage: Social Studies (without Data) .......... 85
- Practice Test Review: Test 5 and Test 6 .......... 90
- Bonus Tip! Questions and Answer Service .......... 96

# LESSON 6: UNDERSTANDING THE CLOCK ............................................................ 97
Option 1: The Time Bank ........................................................................................... 97
Option 2: Going Old-School ..................................................................................... 100
Extra Time? .............................................................................................................. 101
Running Out Of Time ............................................................................................... 101
Practice Test: Official Test 7 .................................................................................... 103

# LESSON 7: MASTERING THE PASSAGES ............................................................. 105
Passage Topics: Literature, History/Social Studies, and Science Passages ............. 105
Passage Features: Data, Paired, and Antiquated English ........................................ 110
Practice Passage: Literature (Antiquated English) .................................................. 119
Passage Type and Features: Extra Passages .......................................................... 122

# LESSON 8: MASTERING THE CLOCK ................................................................... 127
Learning to Focus 13 Minutes At A Time ................................................................. 127
Ten Books to Read for Fun ...................................................................................... 148
Practice Test: Official Test 8 .................................................................................... 151

# LESSON 9: MASTERING KHAN ACADEMY .......................................................... 153
Khan Academy Worksheets ..................................................................................... 153
Five Worksheets ....................................................................................................... 157
Practice Test Review: Test 7 and Test 8 .................................................................. 183

# LESSON 10: UNDERSTANDING THE TEST-MAKERS ........................................... 185
Literature Build-a-Passage: The Minister's Black Veil ............................................. 185
Science Build-a-Passage: Civil War Naval Data ...................................................... 193
Social Studies Build-a-Passage: Real Price Parity .................................................. 201
Paired History Build-a-Passage: Women's Suffrage ............................................... 210
Building Passages and Increasing you Reading Skills ............................................. 218

# LESSON 11: MASTERING THE TEST ..................................................................... 219
How to Review ......................................................................................................... 220
Official Test Review: Tests 1-10 .............................................................................. 223

# LESSON 12: UNDERSTANDING WHAT'S NEXT .................................................... 283
Before You Get Your Scores .................................................................................... 283
After You Get Your Scores ....................................................................................... 284
Taking The Test Again: Studying and Reviewing ..................................................... 285
Taking The Test Again: Doing your best .................................................................. 286

# SOLUTIONS ............................................................................................................ 287

# WELCOME TO *THE ESSENTIAL GUIDE TO SAT READING*

**I started writing this book because I kept encountering students who struggled to take tests strategically.** I've been tutoring the SAT and ACT since 2006 and I've seen all sorts of students, from those trying to get their scores over the 1000 barrier to those demanding a 1500+ from themselves. One thing I've seen across the board, however, is a lack of strategic test-taking.

Many of my students could read at a high level, often taking honors and AP level English classes, but they couldn't translate this knowledge to the test. Even the best students can find themselves struggling to meet their score goals because they aren't sure how to take the test. I've also had students who weren't great readers and had to work twice as hard as their peers to earn a B in English class but learned to take the SAT reading test like a professional. **Taking the test strategically works**.

I've also found that students who study for the SAT strategically find that they are **laying the foundations for success in college**. The critical reading skills you build here will help you beyond the time you put in on a random Saturday afternoon in high school. Ideally, they'll extend to the rest of your academic career. As a result, *this isn't a strictly a reading book*. You'll be building toward achieving success (however you want to define it) on the test while you work on developing the necessary critical thinking and problem-solving skills to make you a better student overall.

This book will reward students who immerse themselves in their studies. The more you put into your practice, the more you'll get out of it. As you read, you'll **understand the passage** by thinking critically about what you are reading. You'll **understand the questions** and recognize what the test makers are asking you. You'll **understand the answers** and narrow down the multiple choices. You'll learn to not only find the correct answer but figure out why the incorrect answers are wrong. You'll also gain confidence and **use time effectively**, making the most of your strategies and knowledge to maximize your score. Not only are these good skills to possess, they are more likely to "stick" on test day than simply taking practice test after practice test and hoping things improve.

After laying these foundations, you'll expand your critical thinking and problem-solving skills by diving deeper into the test. Lessons on **advanced passage types** and **learning to care** will bolster your reading skills, while you work to **master Khan Academy** and get creative with the **Build-a-Passage Workshop**.

I can't promise you that you'll get a perfect score; you wouldn't believe me if I said that I could. What I can tell you, however, is that this book will make you a better test taker and that the skills you build here will help you beyond high school into college.

# HOW TO USE THIS BOOK

Most students fall into one of two groups: those who are preparing for a test that is months away and those who are cramming with weeks to go. In short, some students are looking for a **complete course** and others are looking for a **crash course**.

## Complete Course (Two to Three Months)

For most students, the reading section of the SAT takes the most time to work through. Unlike the grammar section of the test, which involves a little bit of strategy and some grammar and punctuation content mastery, and the math test, which involves a little bit more strategy and a great deal of content mastery, the reading portion of the test involves a lot of strategy and less content mastery.

Each of the ten lessons in this book presents a different element of a cohesive strategy to taking the SAT reading test. Ideally, you'll work through one lesson a week, though you can combine weeks if you're tight on time.

| Timeframe | Strategy | Practice Tests |
|---|---|---|
| Week 1 | Lesson 1: Understanding the Test | Take Test 1 |
| Week 2 | Lesson 2: Understanding the Passages | Take Test 5 |
| Week 3 | Lesson 3: Understanding the Questions and Answers<br>Lesson 4: Mastering the Questions | Take Test 6 |
| Week 4 | Lesson 5: Mastering the Answers | Review Tests 5 and 6 |
| Week 5 | Lesson 6: Understanding the Clock | Take Test 7 |
| Week 6 | Lesson 7: Mastering the Passages | Selections Tests 1-4 and 9-10 |
| Week 7 | Lesson 8: Mastering the Clock | Take Test 8 |
| Week 8 | Lesson 9: Mastering Khan Academy | Review Test 7 and 8 |
| Week 9 | Lesson 10: Understanding the Test-Makers | Selections Tests 1-4 and 9-10 |
| Week 10 | Lesson 11: Mastering your Review | Review Tests 1-10 |
| Aftermath | Lesson 12: Understanding What Is Next | Post-Test Diagnostic |

You can double up some of the weeks if you'd like, but this pace typically has one hour or so per lesson, plus one and half hours of practice tests and review.

## Crash Course (Less Than One Month)

*I get it.* I've had students (and their parents) call me weeks (sometimes even days) before the test looking for help. Maybe you got this book with the intention of studying every day. Maybe you took a dry run at the SAT and didn't like what you saw, so you decided to take things into your own hands. Maybe you just hate the SAT and are taking the test against your will.

Obviously, more time is better than less time. When you're under the gun, the SAT only gets more intimidating. **But you can still become a better strategic test taker with the time you have.**

Here's the crash course curriculum:

| Strategy | Practice Tests |
|---|---|
| Lesson 1: Understanding the Test | Take Test 5 |
| Lesson 2: Understanding the Passages | |
| Lesson 3: Understanding the Questions and Answers | Take Test 6 |
| Lesson 5: Understanding the Clock | Take Test 7 |
| Lesson 12: Taking the Test Again | Post-Test Diagnostic |

After you get your scores back, you can make a decision about taking the test again. If you are signing up for more, you should go back and do the complete curriculum.

# GETTING THE OFFICIAL PRACTICE TESTS

There are **two ways to access the official practice tests**. The first is the College Board's ***Official SAT Study Guide***. It's list price is $30, but you can usually find it for around $20 online. The *Official Guide* has eight practice tests included, plus complete solutions to every problem (about 50 pages per test!). When you see references to page numbers, these references are to the 2020 edition. It is worth noting that the official guide doesn't include a scoring table, so while you will know what the correct and incorrect answers are, you won't know your exact score.

The second way to get the tests is to download them through **Khan Academy or SAT.org**. Khan Academy (www.khanacademy.org/mission/sat) has a lot of free resources for SAT takers, including a printable version of eight practice tests. You can also score your tests on Khan Academy and get personalized recommendations generated from your answers. The same PDF's are available on the College Board's website (www.sat.org), but without Khan's algorithm. They have also posted printable copies of the solutions from *Official Guide* for free download.

You might have noticed that the tests recommended for each week seem out of order. You're not wrong, but I assure you there is a method to the madness. The *Official SAT Study Guide* starts with test 10 and works backwards to test 1 (skipping tests 2 and 4). Khan Academy's diagnostic software works with tests 1, 3, and 5-10. The College Board's website has tests 1, 3, and 5-10, scoring guidelines for tests 1-10, and full solutions, but no algorithm. The College Board also has a "scan and score" feature on their app, but this doesn't work with the algorithm (and will actually prevent you from inputting the answers on Khan Academy).

|         | *Official Guide* pages | Downloadable www.sat.org | Downloadable with Algorithm Khan Academy | Administration Test Date |
|---------|---|---|---|---|
| Test 1  | 1193 | ✓ | ✓ | Not administered |
| Test 2  | Not included | Not included | Not included | Not administered |
| Test 3  | 1081 | ✓ | ✓ | Not administered |
| Test 4  | Not included | Not included | Not included | Not administered |
| Test 5  | 949 | ✓ | ✓ | May 2016 |
| Test 6  | 815 | ✓ | ✓ | April 2016 |
| Test 7  | 689 | ✓ | ✓ | October 2016 |
| Test 8  | 553 | ✓ | ✓ | January 2017 |
| Test 9  | 423 | ✓ | ✓ | October 2017 |
| Test 10 | 295 | ✓ | ✓ | October 2018 |

You'll notice that I have tests 2 and 4 here. These tests are still available in the 2018 edition of the *Official Guide* and online, but know that they don't work with Khan Academy anymore.

If you look over the curricula above, you'll see that the tests assigned focus on tests 5 to 8. You'll also notice that these tests were previously administered. What better way to practice than with the real thing?

# ONLINE BONUS CONTENT

Throughout the book, you'll find call out boxes pointing you to online bonus content. This bonus content includes extended passages (often the full work from which the passages have been excerpted) and extra passages to help you build your reading skills. These passages are available as PDF's you can view on your own device or print at home or school. I'm always adding new bonus content as well, so check back frequently.

You can find these at www.professorscompanion.com/reading.

---

### Online Bonus Content: Treasure Hunt

When I was a kid, my grandparents gave me a subscription to *Games Magazine*. *Games* was filled with things like crossword and Sudoku puzzles along with more complex logic and trivia-style games. One of their staples was a "fake ad" for a product that didn't exist: a USB-powered toaster or a deck of playing cards with irrational numbers like the "pi of spades" and the "root two of hearts" instead of the more familiar aces and jacks).

The editors would hide these ads in with the rest of the real ads for things you could actually buy (fancy tables for games, puzzle books, et cetera). If you spotted the fake ad, you could send them an email with your guess. One winner each month would get a free year's subscription to the magazine.

I *loved* hunting for the fake ad. I would pore over the pages trying to find something that didn't belong. The goal, of course, was to get you to read the magazine's ads more closely. Clever, right? They simply slipped something into the pages and got me to read all those ads intently.

This book doesn't have ads, but I have hidden some grammatical mistakes in the pages. If you find a mistake in the pages, you'll get a discount on another *Professor's Companion* textbook. Just send an email to me at tom@professorscompanion.com with the error you've found and a copy of your receipt for this book and I'll send you a discount code.

Careful reading will make you a better test taker. Plus, finding treasure is always fun!

---

One other thing to note: If you find something in this book that seems out of date, email me. The test makers are always making changes to the test, but they don't always say "hey all, we're changing something." I keep my ear close to the ground, but I'll put updates up on the web if something needs fixing.

# DOING YOUR BEST

Standardized test prep can be a long task for students looking for success. Here are five rules for doing your best.

1. **All that you can ask of yourself is to do your best.** The SAT has a way of making us feel inadequate, like we should have done better. You can't ask more of yourself than your best.

2. **If you put in the work, you will get the best score that you can get.** There isn't some secret to scoring better on the test than doing the work. This book contains a lot of practice passage sets and guidelines for practice tests. I can't promise you an 800, but I can promise you that you won't achieve your best score if you don't put in the work.

3. **You should not let your test prep cause your grades to slip.** In fact, the lessons in this book should help you across your high school curriculum, from English to AP US History to physics. If you have to choose between studying for a physics test or for the SAT you should probably study physics. It isn't worth getting a D on your projectile motion test because of the SAT.

4. **Don't start your test prep after 11 pm.** If you are working on your test prep at 11 pm instead of sleeping, please get some sleep instead. You can always grab a good book and read if you are looking to improve your score at the end of the night. That said, don't start binge-watching *Parks and Recreation* after dinner if you are then going to invoke the 11 pm rule. Rule 4 doesn't supersede Rule 2!

5. **You will keep taking the SAT until you are done taking it.** This can sound somewhat trite: Everything that you do you do until you stop doing it. But it's a nice reminder that if you want to be finished with test prep, you won't be done until you do everything that you're going to do. In other words, procrastinating and postponing just means you have to keep at it for another test cycle.

College admissions tests can be a pressure cooker. All you can ask of yourself is to do your best and work hard for what you want.

Let's start looking at the test.

# LESSON 1: UNDERSTANDING THE TEST

There are a lot of moving parts on the SAT. Before we get too far down the rabbit hole, let's start with a quick overview of the **passages**, the **questions**, the **answers**, the **clock**, and the **scoring**.

## THE PASSAGES

500 to 750 words. That's the length of the passages on the SAT. There are five passages on every test, which can be broken down into four types: Literature, Science, History, and Social Studies. One of these passages will have two "paired" passages that are a combined 500 to 700 words.

**Literature (1):** The first passage of every test is a literature passage. The College Board chooses passages from classic authors, like Charles Dickens or the Brontë sisters, and from modern authors, like Maxine Hong Kingman, Kurt Vonnegut, and Gabriel Garcia Marquez.

**Science (2):** The science passages draw broadly from the science classes typically taught in high school: physics, chemistry, biology (both plant and animal), and earth/space science. Of the two science passages, one will have data to interpret (charts and tables). The one without data is sometime a paired passage.

**Social Studies (1):** The social studies passage cover topics you should be familiar with from your high school curriculum, such as economics and government, as well as some that appear more frequently as electives for seniors or as college courses, such as anthropology, sociology, or psychology. Charts and tables have accompanied these passages on all the official practice tests.

**History (1):** The history passage is typically taken from the "founding documents" of the United States or texts from what the College Board calls "the Great Global Conversation." In practice, these passages primarily deal with the expansion of rights and spreading of democracy. These are often, though not always, paired passages.

The passages are of varying difficulty from texts appropriate from 9th grade through honors-level high school courses. Some passages have a clearer structure and language, while others have a looser structure and complex vocabulary and sentence structure.

| Type | Number |
| --- | --- |
| Literature | 1 Passage without Data |
| Science | 1 Passage with Data |
|  | 1 Passage without Data, occasionally paired |
| Social Studies | 1 Passage with Data |
| History | 1 Passage without Data, frequently paired |

# THE QUESTIONS

The SAT Reading section has fifty-two questions, either ten or eleven per passage. These questions assess **your ability to read the passage critically**. You will be asked to answer questions about what information and ideas are presented in the passage, how the author constructs their argument, and how the information presented relates to other ideas and evidence. You'll also be asked to provide evidence to support your answers.

Unlike the math questions, which are ordered by difficulty, or the grammar questions, which follow the order of the passage, **the reading questions are ordered by their general focus**.

1. **General** questions about the whole passage are first.

2. **Specific** questions about individual parts of the passage follow.

3. **Synthesis** questions about data or compare paired passages, if there are any, will follow.

The questions associated with passages are thematically appropriate. Science passages are likely to ask you about a hypothesis or analysis of data, while literature passages are more likely to have questions about the characters' motivations or the literary tone.

We'll talk more about question types later, but you should get used to "evidence-based reasoning" questions. Each test includes ten of these questions which ask you to justify your answer to the previous question, like #10 below asks you to defend your answer to question #9.

### 9

According to the passage, Leibniz built his machine

A) by himself and at his own expense.

B) on his own, but with the financial assistance of the English and French governments.

C) with a wide variety of assistants.

D) through a grant from the University of Göttingen.

### 10

Which choice provides the best evidence for the answer to the previous question?

A) Lines 6-10 ("Lesser ... thinking")

B) Lines 10-12 ("In 1879 ... Germany").

C) Lines 17-21 ("supported ... butler").

D) Lines 29-31 ("Costing ... issues")

## THE ANSWERS

All of the verbal questions on the SAT are multiple choice. You won't find any short answer questions, let alone essays. You will get to do a lot of bubbling in:

Ⓐ Ⓑ Ⓒ Ⓓ

The College Board states that *all of the information you need to answer the questions comes from the passages themselves*: "Answers are derived from what is stated or implied in the passages and graphics rather than from prior knowledge of the topics." **No outside knowledge is needed.** This is a reading comprehension test, not a test of facts and dates from science or history class.

Each question has an answer bank with four multiple choice options. One choice is correct. Three choices are answers that appear convincing enough for some students to select them but are also wrong enough that they can be eliminated. In other words, **each incorrect answer is wrong**. This means you can use process of elimination to get yourself to the correct answer.

One final thing: Unlike some standardized tests, **there is no penalty for incorrect answers**. The answers are randomly distributed, so there is no answer choice that is correct more frequently than the others.

## THE CLOCK

The SAT is a timed test. You have sixty-five minutes to read five passages. These means that you have about 13 minutes to read each passage and answer the questions associated with it.

In general, you want to **avoid getting too far ahead or too far behind**. If you get too far behind, there are going to be questions (or even passages) that you don't get to on test day. If you get too far ahead, it means that you're leaving valuable time on the table at the end of the test. A good rule of thumb is to try and **keep yourself in the 12- to 14-minute range**.

Time is your most valuable asset on test day. **Use it wisely**.

# THE SCORING

## Raw Score vs. Scaled Score

**The SAT is a standardized test**, meaning that each time the test is offered, the test makers scale the test so that (approximately) the same percentage of students earn the same score as previous tests. Some tests may give you a little extra leeway because they are a little harder than others. The reading test is **half of your total verbal score (200-800)**. The other half is the Writing and Language (grammar) test. The optional **essay does not factor** into your score out of 800.

| Raw Score | Test Score | Raw Score | Test Score |
|---|---|---|---|
| 1 | 10 | 27 | 26 |
| 2 | 10 | 28 | 26 |
| 3 | 10 | 29 | 27 |
| 4 | 11 | 30 | 28 |
| 5 | 12 | 31 | 28 |
| 6 | 13 | 32 | 29 |
| 7 | 14 | 33 | 29 |
| 8 | 15 | 34 | 30 |
| 9 | 16 | 35 | 30 |
| 10 | 17 | 36 | 31 |
| 11 | 17 | 37 | 31 |
| 12 | 18 | 38 | 32 |
| 13 | 19 | 39 | 32 |
| 14 | 19 | 40 | 33 |
| 15 | 20 | 41 | 33 |
| 16 | 20 | 42 | 34 |
| 17 | 21 | 43 | 35 |
| 18 | 21 | 44 | 35 |
| 19 | 22 | 45 | 36 |
| 20 | 22 | 46 | 37 |
| 21 | 23 | 47 | 37 |
| 22 | 23 | 48 | 38 |
| 23 | 24 | 49 | 38 |
| 24 | 24 | 50 | 39 |
| 25 | 25 | 51 | 40 |
| 26 | 25 | 52 | 40 |

To calculate your reading score, you first need to **find your "raw" score**. This raw score is just the number of questions you answered correctly. You get one point for each correct answer. You do not lose any points for an incorrect or omitted answer.

After you have your raw score, you can **convert your raw score to a scaled "test" score** using a table like the one to the left. Let's say you answered 32 questions correctly on this test. For this test, that 32 is converted to a scaled score of 29.

Because your reading score is half your verbal score, you won't have a complete score without your grammar test score (which is calculated with a similar scale). To find this, you add your reading and grammar scores together and multiply by ten. So if your reading test score is a 29 and your grammar test score is a 32, your verbal test score will be a 610. **If you want to estimate your score from just the reading**, you can double it and multiply by ten; a 29 on the reading test is *approximately* a 580. Schools do not, in general, take your best reading and your best grammar test and combine those to find your "super score" for the verbal, so you have to work at both to maximize your score.

## Subscores and Cross-test Scores

The reading test also factors into your verbal **subscores** and **cross-test scores**. These scores do not factor into your score out of 800, and most schools don't take these into account with their admissions choices. You should not worry about these scores; in fact, Khan Academy does not calculate these scores for you when you use their online calculator. The subscores can give you marginal information about your strengths and weaknesses. You will find them on your official score reports, however, and you can calculate them by hand using the scoring tables.

- Your verbal subscores are based on your raw score on ten **words in context** questions and ten **command of evidence** questions. These raw scores are combined with your raw score on similar questions on the Writing and Language test and then scaled 1-15.
- Your cross-test scores in **science** and **history/social studies** are based on the questions on the two passages of each type. These are combined with 14 questions on the Writing and Language test and Math test, and your raw score of 1-35 is then converted to a scaled score of 10-40.

You can find the tables for subscores and cross-test scores in the scoring worksheets posted on Khan Academy. Again, they are not part of what schools use for admission. They can help you figure out which passage types (science or history/social studies) you may want to put a little more effort into, but by and large you don't need to worry about them.

## WHAT ABOUT THE PSAT?

The PSAT is primarily used for the National Merit Award and other scholarship opportunities (especially for students of color, indigenous students, and students from rural communities). All of the reading content on the PSAT is the same as on the SAT, though there are minor variations in length and scoring.

|  | PSAT | SAT |
| --- | --- | --- |
| The Passages | 5 total (1 literature, 2 science, and 2 social studies/history) | 5 total (1 literature, 2 science, and 2 social studies/history) |
| The Questions | 47 | 52 |
| The Answers | All multiple choice | All multiple choice |
| The Clock | 60 minutes | 65 minutes |
| The Scoring | 10-38 (20-76) | 10-40 (200-800) |

If you haven't taken it yet, good news! Studying for the SAT is great practice for the PSAT. If you have already taken the PSAT, then you should have some test taking experience for what to expect on the SAT.

You can learn more about the PSAT and scholarship opportunities at www.collegeboard.com/psat.

# PRACTICE TEST: OFFICIAL TEST 1

**The best way to practice is to take practice tests.** We'll be reading plenty of practice passages and answering lots of practice questions, but there is no substitute for taking official practice tests. Fortunately, the College Board has made practice tests freely available through Khan Academy (and linked at www.professorscompanion.com/reading). You can also buy the College Board's *Official SAT Study Guide*.

Let's try practice test 1 as a diagnostic test (page 1196 in the *Official Guide*). It's helpful to know your score, but for now, the most important thing you can work on is to become familiar with the test:

- What are the passages like?
- What are the questions like?
- What are the answers like?
- What is the clock like?

When you take practice tests, as opposed to practice passages in this book or on Khan Academy, you should keep track of your time. You have 65 minutes total, or about 13 minutes per passage.

After you have finished the test, you have two options for how to score your test. You can simply **copy your answers and input them on Khan's "full tests" page.** Second, you can **score the test by hand using the scoring sheet on Khan Academy** as the answer key. This is a little more tedious, but you will see the questions that you answered incorrectly right away, rather than scrolling through the whole test. Both methods will give you the number of questions you answered right and wrong, though you won't get a score out of 800 with the online calculator until you finish the whole test.

# SELF-EVALUATION TEST 1

| | | | | | | |
|---|---|---|---|---|---|---|
| **Passage 1** | I felt confident during the first passage. | Strongly Agree | Somewhat Agree | No Opinion | Somewhat Disagree | Strongly Disagree |
| | Describe in two to three sentences how you felt on the first passage | | | | | |
| **Passage 2** | I felt confident during the second passage. | Strongly Agree | Somewhat Agree | No Opinion | Somewhat Disagree | Strongly Disagree |
| | Describe in two to three sentences how you felt on the second passage | | | | | |
| **Passage 3** | I felt confident during the third passage. | Strongly Agree | Somewhat Agree | No Opinion | Somewhat Disagree | Strongly Disagree |
| | Describe in two to three sentences how you felt on the third passage | | | | | |
| **Passage 4** | I felt confident during the fourth passage. | Strongly Agree | Somewhat Agree | No Opinion | Somewhat Disagree | Strongly Disagree |
| | Describe in two to three sentences how you felt on the fourth passage | | | | | |
| **Passage 5** | I felt confident during the fifth passage. | Strongly Agree | Somewhat Agree | No Opinion | Somewhat Disagree | Strongly Disagree |
| | Describe in two to three sentences how you felt on the fifth passage | | | | | |
| **Overall** | I felt confident during the reading section. | Strongly Agree | Somewhat Agree | No Opinion | Somewhat Disagree | Strongly Disagree |
| | I had enough time for the reading section. | Strongly Agree | Somewhat Agree | No Opinion | Somewhat Disagree | Strongly Disagree |
| | I cared about the passages I read. | Strongly Agree | Somewhat Agree | No Opinion | Somewhat Disagree | Strongly Disagree |
| | In three to four sentences, describe how you feel about the reading section | | | | | |

Lesson 1: Understanding the Test

# BONUS TIP! REGISTER EARLY

As soon as you are ready, you should register for the SAT to make sure you get a spot near where you live or go to school. Your school may also have vouchers that let you take the test for free. Check with your guidance counselor for more information.

| **2019-2020 SAT Administration Dates and Deadlines** | | | | |
|---|---|---|---|---|
| SAT Date | SAT Subject Tests Available | Registration Deadline | Late Registration Deadline | Deadline for Changes |
| March 14, 2020 | SAT Subject Tests not offered on this date | February 14, 2020 | February 25, 2020 (for mailed registrations)<br><br>March 3, 2020 (for registrations made online or by phone) | March 3, 2020 |
| May 2, 2020 | See www.sat.org for up to date information on Subject tests. | April 3, 2020 | April 14, 2020 (for mailed registrations)<br><br>April 21, 2020 (for registrations made online or by phone) | April 21, 2020 |
| June 6, 2020 | See www.sat.org for up to date information on Subject tests. | May 8, 2020 | May 19, 2020 (for mailed registrations)<br><br>May 27, 2020 (for registrations made online or by phone) | May 27, 2020 |

If you are a *planner* (or if you've picked up a copy of this book from somebody else), here are the anticipated dates through Spring 2023.

| **2020-2021** | **2021-2022** | **2022-2023** |
|---|---|---|
| August 29, 2020 | August 28, 2021 | August 27, 2022 |
| October 3, 2020 | October 2, 2021 | October 1, 2022 |
| November 7, 2020 | November 6, 2021 | November 5, 2022 |
| December 5, 2020 | December 4, 2021 | December 3, 2022 |
| March 13, 2021 | March 12, 2022 | March 11, 2023 |
| May 8, 2021 | May 7, 2022 | May 6, 2023 |
| June 5, 2021 | June 4, 2022 | June 3, 2023 |

# LESSON 2: UNDERSTANDING THE PASSAGES

I want you to think about the differences between the passages you see on the SAT and your textbooks in school. (Feel free to grab a textbook if you want an example for comparison). Try to come up with a handful of differences.

| Textbooks | SAT |
|---|---|
| meant to explain / every thought; doesn't require outside knowledge | complicated; lots of knowledge before |

Here's a few of the things that I've noticed:

| Textbooks | SAT |
|---|---|
| Key terms are bolded | All plain text |
| Part of a larger chapter or discussion you know about | Just the passage (maybe an intro) |
| Call-outs in the margins let you know what's important | No indication what is important |
| Expansive short answer and essay questions | Multiple choice questions |
| Written for high school students | Written for broader audiences |

In general, SAT passages are harder to read that what you are used to reading in school. This means that **the first step to improving your SAT reading score is to understand the passages better.**

I can reasonably infer that you know how to read — you are reading this right now. But to succeed on the Reading portion of the SAT, you are going to need to **relearn to read.**

Lesson 2: Understanding the Passage

# RELEARNING TO READ: UNDERLINE, ANNOTATE, AND IDENTIFY

There are three steps to reading an SAT passage.

1. **Underline** anything that you think might possibly be relevant.

2. **Annotate** the passage.

3. **Identify** the author's purpose.

Students sometimes stress about the amount of time it takes to read the passage. I understand their feelings. It's a timed test, and you may think that the time you spend on the passage is wasted time. However, every second you spend on the passage will save you two seconds when you are reading and answering the questions, so you'll know where to go.

This doesn't mean you should dawdle. You want to read efficiently and with pace, so don't get bogged down on any section of the passage. *Keep yourself moving.* You can come back to anything you miss.

## Step 1: Underline

One of the things I look for when I first meet with a student is whether or not they underlined the passages on their diagnostic test. I've looked at hundreds of diagnostic tests and the data shows that students who underline score higher than students who don't. Here's the weird part: *It doesn't matter what you underline, just that you underline.*

I have found that the more underlining a student does, the better they remember not just the information that they underlined, but the information around the underlining as well. So, while you should try to underline things you think will be useful, you should always err on the side of underlining too much, rather than not enough. Sentences 1 and 3 make 2, 4, and 5 easier.

One other thing: I **circle the names that appear in the passage** to keep track of the various characters, researchers, and historical figures. I'll also **star dates** in case I need to track what happened when.

- You can't overdo this. If you think it might be important, then you should underline it!
- Circle names the first time they appear in the passage and box or star dates.

## Step 2: Annotate

As you go, **annotate the passage so that you know the main ideas of each paragraph**. Keep your annotations brief. Strive for two or three words, four if you must. *Frequent brief annotations are much better than intermittent detailed annotations.*

The goal isn't to cram all the information into the margins that you can or satisfy your English teacher by reading the passage. Rather, you are setting yourself up so that you can answer the questions that follow quickly, sketching out the passage for yourself so you can bounce back and forth between the questions and the passage. **Bullet points** are fine.

Your annotations can also help you answer questions that deal with smaller segments of the passage. If they ask you about the main idea of the fourth paragraph, and you've already written down some keywords in the margins, it makes sorting between the correct and incorrect answers that much faster. If you need to identify where the author talks about virtue ethics, your notations can tell you where to go.

If the passage has a graph or chart (two passages per test will), you'll want to give the briefest of descriptions of what the data indicate. If you're asked for a specific number, you can always go find it in the table later. For now, spend 15 to 30 seconds looking at the caption, the variables, and what the data measure.

- Keep your annotations brief: 2-4 words [*frequent*] [*independent/dependent variables*]
- Annotate frequently: 1-2 annotations per paragraph
- Write down a general sense of the data (trends)

## Step 3: Identify

The last and most important annotation that you will make is identifying the author's purpose in writing this passage. **Why did the author write this?**

There are three main reasons that the authors of SAT passages write the things that they write.

1. **To explain something**: the ethics of economics; DNA; flight and bird physiology. Science and Social Studies passages are well suited to explanatory passages.

2. **To argue something**: women should be educated like men; public transportation can be better; civil disobedience is good. The paired passages are often argument passages—two authors debating each other—though you will also find them on Social Studies and History passages.

3. **To describe literary characters**: a man asks a woman for her daughter's hand in marriage; a man hates his boss; a woman pretends to be somebody she is not. The literature passages, which typically focus on the interactions of two or three characters, are descriptive passages.

If you're looking for help identifying the author's purpose, read line 0. *Where is line zero?* That's the blurb in the paragraph before the passage itself begins. It will be in a different font to separate it out.

Reading for purpose helps with a lot of questions on the test. Many passages will have questions that straight up ask you "What's the purpose of the passage?" Others will ask you to identify the function of a word or image as it relates to the author's argument. It is a lot easier to identify why an author used some phrase or metaphor if you look for what they are trying to do overall.

## Practice Passage

*Ready for a practice passage?* Here's a passage about Gottfried Wilhelm Leibniz (rhymes with "tribe-nits"), the German mathematician and inventor of differential calculus. Focus on the steps for reading: **underline**, **annotate**, and **identify**. You can find my annotations in the solution manual on page S-4.

# PRACTICE PASSAGE: SOCIAL STUDIES

This passage is adapted from Jonathan Gray, "'Let Us Calculate!' Leibniz, Llull, and the Computational Imagination." 2016, Public Domain Review. Gottfried Wilhelm Leibniz (1646-1716) was a German mathematician and philosopher.

The seventeenth-century German polymath Gottfried Wilhelm Leibniz is best known for developing differential calculus, a mathematical innovation independent from that of the more famous
5   English mathematician and scientist Isaac Newton. Lesser known, however, are Leibniz's invention of the "stepped reckoner," an early precursor of the modern computer, and the crucial role Leibniz played in the history of computation and computational thinking.
10  In 1879, workmen fixing a leaking roof discovered a mysterious machine discarded in the corner of an attic at the University of Göttingen, Germany. With its cylinders of polished brass and oaken handles, the artifact was identified as one of a number of early
15  mechanical calculating devices that an aged Leibniz invented.

Supported by a network of professors, preachers, and friends—and developed with the technical assistance of a series of itinerant and precariously
20  employed clockmakers, mechanics, artisans, and even a butler—Leibniz's instrument aspired to provide less function than even the most basic of today's calculators. Through an intricate system of different sized wheels, the hand-crank operated device modestly
25  expanded the repertoire of possible operations to include multiplication and division as well as addition and subtraction.

The machine faltered through live demonstrations in London and Paris. Costing a small fortune to
30  construct, it suffered from a series of financial setbacks and technical issues. The Royal Society invited Leibniz to come back once it was fully operational. There is even speculation that—despite Leibniz's rhetoric spanning an impressive volume of letters and
35  publications—the machine never actually worked as intended.

Nevertheless, the instrument exercised a powerful grip on the imagination of later technicians. Leibniz's machine became part of textbook and industry
40  narratives about the development of computation. It was retrospectively integrated into the way that practitioners envisaged the history of their work. IBM acquired a functioning replica for their "antiques attic" collection. Scientist and inventor Stephen Wolfram
45  credits Leibniz with anticipating contemporary projects by "imagining a whole architecture for how knowledge would … be made computational." Recent writers have called Leibniz the "patron saint" of cybernetics and the "godfather of the modern
50  algorithm."

While Leibniz made groundbreaking contributions towards the modern binary number system as well as integral and differential calculus, his role in the history of computing amounts to more than the sum of his
55  scientific and technological accomplishments. He also advanced what we might consider a kind of "computational imaginary"—reflecting on the analytical and generative possibilities of rendering the world computable.

60  Leibniz believed that, just as all words in a language could be represented by the comparatively small number of letters in an alphabet, so the whole world of nature and thought could be considered in terms of a number of fundamental elements—an "alphabet of
65  human thought." By reformulating arguments and ideas in terms of a *characteristica universalis*, or universal language, all could be rendered computable. The combinatorial art would not only facilitate such analysis, but would also provide means to compose
70  new ideas, entities, inventions, and worlds.

Ultimately Leibniz hoped that a thought language of "pure" concepts, combined with formalized processes and methods akin to those used in mathematics, would lead to the mechanization and automation of reason itself. By means of new artificial languages and methods, our ordinary and imperfect ways of reasoning with words and ideas would give way to a formal, symbolic, rule-governed science conceived of as a computational process. Disputes, conflict, and grievances arising from ill-formed opinions, emotional hunches, biases, prejudices, and misunderstandings would give way to consensus, peace, and progress.

**Let's break down the passage.** You should be able to use your underlining and annotating to help you answer these free-response questions. Try to limit yourself to the space provided on each line. You will get more out of a compact answer that distills your thoughts than a longer answer. **Concision is more important than precision!**

| | Annotate |
|---|---|
| What is the main idea of the first paragraph (lines 1-9)? | Leibniz and the legacy he had |
| What is the main idea of the second paragraph (lines 10-16)? | Discovery! |
| What is the main idea of the third paragraph (lines 17-27)? | the calculator |
| What is the main idea of the fourth paragraph (lines 28-36)? | Didn't work |
| What is the main idea of the fifth paragraph (lines 37-50)? | example for future |
| What is the main idea of the sixth paragraph (lines 51-59)? | binary system |
| What is the main idea of the seventh paragraph (lines 60-71)? | Universal language = math |
| What is the main idea of the eighth paragraph (lines 72-84)? | hopes/dreams/ effects |

Let's also go through some big picture questions. Why did the author write this? What is the main idea or thesis of the passage? What is the author's attitude toward the topic? Once again, **shorter compact answers are best.**

| | Identify |
|---|---|
| What is the main purpose of the passage overall? | To explain Leibniz and his accomplishments |
| What is the main idea (or thesis) of the passage? | Stepped reckoner no work, important! |
| What is the author's attitude toward Leibniz? | enjoys / positive |

Lesson 2: Understanding the Passage

Ready for some SAT-style questions? Use your **underline**, **annotate**, and **identify** skills to help you answer these questions. (You can find solutions on the solution manual starting on page S-5).

### 1

The primary purpose of the passage is

A) to explore the intersection of mathematics and philosophy.

B) to investigate ancient precursors to modern computers.

C) to discuss Leibniz's contributions to computation.

D) to expose the technical flaws of pre-modern machinery.

### 2

The passage implies that Leibniz

A) never successfully demonstrated his calculator to the public.

B) wrote textbooks on machinery still used today.

C) once worked as a clockmaker.

D) created a new alphabet for mathematicians.

### 3

Which choice provides the best evidence for the answer to the previous question?

A) Lines 17-21 ("supported ... butler")

B) Lines 32-36 ("there is ... intended")

C) Lines 38-42 ("Leibniz's machine ... work")

D) Lines 60-65 ("Leibniz ... thought")

### 4

The primary function of the third paragraph (lines 17-27) is to

A) describe the technological capabilities and limitations of Leibniz's machine.

B) denigrate the calculations of Leibniz's machine.

C) suggest improvements Leibniz could have implemented.

D) reject the importance of Leibniz's work.

### 5

As used in line 37, the word "exercised" most nearly means

A) supported.

B) worked.

C) lifted.

D) held.

### 6

The final paragraph (lines 72-84) implies that

A) previous calculators had caused military conflict.

B) science has an unlimited potential to concentrate wealth and power.

C) Leibniz believed that rational thinking could solve social and global problems.

D) the failures of Leibniz's invention held society back.

**7**

The attitude of the scientist and writers mentioned in lines 44-50 ("Scientist ... algorithm") is one of

A) reflection.
B) awe.
C) superiority.
D) whimsy.

**8**

The main idea of the fifth paragraph (lines 37-50) is that

A) Leibniz was famous for his mathematical skills.
B) subsequent calculating machines were modeled on Leibniz's invention.
C) modern calculators are superior to those of Leibniz's machine.
D) Leibniz's machine has historical importance in computer science despite its failures.

**9**

According to the passage, Leibniz built his machine

A) by himself and at his own expense.
B) on his own, but with the financial assistance of the English and French governments.
C) with a wide variety of assistants.
D) through a grant from the University of Göttingen.

**10**

Which choice provides the best evidence for the answer to the previous question?

A) Lines 6-10 ("Lesser ... thinking")
B) Lines 10-12 ("In 1879 ... Germany").
C) Lines 17-21 ("supported ... butler").
D) Lines 29-31 ("Costing ... issues")

Did you notice how many questions you could answer using your annotations and identifications? **Question 1** asks what the purpose of the passage is. You already wrote that down, and if even if your answer isn't the exact same as the answer choices (and it rarely is), it will lead you to the right answer.

**Question 6, 7, and 8** ask you what sections of the passage are about (6 and 8) or how they contribute to the author's overall point (7). Your marginal annotations will lead you to the correct answers here.

The paired sets, **questions 2-3** and **9-10**, can be solved using your underlining. You may have answers to 2 and 9, but you can also work backward if you're stuck. You can read through your underlining and annotations for the lines indicated in questions 3 and 10. Within these sets of lines, you'll find the answers for 2 and 9. There's a fun little trap in question 2. A lot of students want to say that Leibniz invented a new alphabet for mathematicians. This answer is wrong because it uses the right words but is not true. Leibniz was a mathematician, and lines 60-65 describe "an alphabet of human thought," but this doesn't mean he created an alphabet for mathematicians.

Even the questions that don't seem to have line numbers associated with them can be answered using your annotations and identification. **Question 4** on the attitude of the scientist and writers and **question 5** on the word "exercised" can be answered more easily by considering the whole passage. The scientist and writers have a *positive* opinion of Leibniz. The word "exercised" indicates that Leibniz's instrument had importance beyond its functionality.

Lesson 2: Understanding the Passage

One other thing to note: A lot of time, students slow down when they find words that they don't know or phrases they don't understand. This is normal, but you should fight the urge to try and get all of the details figured out right away. For example, the author refers to Leibniz as a "polymath" in the very first line. Instead of stopping to figure out what it means to be a polymath, your time is better spent getting a sense for the passage overall. From the context, it sounds like being a polymath is a good thing. But you don't need to know the precise definition (somebody who has expertise in a wide range of topics) in order to understand that first paragraph or the entire passage.

**Online Bonus Content**
When Google wanted to recognize Leibniz's birthday with a doodle, they chose to celebrate Leibniz's contributions to computation (represented by the binary code for the letters G-O-O-G-L-E). Even if the calculator never worked, Leibniz's legacy matters as much to computer scientists as his invention of calculus matters to mathematicians. You can find a full copy of Jonathan Gray's essay "Let us Calculate!": Leibniz, Llull, and the Computational Imagination" and other essays online at www.professorscompanion.com/reading.

Ready for another passage? Let's try a **literature** passage. Work on **underlining** and **annotating** the passage and **identifying** the author's purpose (**explain**, **argue**, or **describe**).

My solutions to this passage and its questions are in the solution manual on page S-8.

# PRACTICE PASSAGE: LITERATURE

This passage is adapted from Susan Glaspell, "A Jury of Her Peers," written in 1917. The story takes place in early twentieth-century Iowa.

When Martha Hale opened the storm-door and got a cut of the north wind, she ran back for her big woolen scarf. As she hurriedly wound that round her head her eye made a scandalized sweep of her kitchen. [5] It was no ordinary thing that called her away--it was probably further from ordinary than anything that had ever happened in Dickson County. But what her eye took in was that her kitchen was in no shape for leaving: her bread all ready for mixing, half the flour [10] sifted and half unsifted.

She hated to see things half done; but she had been at that when the team from town stopped to get Mr. Hale, and then the sheriff came running in to say his wife wished Mrs. Hale would come too—adding, with [15] a grin, that he guessed she was getting scared and wanted another woman along. So she had dropped everything right where it was.

"Martha!" now came her husband's impatient voice. "Don't keep folks waiting out here in the cold."

[20] She again opened the storm-door, and this time joined the three men and the one woman waiting for her in the big two-seated buggy.

After she had the robes tucked around her, she took another look at the woman who sat beside her on [25] the back seat. She had met Mrs. Peters the year before at the county fair, and the thing she remembered about her was that she didn't seem like a sheriff's wife. She was small and thin and didn't have a strong voice. Mrs. Gorman, sheriff's wife before Gorman went out and [30] Peters came in, had a voice that somehow seemed to be backing up the law with every word. But if Mrs. Peters didn't look like a sheriff's wife, Peters made it up in looking like a sheriff. He was to a dot the kind of man who could get himself elected sheriff—a heavy man [35] with a big voice, who was particularly genial with the law-abiding, as if to make it plain that he knew the difference between criminals and non-criminals. And right there it came into Mrs. Hale's mind, with a stab, that this man who was so pleasant and lively with all of [40] them was going to the Wrights' now as a sheriff.

"The country's not very pleasant this time of year," Mrs. Peters at last ventured, as if she felt they ought to be talking as well as the men.

Mrs. Hale scarcely finished her reply, for they had [45] gone up a little hill and could see the Wright place now, and seeing it did not make her feel like talking. It looked very lonesome this cold March morning. It had always been a lonesome-looking place. It was down in a hollow, and the poplar trees around it were [50] lonesome-looking trees. The men were looking at it and talking about what had happened. The county attorney was bending to one side of the buggy, and kept looking steadily at the place as they drew up to it.

"I'm glad you came with me," Mrs. Peters said [55] nervously, as the two women were about to follow the men in through the kitchen door.

Even after she had her foot on the door-step, her hand on the knob, Martha Hale had a moment of feeling she could not cross that threshold. And the [60] reason it seemed she couldn't cross it now was simply because she hadn't crossed it before. Time and time again it had been in her mind, "I ought to go over and see Minnie Foster"—she still thought of her as Minnie Foster, though for twenty years she had been Mrs. [65] Wright. And then there was always something to do and Minnie Foster would go from her mind. But now she could come.

The men went over to the stove. The women stood close together by the door. Young Henderson, the [70] county attorney, turned around and said, "Come up to the fire, ladies."

Mrs. Peters took a step forward, then stopped. "I'm not—cold," she said.

And so the two women stood by the door, at first [75] not even so much as looking around the kitchen.

The men talked for a minute about what a good thing it was the sheriff had sent his deputy out that morning to make a fire for them, and then Sheriff Peters stepped back from the stove, unbuttoned his [80] outer coat, and leaned his hands on the kitchen table in a way that seemed to mark the beginning of official business. "Now, Mr. Hale," he said in a sort of semi-official voice, "before we move things about, you tell Mr. Henderson just what it was you saw when you [85] came here yesterday morning."

Lesson 2: Understanding the Passage

**Now, let's break down the passage.** With the literature passages, sometimes annotating every paragraph can get unwieldy, since dialogue breaks up paragraphs. I try to "chunk" the passage together when I am doing my annotations, so that's what I have below. These are my chunks, so it's OK if you have different chunks. Remember, **these annotations aren't really right or wrong**. Their goal is to lead you to the right answers. There isn't going to be an English teacher reading over your shoulder. (My annotations are on page S-4 in the solution manual.

|  | Annotate |
|---|---|
| What is the main idea of lines 1-10? | Hurrying to leave |
| What is the main idea of lines 11-22? | |
| What is the main idea of lines 23-40? | |
| What is the main idea of lines 41-43? | |
| What is the main idea of lines 44-56? | |
| What is the main idea of lines 57-67? | |
| What is the main idea of lines 68-75? | |
| What is the main idea of lines 76-85? | |

With literature passages, it's sometimes a good idea to identify any **conflicts** in the passages in addition to the author's **purpose**.

|  | Identify |
|---|---|
| What is the main purpose of the passage overall? | To describe Mrs. Hale and |
| What is the main idea (or thesis) of the passage? | |
| What is the tone of the passage | |
| What is the conflict in the narrative? | |

Now that you've mapped the passage, let's try some SAT questions. Remember to use your underlining, annotations, and identifications when answering these questions.

### 1

The passage can be best described as

A) a woman cooks breakfast and brings it to an old friend.

B) a woman leaves her home and accompanies a group of investigators to another house.

C) a woman joins her friends at a party at a house on the outskirts of town.

D) a woman enjoys a ride in the county with her husband and the sheriff.

### 2

The second paragraph (lines 11-17) indicates that

A) Mr. Hale requested that his wife join him on his trip with the sheriff.

B) the sheriff was prepared to arrest Mrs. Hale if she did not cooperate.

C) Mr. Hale was fond of telling humorous stories.

D) Mrs. Hale left her home hurriedly.

### 3

As used in line 16, the word "dropped" most nearly means

A) declined.

B) lowered.

C) abandoned.

D) threw.

### 4

The word "plain" in line 36 most nearly means

A) obvious.

B) simple.

C) pure.

D) flat.

### 5

The description of the voices in lines 27-31 ("She ... word") primarily serves to

A) emphasize the authority Mrs. Peters commands.

B) describe the lawlessness of the town's residents.

C) indicate Mrs. Gorman's vitality.

D) contrast Mrs. Peters with Mrs. Gorman.

### 6

Lines 41-43 ("The country's ... men") imply that

A) Mrs. Hale and Mrs. Peters had been silent while the men were talking among themselves.

B) Mrs. Hale and Mrs. Peters had been answering the sheriff's questions.

C) Mrs. Hale refused to talk to Mrs. Peters.

D) Mrs. Gorman found the cold weather disagreeable.

Lesson 3: Understanding the Questions

### 7

Mrs. Hale's attitude toward entering the Wrights' house is one of

A) apprehension.
B) regret.
C) nostalgia.
D) suspicion.

### 8

It can be inferred from the ninth paragraph (lines 57-67) that Mrs. Hale and Mrs. Wright

A) visited each other frequently.
B) refused to speak to each other.
C) had a history of animosity.
D) had known each other before Mrs. Wright was married.

### 9

It can be inferred from the passage that the Wrights' house

A) was only warmed by a recently lit fire.
B) had been damaged by an arsonist.
C) was abandoned throughout the cold spring.
D) frequently hosted lavish parties for the town's dignitaries.

### 10

Which choice provides the best evidence for the answer to the previous question?

A) Lines 46-47 ("It looked … morning")
B) Lines 68-72 ("The women … fire")
C) Lines 76-78 ("The men … them")
D) Lines 82-85 ("Now … morning")

---

Once again, your underlining, annotating, and identifying will help you with the answers. For literature passages, it is important to keep track of the overall narrative and the attitudes of the characters.

**Question 1** asks about the events of the passage: the beginning of an investigation of events at the Wright's house. **Question 2, 5, 6 and 8** ask you about the paragraphs or line numbers and how they contribute to the narrative overall.

This passage has only one paired set (**questions 9 and 10**), but it is trickier than those in the previous passage. There are half-correct elements in the incorrect answers to 9 (Mrs. Hale grabs a scarf in lines 1-3, but it's not clear the scarf keeps her warm; the spring had been cold, but the springs were usually cold). If, however, you work through the line numbers given in 10, you'll get to the correct answer for 9.

Identifying Mrs. Hale's attitude toward Mrs. Wright (her old friend Minnie Foster) will help you with **question 7**. Similarly, **questions 3 and 4**, which ask about vocabulary, are more easily resolved by identifying Mrs. Hale's attitude toward her unexpected departure (she doesn't like *abandoning* things) and Mr. Gorman's demeanor (it's *obvious* he knows the difference between criminals and upstanding citizens).

---

**Online Bonus Content**

Susan Glaspell's "A Jury of Her Peers," based upon a story Glaspell covered for a Des Moines newspaper, is one of the first true crime stories, made popular again with podcasts like *Serial* and television series like *American Crime Story*, *Making a Murderer*, and the satirical *American Vandal*. Do you want to find out what Mrs. Hale and Mrs. Peters discovered at Minnie Foster's house? You can find a full copy of *A Jury of Her Peers* and other stories online at www.professorscompanion.com/reading.

## THE BEST WAY TO IMPROVE IS TO ENGAGE

We'll talk more about this throughout the book, but you will do better on the test by engaging each passage, even if only for thirteen minutes. **Underlining**, **Annotating**, and **Identifying** are ways to keep your brain engaged as you read (this is sometimes called "active reading"). It may feel tedious, but it is the best way to improve. Also: *nothing is more tedious than having to take these tests a second time because you aren't happy with how you did the first time.*

## PRACTICE TEST: OFFICIAL TEST 5

Let's try practice test 5. If you have the *Official SAT Study Guide*, section 1 of test 5 is on page 952. You can find a free PDF on Khan Academy's website. There is a mirrored copy of the test as well at www.professorscompanion.com/sat.

For this test, work on the skills you've learned in this lesson:

1. **Underline the passage.** Again, it doesn't matter what you underline as much as it matters *that* you underline. I like to circle the names and star the dates as well to things organized in my head.

2. **Annotate the passage.** Give *brief* (2-4 word) summaries of the paragraphs as you read to help you answer the questions. Don't try to impress your teacher with all that you have gleaned from the passage. This isn't a short answer question, but rather a guide to get yourself to the right answer when you are bubbling in.

3. **Identify the passage's purpose.** Why did the author bother to write this? You can use the guidelines of *explain*, *argue*, and *describe* to focus your identification. Don't forget to read line zero for a hint at this as well.

On these practice tests, you should keep track of your total time spent. We'll work on pacing in a couple of lessons, but keep in mind that you've got 65 minutes for the whole reading test, or an average of 13 minutes per passage.

One final note: Make sure you fill out the post-test self-diagnostic form. You want to see your improvements both in terms of score as well as in confidence.

# SELF-EVALUATION TEST 5

| | | | | | | |
|---|---|---|---|---|---|---|
| **Passage 1** | I felt confident during the first passage. | Strongly Agree | Somewhat Agree | No Opinion | Somewhat Disagree | Strongly Disagree |
| | Describe in two to three sentences how you felt on the first passage | | | | | |
| **Passage 2** | I felt confident during the second passage. | Strongly Agree | Somewhat Agree | No Opinion | Somewhat Disagree | Strongly Disagree |
| | Describe in two to three sentences how you felt on the second passage | | | | | |
| **Passage 3** | I felt confident during the third passage. | Strongly Agree | Somewhat Agree | No Opinion | Somewhat Disagree | Strongly Disagree |
| | Describe in two to three sentences how you felt on the third passage | | | | | |
| **Passage 4** | I felt confident during the fourth passage. | Strongly Agree | Somewhat Agree | No Opinion | Somewhat Disagree | Strongly Disagree |
| | Describe in two to three sentences how you felt on the fourth passage | | | | | |
| **Passage 5** | I felt confident during the fifth passage. | Strongly Agree | Somewhat Agree | No Opinion | Somewhat Disagree | Strongly Disagree |
| | Describe in two to three sentences how you felt on the fifth passage | | | | | |
| **Overall** | I felt confident during the reading section. | Strongly Agree | Somewhat Agree | No Opinion | Somewhat Disagree | Strongly Disagree |
| | I had enough time for the reading section. | Strongly Agree | Somewhat Agree | No Opinion | Somewhat Disagree | Strongly Disagree |
| | I cared about the passages I read. | Strongly Agree | Somewhat Agree | No Opinion | Somewhat Disagree | Strongly Disagree |
| | In three to four sentences, describe how you feel about the reading section | | | | | |

# LESSON 3: UNDERSTANDING THE QUESTIONS AND ANSWERS

### RESTATE, RECALL, AND RESOLVE

Do you remember learning to ride a bike? What about serving a tennis ball, reading music, holding your breath underwater, or tying your shoes? We have all sorts of skills that you learned that were at one point difficult for us to do, but we now find easy. You don't think about how to pedal or stabilize the handlebar when you jump on your bike. You just go.

Answering standardized test questions is one of these skills. It takes some time to get used to the process, but soon you'll be doing it without thinking about it. There are three steps to answering every test question.

1. **Restate:** What question is it that the prompt is asking you?

2. **Recall:** How would you answer the question?

3. **Resolve:** Which of the choices in the answer bank gives the best answer?

This lesson is about learning to answer test questions with the same kind of ease you now ride your bicycle. It will take some effort on your part, but the rewards awaiting you are an increased score on the reading portion of the test and an increased confidence in your test-taking abilities overall.

Let's take a look at each of these steps in order with some of the questions from the Leibniz passage.

| SAT Prompt | Restate | Recall | Resolve |
|---|---|---|---|
| According to the passage, Leibniz built his machine | → | → | →   ⒶⒷⒸⒹ <br> Confidence __/5 |
| Which choice provides the best evidence for the answer to the previous question? | → | → | →   ⒶⒷⒸⒹ <br> Confidence __/5 |
| The primary function of the third paragraph is | → | → | →   ⒶⒷⒸⒹ <br> Confidence __/5 |
| As used in line 36, the word "exercised" most nearly means | → | → | →   ⒶⒷⒸⒹ <br> Confidence __/5 |

## Step 1: Restate

The first step is to **restate** what the prompt is asking you. This can sometimes be difficult since the test often gives open-ended or fill-in-the-blank statements. But all prompts have a "core" question that they are asking you. These core questions can be described using the interrogative words of **Who, What, Why, When, Where, and How.**

If you can recognize the question type of the prompt, you are most of the way there. Learning to restate what you are being asked will likely take some time. Be generous with yourself. Your ultimate goal is to start recognizing the question types and the simplified prompt without thinking about it.

Remember: You are jotting down the question. Don't try to pretty it up. I sometimes try the "Incredible Hulk Test."

**The more your question sounds like the Incredible Hulk, the better it is.**

For these examples, "How did Leibniz build his machine" is better than "What does the passage say about how Leibniz built his machine." Similarly, "Why did the author write paragraph 3?" will lead to a more accurate answer than "What is the purpose of including paragraph 3 in the author's overall argument?" You're doing this for yourself, not your English teacher.

| SAT Prompt | Restate | Recall | Resolve |
|---|---|---|---|
| According to the passage, Leibniz built his machine | → How did Leibniz build his machine? | → | → Ⓐ Ⓑ Ⓒ Ⓓ  Confidence _/5 |
| Which choice provides the best evidence for the answer to the previous question? | → How did you know the answer? | → | → Ⓐ Ⓑ Ⓒ Ⓓ  Confidence _/5 |
| The primary function of the third paragraph is | → Why did the author write paragraph 3? | → | → Ⓐ Ⓑ Ⓒ Ⓓ  Confidence _/5 |
| As used in line 36, the word "exercised" most nearly means | → What does the word "exercised" mean in line 36? | → | → Ⓐ Ⓑ Ⓒ Ⓓ  Confidence _/5 |

## Step 2: Recall

The next step is to **recall** the answer to the core question. The goal is not to craft the perfect short answer for your English or History teacher to grade. This can be hard for a lot of students. Fear not! Focus on being clear, not comprehensive. Try to jot down your best answer *without looking at the answer bank*. There are two primary reasons to avoid using the answer bank.

First, by waiting until you have your answer, **you are focusing on the things that are true** (the passage) rather than the things that are false (three of the four answer choices). Sometimes, students can get tripped up by things that seem true because of the passage, answers that appear in the test but don't answer the question that is being asked. By answering first and then looking, you increase your accuracy.

Second, **it makes it easier to check your answer to the question**. It can often be difficult to check your reading answers since you already decided that answer choice (A) is correct (or whatever answer you actually choose). Avoiding the answer bank means that when you do look at the answers, it will be easier to separate the correct choice from the three incorrect ones.

**Keep it short and sweet.** Again, your goal is to guide yourself to the right answer choice, not "guess" the right answer. You'll do that in the resolve step.

| SAT Prompt | Restate | Recall | Resolve |
|---|---|---|---|
| According to the passage, Leibniz built his machine | → How did Leibniz build his machine? | → He had help | → Ⓐ Ⓑ Ⓒ Ⓓ  Confidence _/5 |
| Which choice provides the best evidence for the answer to the previous question? | → How did you know the answer? | → Paragraph 2 | → Ⓐ Ⓑ Ⓒ Ⓓ  Confidence _/5 |
| The primary function of the third paragraph is | → Why did the author write paragraph 3? | → Explains what the machine did | → Ⓐ Ⓑ Ⓒ Ⓓ  Confidence _/5 |
| As used in line 36, the word "exercised" most nearly means | → What does the word "exercised" mean in line 36? | → had | → Ⓐ Ⓑ Ⓒ Ⓓ  Confidence _/5 |

Lesson 3: Understanding the Questions and Answers

## Step 3: Resolve

The final step is to **resolve** the prompt and answer using the answer bank. Having identified the question and give your answer, select the best answer choice and bubble that in.

As you resolve the prompt, think about how confident you are in your answer. **I grade my confidence on a scale of 1 to 5.**

| Grade | | Meaning |
|---|---|---|
| 1/5 | → | I have no idea. This is just a guess. |
| 2/5 | → | I have an idea, but this is only an educated guess. |
| 3/5 | → | I narrowed it down to a 50/50. |
| 4/5 | → | I like this answer, and I'm about 80% confident that it is correct. |
| 5/5 | → | This *is* the answer; indeed, if it's wrong, I'll scream. |

If your confidence level is a three or below, try writing out your paraphrased core question, and then tailor your answer to the paraphrased question. Over time, you'll start to do this in your head, but, like riding a bike, it takes some practice.

| SAT Prompt | Restate | Recall | Resolve |
|---|---|---|---|
| According to the passage, Leibniz built his machine | → How did Leibniz build his machine? | → He had help | → with a wide variety of assistants. <br> Ⓐ Ⓑ ● Ⓓ <br> Confidence 4/5 |
| Which choice provides the best evidence for the answer to the previous question? | → How did you know the answer? | → Paragraph 2 | → Lines 17-21 ("supported … butler"). <br> Ⓐ ● Ⓒ Ⓓ <br> Confidence 5/5 |
| The primary function of the third paragraph is | → Why did the author write paragraph 3? | → Explains what the machine did | → describe the technological advancements and limitations of Leibniz's machine. <br> ● Ⓑ Ⓒ Ⓓ <br> Confidence 4/5 |
| As used in line 36, the word "exercised" most nearly means | → What does the word "exercised" mean in line 36? | → Exerted | → held <br> ● Ⓑ Ⓒ Ⓓ <br> Confidence 5/5 |

## Reset

Once you have resolved the question, reset and continue. Keep yourself moving so you don't dwell too long on any one question. You can (and should) make sure your answer is correct, but give yourself credit for your work restating, recalling, and resolving the prompt.

One note: If reviewing the answer choices in question 17 lead you to reconsider your answer to question 12, feel free to change your answer. *Don't overdo this*. If you aren't confident in your new answer, keep things the way they were. But realizing that you've made a mistake is a good thing.

The goal here is to work on the three elements of understanding the questions:

1. **Restate:** What is it that the prompt is asking you (paraphrase)?

2. **Recall:** How would you answer your paraphrased question (answer)?

3. **Resolve:** Which of the four answer choices gives the best answer to the prompt (match with answer bank)?

Don't forget to practice your reading skills from the last chapter as well. **Underline**, **Annotate**, and **Identify** the following history passage.

You can find my marked up passage and solutions for all the questions accompany the passage, including my notes for **restate**, **recall**, and even **resolve**, on page S-12 in the solution manual.

# PRACTICE PASSAGE: HISTORY

The following passage is adapted from President John F. Kennedy, "Civil Rights Address," originally delivered 11 June 1963. Kennedy addressed the nation after he federalized the Alabama National Guard to enforce the desegregation of the University of Alabama against the wishes of Alabama governor George Wallace.

This Nation was founded by men of many nations and backgrounds. It was founded on the principle that all men are created equal, and that the rights of every man are diminished when the rights of one man are threatened.

Today we are committed to a worldwide struggle to promote and protect the rights of all who wish to be free. And when Americans are sent to Vietnam or West Berlin, we do not ask for whites only. It ought to be possible, therefore, for American students of any color to attend any public institution they select without having to be backed up by troops.

It ought to be possible for American consumers of any color to receive equal service in places of public accommodation, such as hotels and restaurants and theaters and retail stores, without being forced to resort to demonstrations in the street, and it ought to be possible for American citizens of any color to register and to vote in a free election without interference or fear of reprisal.

It ought to be possible, in short, for every American to enjoy the privileges of being American without regard to his race or his color. In short, every American ought to have the right to be treated as he would wish to be treated, as one would wish his children to be treated. But this is not the case.

The Negro baby born in America today, regardless of the section of the Nation in which he is born, has about one-half as much chance of completing a high school as a white baby born in the same place on the same day, one-third as much chance of completing college, one-third as much chance of becoming a professional man, twice as much chance of becoming unemployed, about one-seventh as much chance of earning $10,000 a year, a life expectancy which is 7 years shorter, and the prospects of earning only half as much.

This is not a sectional issue. Difficulties over segregation and discrimination exist in every city, in every State of the Union, producing in many cities a rising tide of discontent that threatens the public safety. Nor is this a partisan issue. In a time of domestic crisis men of good will and generosity should be able to unite regardless of party or politics. This is not even a legal or legislative issue alone. It is better to settle these matters in the courts than on the streets, and new laws are needed at every level, but law alone cannot make men see right.

We are confronted primarily with a moral issue. It is as old as the scriptures and is as clear as the American Constitution.

The heart of the question is whether all Americans are to be afforded equal rights and equal opportunities, whether we are going to treat our fellow Americans as we want to be treated. If an American, because his skin is dark, cannot eat lunch in a restaurant open to the public, if he cannot send his children to the best public school available, if he cannot vote for the public officials who represent him, if, in short, he cannot enjoy the full and free life which all of us want, then who among us would be content to have the color of his skin changed and stand in his place? Who among us would then be content with the counsels of patience and delay?

One hundred years of delay have passed since President Lincoln freed the slaves, yet their heirs, their grandsons, are not fully free. They are not yet freed from the bonds of injustice. They are not yet freed from social and economic oppression. And this Nation, for all its hopes and all its boasts, will not be fully free until all its citizens are free.

We preach freedom around the world, and we mean it, and we cherish our freedom here at home, but are we to say to the world, and much more importantly, to each other that this is a land of the free except for the Negroes; that we have no second-class citizens except Negroes; that we have no class or caste system, no ghettoes, no master race except with respect to Negroes?

Now the time has come for this Nation to fulfill its promise. The events in Birmingham and elsewhere have so increased the cries for equality that no city or State or legislative body can prudently choose to ignore them.

For each of these questions, try to **restate** (paraphrase) what they are asking you, **recall** your answer to this question, and **resolve** the prompt by giving your best answer and your confidence from 1 to 5. Be brief: Try to write down six or fewer words. Nobody's giving you partial credit; this is a tool to get you to full credit on each questions. After each question, **reset** for the next one.

## 1

The passage is primarily concerned with

Restate: What is this passage about?

Recall: black people facing injustice

A) racial inequality in the United States. *(circled)*
B) desegregation in the American South.
C) defending the legacy of Abraham Lincoln.
D) the infringement of states' rights.

Resolve  (A)BCD    Confidence 4/5

## 2

The primary purpose of the phrase "it ought to be possible" in lines 9-24 is to

Restate: What is "it ought to be possible"? *(the function of)*

Recall: to argue it should be a different way

A) emphasize the disparities between Northerners and Southerners.
B) attack those who oppose desegregation.
C) highlight injustices faced by black Americans. *(circled)*
D) defend the legal status of demonstrators.

Resolve  AB(C)D    Confidence 4/5

## 3

The fifth paragraph (lines 27-37) mainly deals with

Restate: what is the 5th paragraph about?

Recall: statistics between blacks and whites

A) social and economic inequalities between black and white Americans. *(circled)*
B) rising birthrates in impoverished cities.
C) the effects of desegregation.
D) the need for greater political freedom.

Resolve  (A)BCD    Confidence 1/5

## 4

The phrase "rising tide of discontent" in line 41 most nearly refers to

Restate: what does it mean

Recall: increasing protests/demonstrations

A) an increase in restlessness. *(circled)*
B) the likelihood of exploitation.
C) the propensity for economic advancement.
D) an awakening within moderates.

Resolve  (A)BCD    Confidence 1/5

### 5

Lines 49-51 ("We are ... Constitution") suggest that Kennedy believes that

Restate: What does Kennedy believe?

Recall: the problem is old and simple

A) segregation transcends political categories.
B) history will provide a solution to America's problems.
C) religion is as likely to divide people as to unite them.
D) segregation is ethically unambiguous.

Resolve  Ⓐ B C Ⓓ   Confidence 3/5

### 6

Kennedy refers to Lincoln in lines 65 in order to

Restate: Why does Kennedy mention Lincoln

Recall: highlight how long the issue has been going on

A) suggest that America's racial struggles are in its past.
B) warn of impending civil strife.
C) highlight America's failure to uphold its promises.
D) implicate previous presidents for their lack of leadership.

Resolve  A B Ⓒ D   Confidence 2/5

### 7

In lines 52-64, Kennedy uses rhetorical questions to encourage his audience to

Restate: Why does Kennedy say that

Recall: to cause empathy?

A) work toward gradual reconciliation of whites and blacks.
B) oppose unjust desegregation laws.
C) imagine themselves as the victims of discrimination
D) fight against racial integration.

Resolve  A B Ⓒ D   Confidence 2/5

### 8

The passage indicates that problems arising from desegregation were

Restate: _____

Recall: _____

A) primarily located in partisan strongholds.
B) found across the United States.
C) beyond the government's ability to legislate.
D) the result of judicial overreach.

Resolve  A B C D   Confidence __/5

**9**

Which choice provides the best evidence for the answer to the previous question?

Restate: Whats your evidence

Recall: _____

A) Lines 23-26 ("In short ... treated") ✓
B) Lines 38-40 ("Difficulties ... Union") ⓑ
C) Lines 45-48 ("It is ... right") ✗
D) Lines 72-73 ("We preach ... home.") ✗

Resolve  Ⓐ Ⓑ Ⓒ Ⓓ    Confidence ___/5

**10**

The overall tone of the passage is

Restate: Whats the tone of the passage

Recall: Serious and idealistic

A) principled. ⓐ
B) radical.
C) resigned.
D) dispassionate.

Resolve  Ⓐ Ⓑ Ⓒ Ⓓ    Confidence ___/5

A lot of students, *especially good ones*, struggle with keeping their **restate** and **recall** answers short. I suppose this results from good teachers wanting you to give complete answers. Were the SAT not a multiple choice test, these teachers would be right. But the SAT doesn't need you to come up with complete answers. Rather, you need to find your answer in the bank so that you can **resolve** the prompt and get the points you have earned.

---

**Online Bonus Content**
The SAT likes to give passages about the expansion of human rights. Three of the published passages deal with the abolitionist movement, and the May 2018 test included a passage written by Frederick Douglass. The College Board has suggested that future history or social studies passages will be based around "the Great Global conversation," a term that they have invented, but they give as an example a speech from Nelson Mandela, former leader of the anti-Apartheid African National Congress in South Africa and Nobel Prize. You can find more passages on African American history at www.professorscompanion.com/reading

---

In the next lesson, we're going to look at question types a little more closely. It's a section that can really up your **restate**, **recall**, and **resolve** game, but if you're cramming (as in, "the test is this Saturday" cramming), you may just want to read the first page. If you've got the time, however, it's one of the most important sections in the book.

Lesson 3: Understanding the Questions and Answers

# PRACTICE TEST REVIEW: RESTATE, RECALL, AND RESOLVE FOR TESTS 1 AND 5

Let's take a look at tests 1 and 5. For each question that you answered incorrectly, try to **restate** their prompt as a question. Then, **recall** the answer to that question. Finally, **resolve** the question by finding the answer choice that best matches your recalled answer.

If their correct answers are still eluding you, check out the test maker's explanations on Khan Academy or in the *Official Guide* (the solutions for test 1 start on page 1267 and the solutions for test 5 start on page 1035). You can also find mirrored solutions on professorscompanion.com/reading.

## Test 1 Review: Restate, Recall, and Resolve

| Restate | Recall | Resolve |
|---|---|---|
| 1 What is the best summary? | Woman pretends to someone else | Ⓐ Ⓑ Ⓒ Ⓓ |
| 2 What does "turn" mean here? | to take a look around | Ⓐ Ⓑ Ⓒ Ⓓ |
| 3 How to describe Lady Carlotta? | confident/quick | Ⓐ Ⓑ Ⓒ Ⓓ |
| 4 What best supports Q3? | | Ⓐ Ⓑ Ⓒ Ⓓ |
| 5 What do lines (14-15) show? | to do nothing | Ⓐ Ⓑ Ⓒ Ⓓ |
| 6 What does "charge" mean here? | expectation | Ⓐ Ⓑ Ⓒ Ⓓ |
| 7 What are they like? | privileged | Ⓐ Ⓑ Ⓒ Ⓓ |
| 8 How does Mrs. Quabarl like school? | traditional | Ⓐ Ⓑ Ⓒ Ⓓ |
| 9 How is Mrs. Quabarl described? | traditional and cruel | Ⓐ Ⓑ Ⓒ Ⓓ |
| 10 What best supports Q9? | | Ⓐ Ⓑ Ⓒ Ⓓ |
| 11 What does the third paragraph prove? | American public transit is bad | Ⓐ Ⓑ Ⓒ Ⓓ |
| 12 What is an advantage of driving in north America? | ease | Ⓐ Ⓑ Ⓒ Ⓓ |
| 13 What best supports Q12? | | Ⓐ Ⓑ Ⓒ Ⓓ |
| 14 What is the main point of paragraph 4? | places and pros to public transportation | Ⓐ Ⓑ Ⓒ Ⓓ |
| 15 What best supports Q14 | | Ⓐ Ⓑ Ⓒ Ⓓ |
| 16 What does "credit" mean here? | rightfully give ownership to | Ⓐ Ⓑ Ⓒ Ⓓ |
| 17 What does "favor" mean here? | to like over others | Ⓐ Ⓑ Ⓒ Ⓓ |
| 18 What best supports personal electronic devices make public transportation easier? | 63-67 | Ⓐ Ⓑ Ⓒ Ⓓ |
| 19 What statement makes sense with the graphs? | D? | Ⓐ Ⓑ Ⓒ Ⓓ |
| 20 Who uses public transportation the most? | working people outside the home | Ⓐ Ⓑ Ⓒ Ⓓ |
| 21 What best summarizes the events? | question, experiment, chance, new outcome | Ⓐ Ⓑ Ⓒ Ⓓ |

| Restate | Recall | Resolve |
|---|---|---|
| 22. What does "challenged" mean here? | asked | A B C D |
| 23. What does Kendial think while setting up research? | birds like the ground and climbing | A B C D |
| 24. What best supports Q23? | | A B C D |
| 25. Why do we have lines 12-32? | unexpected information is helpful? | A B C D |
| 26. What did Kendial do after line 41? | changed his experiment to fit his new idea | A B C D |
| 27. How could the birds stay on steep things? | their wings flapped at an angle | A B C D |
| 28. What does "document" mean here? | record | A B C D |
| 29. What do we know about sliding birds? | the ground is used very little | A B C D |
| 30. What best supports Q29? | | A B C D |
| 31. What does "common" mean here? | similar/shared | A B C D |
| 32. What does the author think about running a household? | women should do it because they are less than | A B C D |
| 33. What best supports Q32? | | A B C D |
| 34. What should women do for society to progress? | they must learn | A B C D |
| 35. What does "reason" mean here? | motivator | A B C D |
| 36. What has the author claimed about society header freedoms | favors one gender over another | A B C D |
| 37. What best supports Q36. | | A B C D |
| 38. Why does P2 refer to P1? | show an assumption about women to prove it wrong | A B C D |
| 39. What connects P1 and P2? | Passage 2 is opposite of P1 | A B C D |
| 40. What would both authors agree on? | women need education | A B C D |
| 41. How would P1 authors react to P2 final points? | women can't do it | A B C D |
| 42. How do those words help the argument? | to indicate they are not sure | A B C D |
| 43. Which choice is a hypothesis authors could test? | B | A B C D |
| 44. What best supports Q43? | | A B C D |
| 45. What did insecticides do? | It kills good bacteria | A B C D |
| 46. What best supports Q45? | | A B C D |
| 47. What does "postulate" mean here? | investigate/think | A B C D |
| 48. What does the 4th paragraph do? | | A B C D |
| 49. What can we assume about dover? | could be toxic if eaten too much | A B C D |
| 50. What % of the failed colonies had all 4 pathogens | 77% | A B C D |
| 51. Based on the data, which pathogen affected the most without others | D | A B C D |
| 52. Does the data support the claim? | No, doesn't talk about mites | A B C D |

Lesson 3: Understanding the Questions and Answers

## Test 5 Review: Restate, Recall, and Resolve

| Restate | Recall | Resolve |
|---|---|---|
| 1 | | Ⓐ Ⓑ Ⓒ Ⓓ |
| 2 | | Ⓐ Ⓑ Ⓒ Ⓓ |
| 3 | | Ⓐ Ⓑ Ⓒ Ⓓ |
| 4 | | Ⓐ Ⓑ Ⓒ Ⓓ |
| 5 | | Ⓐ Ⓑ Ⓒ Ⓓ |
| 6 | | Ⓐ Ⓑ Ⓒ Ⓓ |
| 7 | | Ⓐ Ⓑ Ⓒ Ⓓ |
| 8 | | Ⓐ Ⓑ Ⓒ Ⓓ |
| 9 | | Ⓐ Ⓑ Ⓒ Ⓓ |
| 10 | | Ⓐ Ⓑ Ⓒ Ⓓ |
| 11 | | Ⓐ Ⓑ Ⓒ Ⓓ |
| 12 | | Ⓐ Ⓑ Ⓒ Ⓓ |
| 13 | | Ⓐ Ⓑ Ⓒ Ⓓ |
| 14 | | Ⓐ Ⓑ Ⓒ Ⓓ |
| 15 | | Ⓐ Ⓑ Ⓒ Ⓓ |
| 16 | | Ⓐ Ⓑ Ⓒ Ⓓ |
| 17 | | Ⓐ Ⓑ Ⓒ Ⓓ |
| 18 | | Ⓐ Ⓑ Ⓒ Ⓓ |
| 19 | | Ⓐ Ⓑ Ⓒ Ⓓ |
| 20 | | Ⓐ Ⓑ Ⓒ Ⓓ |
| 21 | | Ⓐ Ⓑ Ⓒ Ⓓ |
| 22 | | Ⓐ Ⓑ Ⓒ Ⓓ |
| 23 | | Ⓐ Ⓑ Ⓒ Ⓓ |
| 24 | | Ⓐ Ⓑ Ⓒ Ⓓ |
| 25 | | Ⓐ Ⓑ Ⓒ Ⓓ |
| 26 | | Ⓐ Ⓑ Ⓒ Ⓓ |
| 27 | | Ⓐ Ⓑ Ⓒ Ⓓ |
| 28 | | Ⓐ Ⓑ Ⓒ Ⓓ |
| 29 | | Ⓐ Ⓑ Ⓒ Ⓓ |
| 30 | | Ⓐ Ⓑ Ⓒ Ⓓ |
| 31 | | Ⓐ Ⓑ Ⓒ Ⓓ |
| 32 | | Ⓐ Ⓑ Ⓒ Ⓓ |

| Restate | Recall | Resolve |
|---|---|---|
| 33 | | Ⓐ Ⓑ Ⓒ Ⓓ |
| 34 | | Ⓐ Ⓑ Ⓒ Ⓓ |
| 35 | | Ⓐ Ⓑ Ⓒ Ⓓ |
| 36 | | Ⓐ Ⓑ Ⓒ Ⓓ |
| 37 | | Ⓐ Ⓑ Ⓒ Ⓓ |
| 38 | | Ⓐ Ⓑ Ⓒ Ⓓ |
| 39 | | Ⓐ Ⓑ Ⓒ Ⓓ |
| 40 | | Ⓐ Ⓑ Ⓒ Ⓓ |
| 41 | | Ⓐ Ⓑ Ⓒ Ⓓ |
| 42 | | Ⓐ Ⓑ Ⓒ Ⓓ |
| 43 | | Ⓐ Ⓑ Ⓒ Ⓓ |
| 44 | | Ⓐ Ⓑ Ⓒ Ⓓ |
| 45 | | Ⓐ Ⓑ Ⓒ Ⓓ |
| 46 | | Ⓐ Ⓑ Ⓒ Ⓓ |
| 47 | | Ⓐ Ⓑ Ⓒ Ⓓ |
| 48 | | Ⓐ Ⓑ Ⓒ Ⓓ |
| 49 | | Ⓐ Ⓑ Ⓒ Ⓓ |
| 50 | | Ⓐ Ⓑ Ⓒ Ⓓ |
| 51 | | Ⓐ Ⓑ Ⓒ Ⓓ |
| 52 | | Ⓐ Ⓑ Ⓒ Ⓓ |

Lesson 3: Understanding the Questions and Answers

## BONUS TIP! FIND A STUDY-BUDDY

It can be hard to study for the SAT. It's hard to keep yourself motivated when you feel like the test is a weight upon your shoulders.

One way to decrease your stress and keep yourself going when the test is feeling oppressive is find somebody to study with. A friend can help keep you accountable for getting through the material when all you want to do is curl up with a blanket (or cat or dog) and watch TV or see what's happening online.

It's up to you whether or not you want to share scores with your buddy. There's enough pressure to succeed that I typically recommend you keep your scores to yourself, but you can talk about the gains you're making each practice test, rather than worrying about who is scoring higher.

# LESSON 4: MASTERING THE QUESTIONS

When you're just getting used to the SAT, it's enough to translate the prompt into a question and then answer that question. In fact, if I have a student that comes to me for a quick session or two to get ready for the test, they don't typically get beyond that stage. But, if you have the time to really dive into the questions, there's a lot more you can do with the questions when you **recognize** question types. So let's look at the question types.

## RECOGNIZING QUESTION TYPES

Questions can be roughly divided into three overarching categories.

- **General** questions focus on the passage overall.

- **Specific** questions focus on words, lines, and paragraphs in the passage.

- **Synthesis** questions ask you to compare the data and the passage or the two authors to each other. (These only appear on data and paired passages).

We'll look at each of these question types over the next pages, but here's a master listing of all of them and the "core questions" that they ask.

|  | Recognize (Recognizes) | | | Restate (Core Questions) |
|---|---|---|---|---|
|  | General | Specific | Synthesis |  |
| Main Purpose | Purpose | Function |  | → Why did they write this? |
| Main Idea | Thesis | Topic |  | → What is this all about? |
| Tone | Tone | Attitude |  | → How do they feel? |
| Rhetoric | Structure | Argument |  | → How do they support the thesis? |
| Vocabulary |  | Vocabulary |  | → What does this mean? |
| Evidence |  | Evidence |  | → Where do they say? |
| Detail |  | Detail |  | → What do they say? |
| Inference |  | Inference |  | → What if...? |
| Data |  | Data Specific | Data Synthesis | → What are the numbers? |
| Paired |  | Paired Specific | Paired Synthesis | → How are these things related? |

Each of the question types will get a summary of the ways the question has appeared on the passages in this book and official practice tests. The Leibniz, *A Jury of Her Peers*, and Kennedy passages are abbreviated L, J, and K respectively, so J.4 is the fourth question that accompanies *A Jury of Her Peers* and K.2 is the second question on the Kennedy passage. You'll also see numbers like 1.32, which means question 32 on test 1. Following the sample prompts, we'll walk through the basics of answering each question type.

After looking at the question prompts and strategies, you'll have a chance to practice with some sample questions. As you answer these questions, don't forget to develop your **restate** and **recall** skills. You'll get the same lines to write in your paraphrasing and answering that we had last section.

At the end of the sample question set, you'll be asked to write your own SAT question of that type.

1. Start by using writing down the core question (**Restate**).

2. Then, write the **prompt** for your question. No need to get creative: You can use the sample prompts provided in the question type analysis on the facing page.

3. Lastly, give the answer to your question (**Recall**).

Don't worry about writing your own multiple choice answers (**Resolve**); we'll get to the answer choices in the next section.

### 4
Write your own **vocabulary-in-context** question

Restate — what does "exercised" mean here?

Prompt — As used in line 36, the word "exercised" most nearly means

Recall — held

### 5
Write your own **function** question

Restate — why does the author talk about the problems with the device?

Prompt — The primary purpose of the fourth paragraph is to

Recall — explain that the machine didn't work

Ready for a science passage with data? We're going to use it for the next 21 questions, plus the dozen or so that you will write. **Underline, Annotate,** and **Identify,** and don't forget to annotate the figure!

You can find my marked up passage and solutions for all the questions accompany the passage, including full solutions for **restate, recall,** and **resolve,** on page S-16 in the solution manual.

# PRACTICE PASSAGE: SCIENCE (WITH DATA)

This passage is adapted from "NASA Mars Rover's Weather Data Bolster Case for Brine." 2015, NASA. Brines are salt-liquid solutions.

Martian weather and soil conditions that NASA's Curiosity rover has measured, together with a type of salt found in Martian soil, could put liquid brine in the soil at night.

[5] Calcium perchlorate identified in Martian soil by the Curiosity mission, and previously by NASA's Phoenix Mars Lander mission, has properties of absorbing water vapor from the atmosphere and lowering the freezing temperature of water. This has [10] been proposed for years as a mechanism for the possible presence of transient liquid brines at higher latitudes on modern Mars, despite the Red Planet's cold and dry conditions.

New calculations were based on more than a full [15] Mars year of temperature and humidity measurements by Curiosity. They indicate that conditions at the rover's near-equatorial location were favorable for small quantities of brine to form during some nights throughout the year, drying out again after sunrise. [20] Conditions should be even more appropriate at higher latitudes, where colder temperatures and more water vapor can result in higher relative humidity more often.

"Liquid water is a requirement for life as we know [25] it, and a target for Mars exploration missions," said the report's lead author, Javier Martin-Torres of the Spanish Research Council, Spain, and Lulea University of Technology, Sweden. "Conditions near the surface of present-day Mars are hardly favorable for microbial [30] life as we know it, but the possibility for liquid brines on Mars has wider implications for habitability and geological water-related processes."

Curiosity is the first mission to measure relative humidity in the Martian atmosphere close to the [35] surface and ground temperature through all times of day and all seasons of the Martian year. Relative humidity depends on the temperature of the air, as well as the amount of water vapor in it. Curiosity's measurements of relative humidity range from about [40] five percent on summer afternoons to 100 percent on autumn and winter nights.

The air that fills pores in the soil encounters the air just above the ground. When its relative humidity gets above a threshold level, salts can absorb enough water [45] molecules to become dissolved in liquid, a process called deliquescence. Perchlorate salts are especially good at this. Since perchlorate has been identified both at near-polar and near-equatorial sites, it may be present in soils all over the planet.

[50] "Gale Crater is one of the least likely places on Mars to have conditions for brines to form, compared to sites at higher latitudes or with more shading. So if brines can exist there, it strengthens the case they could form and persist even longer at many other [55] locations," said Alfred McEwen of the University of Arizona, who co-authored the new report.

Following its August 2012 landing, Curiosity found evidence for ancient streambeds and a lakebed environment more than three billion years old that [60] offered conditions favorable for microbial life. Now, the rover is examining a layered mountain inside Gale Crater for evidence for how ancient environmental conditions evolved.

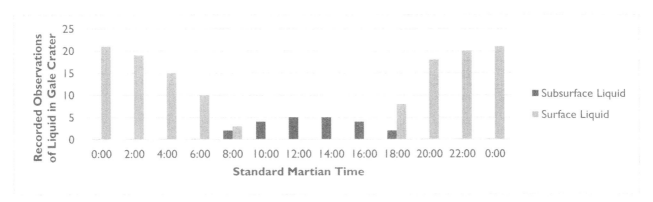

Figure 1 - Time of liquid found in Gale Crater. Adapted from Javier Martin-Torres et al.

# Why Did the Author Write This? Purpose and Function Questions

Identifying the author's purpose is crucial to answering many of the questions on the test, but you will also come across questions that ask you to identify the purpose directly.

**Purpose** questions ask you what the purpose of the passage directly.

| L.1 | 1.32 |
|---|---|
| The primary purpose of the passage is | The main purpose of the passage is to |

Remember that there are three prima cry purposes on the SAT:

- to **explain** something (generally science and social studies)

- to **argue** something (generally history, sometimes social studies or science)

- to **describe** literary characters (generally literature)

If you annotated the passage with an eye to purpose, you can answer these questions immediately. This passage *explains* something about the discovery of calcium perchlorate (per-chlorate, like per-oxide) on Mars.

**Function** questions are localized purpose questions. The stock prompts typically use keywords like "purpose" and "function," or what grammar nerds call "purpose clauses" (in order to, so that, etc.).

| J.3 | K.2 |
|---|---|
| The description of the voices in lines 27-31 ("She ... word") primarily serves to | The primary purpose of the phrase "it ought to be possible" in lines 9-24 is to |

In order to resolve a function question, ask yourself how the word, imagery, or paragraph supports the author's overall purpose. In a passage on abolition, the author may describe the conditions of slaves *in order to incite the reader to action*. A social studies passage on ethics in business may demonstrate the antiquity or ubiquity of various positions.

|  | Recognize (Question Type) | Restate (Core Questions) |
|---|---|---|
| General | Purpose | • Why did the author write this? <br> • What is the main purpose of the passage? |
| Specific | Function | • What is the function of paragraph # in the author's argument? <br> • What is the function of the word/imagery/metaphor in lines ##? |

**1**

The main purpose of the passage is to

Restate _____

_____

Recall _____

_____

A) discuss the discovery of liquid brine on Mars.

B) disprove scientific assumptions about Martian weather and soil.

C) investigate the implications of liquid brine on the Martian surface.

D) examine the conditions necessary for the development of microbial life.

Resolve   Ⓐ Ⓑ Ⓒ Ⓓ   Confidence ___/5

**2**

The primary function of the final paragraph (lines 57-63) is to

Restate _____

_____

Recall _____

_____

A) indicate the scale of Curiosity's mission.

B) provide the date of Curiosity landed on Mars.

C) explain how Martian lakes form.

D) summarize the effects of Calcium perchlorate on water.

Resolve   Ⓐ Ⓑ Ⓒ Ⓓ   Confidence ___/5

Write your own **function** question (use the core question prompts on the previous page to help)

Restate _____

_____

Prompt _____

_____

Recall _____

_____

Lesson 4: Mastering the Questions

# What Is This All About? Thesis and Topic Questions

Questions about the thesis and topic are probably the questions you are most prepared to answer, as your English and history teachers have drilled thesis construction deep inside your brain.

The College Board describes **thesis** questions as "determining central ideas and themes." The test will ask thesis questions with standard question formats.

`K.1`

The passage is primarily concerned with

`1.47`

The central claim of Passage 2 is that space mining has positive potential but

An author's **thesis should be evident in the first paragraph** of the passage. The **final paragraph will often recapitulate the thesis** or suggest further conclusions that could be drawn from the passage (remember that the passages are frequently excerpted from longer works, and so cannot contain the entirety of an author's argument).

**Passage titles frequently hint at the author's thesis** as well. The introductory material (Line Zero) may expand as needed to give you a better sense of the passage going into your reading. "Woolf considers the situation of women in English society" gives the topic, and the thesis follows soon after in the first paragraph.

Much like the main purpose, noting the thesis will help you answer questions about how the various parts of the passage construct a more coherent argument.

**Topic** questions ask about the claim or topic of a specific paragraph.

`L.4`

The main idea of the fifth paragraph (lines 37-50) is that

`5.8`

The main idea of the last paragraph is that Mr. Peters

Your annotations will be your best guide in answering these questions. Don't allow yourself to be swayed by answers that are "true, but irrelevant" or that deal with other paragraphs or sections of the passage. Stay focused!

|  | Recognize (Question Type) | Restate (Core Questions) |
|---|---|---|
| General | Thesis | • What is the author's thesis? <br> • What is this passage about? |
| Specific | Topic | • What is this paragraph about? |

### 3

The main idea of the passage is that

Restate _____

Recall _____

A) liquid brine may indicate the presence of drinkable water.
B) the weather and soil on Mars are incapable of supporting life.
C) researchers have uncovered evidence of life on Mars.
D) liquid brine has been discovered on Mars.

Resolve  Ⓐ Ⓑ Ⓒ Ⓓ   Confidence ___/5

### 4

The sixth paragraph (lines 42-49) primarily discusses

Restate _____

Recall _____

A) the impact of relative humidity on the Martian atmosphere.
B) the process by which liquid brines form on Mars.
C) the location of perchlorate salt deposits.
D) the potential for growing plants in Martian soil.

Resolve  Ⓐ Ⓑ Ⓒ Ⓓ   Confidence ___/5

### 5

The main idea of the second paragraph (lines 5-13) is that

Restate _____

Recall _____

A) water on Mars freezes at higher temperatures than on Earth.
B) previous studies hypothesized that Calcium perchlorate could produce liquid brine on Mars.
C) the Curiosity mission is the second mission to Mars.
D) Mars is inhospitable to human life.

Resolve  Ⓐ Ⓑ Ⓒ Ⓓ   Confidence ___/5

---

Write your own **topic** question (use the core question prompt on the previous page to help)

Restate _____

Prompt _____

Recall _____

Lesson 4: Mastering the Questions

## How Do They Feel? Tone and Attitude Questions

Tone and Attitude questions ask you to identify the overall tone of the passage or a character's attitude toward another character or event, what the test makers call "point-of-view" questions.

**Tone** questions have simple stock phrases. They are not particularly common but appear frequently enough that you should be prepared to answer them.

> **K.10**
>
> The overall tone of the passage is one of

When I am taking a test, I frequently jot down the **tone** of the passage when I am identifying the author's purpose, because it forces me to think about how the author treats their subject. If the author is arguing that people care too much about the value of the gifts they purchase, then a passage may have a conversational or even combative tone. If the author is explaining the psychology of gift giving, however, they may adopt a more academic or descriptive tone. The tone thus leads me toward a better understanding of the passage on the whole.

A person (real or fictional) can have an **attitude** toward things as well. On the literary fiction passages, I always jot the relationship between the characters. If all narratives have conflict (and they do, whether that conflict is between the Montagues and the Capulets, between a man and his conscience, or between Godzilla and Tokyo), then you should expect to answer questions about that conflict.

> **L.7**
>
> The attitude of the scientist and writers mentioned in lines 44-50 ("Scientist … algorithm") is one of

> **J.7**
>
> Mrs. Hale's attitude toward entering the Wright's house is one of

> **1.6**
>
> In the passage, Akira addresses Chie with

> **5.4**
>
> Lymie's primary impression of the "party of four" (line 42) is that they

In the first passage of test 1, Akira treats Chie with respect, Chie looks down upon Akira, and Naomi defies her mother. Similarly, on the first passage in test 5, Lymie is irritated with the other guests at the restaurant and finds his father aged and vain.

|          | Recognize (Question Type) | Restate (Core Questions) |
|----------|---------------------------|--------------------------|
| General  | Tone                      | • What is the tone of the passage?<br>• What is the author's attitude toward [topic]? |
| Specific | Attitude                  | • What is the attitude of [character A] toward [something]?<br>• What is the opinion of [scientist/researcher X] on [something]? |

### 6

The overall tone of the passage is of

Restate _____

Recall _____

A) outright skepticism.

B) measured enthusiasm.

C) begrudging agreement.

D) overall ambivalence.

Resolve  Ⓐ Ⓑ Ⓒ Ⓓ     Confidence ___/5

### 7

The scientist quoted in lines 50-56 ("Gale Crater…locations") primarily regards the discovery of brine with

Restate _____

Recall _____

A) surprise.

B) suspicion.

C) optimism.

D) exuberance.

Resolve  Ⓐ Ⓑ Ⓒ Ⓓ     Confidence ___/5

### 6

Write your own **attitude (person)** question (use the core question prompts on the previous page to help)

Restate _____

Prompt _____

Recall _____

Lesson 4: Mastering the Questions

## How Does the Author Support Their Thesis? Rhetoric Questions

Rhetoric questions look at how authors structure and support their arguments. **Structure** questions are the most basic rhetoric questions. These questions are about passage organization, what the test makers call "analyzing text structure." The stock prompts tend to be phrased as questions.

**1.1**
Which choice best describes the developmental pattern of the passage?

**5.1**
Over the course of the passage, the primary focus shifts from

For the more straightforward structure questions, strip away as much of the detail as you can from the passage to get to the bare-bones description. Tolstoy once said that all great literature is one of two stories: a person goes on a journey or a stranger comes to town. The SAT will ask for a little more specificity than this, but you should take Tolstoy to heart. Get to the generalized description of the passage that would distinguish it from the other passages on the test:

- An invention is discussed and its legacy examined ("Let Us Calculate")
- A woman journeys to her friend's house with the sheriff (A Jury of Her Peers)

Once you have this distilled structure, answer the question accordingly.

**Argument** questions are more advanced. These questions explore the author's argument and ask you to "analyze claims and counterclaims, reasoning, and evidence." Here are some stock prompts they use.

**1.23**
A student claims that nitrogenous bases pair randomly with one another. Which of the following statements in the passage contradicts the student's claim?

**K.7**
In lines 52-64, the use of rhetorical questions suggests that some of Kennedy's audience

When you are asked to analyze an author's evidence, look at how the author defends their thesis. What are the logical steps that went into their argument? If they argue that women should not have equal educational opportunities as men, what are the grounds on which they make this argument? Unpack their logic and answer. If the question asks what objection the author anticipates, ask yourself what they are arguing *for* to see what they are arguing *against*.

|  | Recognize (Question Type) | Restate (Core Questions) |
|---|---|---|
| General | Structure | • How is the passage organized? |
| Specific | Argument | • What evidence would support/contradict the author's point? <br> • What assumptions does the author make? |

### 8

Which choice summarizes the passage?

Restate _____

_____

Recall _____

_____

A) Recent studies disprove an existing hypothesis.
B) An unexpected discovery leads to new avenues of research.
C) A routine experiment revolutionizes scientific consensus.
D) New data support a long-held belief.

Resolve   Ⓐ Ⓑ Ⓒ Ⓓ      Confidence ___/5

### 9

The passage assumes that

Restate _____

_____

Recall _____

_____

A) liquid water is a necessary precondition for microbial life.
B) Gale Crater will become the predominant location for research.
C) calcium perchlorate is found exclusively in Martian soil.
D) Martian weather precludes the existence of liquid water.

Resolve   Ⓐ Ⓑ Ⓒ Ⓓ      Confidence ___/5

### 10

Which choice best describes the structure of the passage?

Restate _____

_____

Recall _____

_____

A) Competing evidence for a scientific hypothesis is presented by advocates and detractors of a theory.
B) Two hypotheses explaining new data are presented and considered.
C) A discovery is outlined and its implications investigated.
D) An innovative experiment is critiqued and revised in response to criticism.

Resolve   Ⓐ Ⓑ Ⓒ Ⓓ      Confidence ___/5

---

Write your own **argument** question (use the core question prompts on the previous page to help)

Restate _____

_____

Prompt _____

_____

Recall _____

_____

Lesson 4: Mastering the Questions

# What Does the Author Mean by This? Vocabulary-in-Context Question

In ancient United States, the vocabulary questions reigned over the SAT. Before 2005, about 50% of the points came from sentence completions, antonyms, or analogy questions. In 2005, they eliminated the antonyms and analogies; in 2016, the sentence completions bit the dust. Students today will never know the sheer joy of hours upon hours of memorizing hundreds if not thousands of words in the hopes that one of them may appear on the test.

I still remember the word on the SAT that I had never seen before: "obstreperous" (*syn.* boisterous, booming, or unruly). My parents found it funny that this word (which may or may not have been a good way of describing me in high school) was the word that tripped me up. I did get the question right (the correct answer was "nitpicking"), but the frustration of studying vocabulary words is thankfully a thing of the past.

Mind you, the vocabulary hasn't disappeared from the test, it has simply moved to passage-based questions, or what the test makers describe as "interpreting words and phrases in context." On any given test, you should expect seven or eight vocabulary-in-context questions. Most **vocab** questions have a simple stock prompt.

### J.4
The word "plain" in line 36 most nearly means

### 5.10
As used in line 93, "becoming" most nearly means

Rare, more complex vocabulary questions may ask you about a figurative expression:

### 1.40
Which choice most closely captures the meaning of the figurative "sixpence" referred to in lines 70 and 71?

### K.4
The phrase "rising tide of discontent" in line 41 most nearly refers to

To answer vocabulary questions, try to isolate the word from its dictionary definition and focus on what the word means in context. Here's an example:

```
5    Calcium perchlorate identified in Martian soil by
     the Curiosity mission, and previously by NASA's
     Phoenix Mars Lander mission, has properties of
     absorbing water vapor from the atmosphere and
     lowering the freezing temperature of water. This has
10   been proposed for years as a mechanism for the
     possible presence of transient liquid brines at higher
     latitudes on modern Mars, despite the Red Planet's
     cold and dry conditions.
```

### 1
As used in line 10, the word "mechanism" most nearly means

A) machinery.
B) instrument.
C) method.
D) routine.

To start, **cross off the word** in question as it appears in the passage. Actually cross it out. You do not want yourself to get trapped by the connotations the word may have, in this case, something having to do with machinery.

**Now, try to find your own word to replace the crossed out word.** Choose a simple word: You're trying to get close, not guess the answer. In this passage, the absorption of water by perchlorate salts has been a proposed way that liquid brines could be found to exist on Mars. So, the word should have a meaning something like "process" or "way." You don't have to be correct but get yourself as close to the contextual meaning of the word as you can. I'll write the word down to the right of the choices, as below.

5　　Calcium perchlorate identified in Martian soil by the Curiosity mission, and previously by NASA's Phoenix Mars Lander mission, has properties of absorbing water vapor from the atmosphere and lowering the freezing temperature of water. This has
10　been proposed for years as a ~~mechanism~~ for the possible presence of transient liquid brines at higher latitudes on modern Mars, despite the Red Planet's cold and dry conditions.

As used in line 10, the word "mechanism" most nearly means

A) machinery.　　　*process*
B) instrument.
C) method.
D) routine.

In general, the dictionary definition of the word in context does not matter much. "Mechanism" does not mean "way," but "way" is still the right answer. In fact, **if you rely on the dictionary meaning, you will frequently end up with an incorrect answer.** For example, test 5, section 1, question 10 gives "emerging," "developing," and "happening" as wrong answers for the vocab word "becoming." Stick to the context.

Finally, resolve the question. **Match your word to the answer choice** that is closest to the contextual meaning, which in this case is "method."

Ⓐ Ⓑ ● Ⓓ

|  | Recognize (Question Type) | Restate (Core Questions) |
|---|---|---|
| General |  | (Specific only) |
| Specific | Vocab | • What does [word] mean here? |

Lesson 4: Mastering the Questions

## 11

In line 25, the word "target" most nearly means

Restate _____

Recall _____

A) landing site.
B) local area.
C) financial constraint.
D) research goal.

Resolve  Ⓐ Ⓑ Ⓒ Ⓓ    Confidence __/5

## 12

The word "encounter" in line 42 most nearly means

Restate _____

Recall _____

A) interacts with.
B) adds to.
C) dissolves into.
D) cools down.

Resolve  Ⓐ Ⓑ Ⓒ Ⓓ    Confidence __/5

---

Write your own **vocabulary-in-context** question (use the core question prompts on the previous page to help)

Restate _____

Prompt _____

Recall _____

## Where Do They Say? How Do You Know? Evidence Questions

The evidence-based reasoning questions give many students trouble. Most standardized tests don't include questions that directly ask you for the line numbers to support your answer, but the SAT does. The test makers describe these questions as proof that students can "cite textual evidence."

There is only one stock prompt for these evidenced-based reasoning questions.

**L.2**

Which choice provides the best evidence for the answer to the previous question?

**J.10**

Which choice provides the best evidence for the answer to the previous question?

Sometimes, you'll know the answer to these questions immediately. This is part of the reason you should **underline** and **annotate** the passages, so you know where to find the evidence to support your answers. If the correct answer doesn't just pop out at you, however, you can always resolve the question by working your way through the four answer sections and seeing which contains the information you used to answer the previous question.

I get the following questions from students a lot:

- My answer for question 14 doesn't appear in question 15. What should I do?

- I think question 14 is C, but for 15 I like A, which would make 14 be D. What do I do?

- I don't know the answer to 14, and question 15 is about 14. What do I do?

These are good questions to be asking yourself when you are taking the test. Remember when I said that 75% of the answer choices are lies? These questions are a little bit different since the answer choices are really just sentences from the passage. That doesn't mean that they don't have the potential to mislead you, but you can trust your intuition on these. *If question 15 leads you to change your opinion on question 14, change your answer on 14 to match.* In other words, you can change your answer when you have new evidence.

We'll be looking at evidence questions on each of the next two question types, as they appear most frequently following detail and inference.

|  | Recognize (Question Type) | Restate (Core Questions) |
|---|---|---|
| General |  | (Specific only) |
| Specific | Evidence | • Where does the passage talk about this? <br> • What led you to your last answer? <br> • How do you know the previous question? |

Lesson 4: Mastering the Questions

## What Do They Say? Detail Questions

Detail questions abound on the SAT. The test makers describe this as "explicit meaning" questions, as they ask you about what the passage actually says ("information and ideas"), rather than your logical conclusions about the passage.

**Detail** questions can frequently be recognized by their question stems.

> **5.42**
> According to the passage, Maguire's findings regarding taxi drivers are significant because they

> **K.8**
> The passage indicates that problems arising from desegregation were

Though they don't follow the same question stem, detail questions can also be phrased as direct questions.

> **5.26**
> Which statement best expresses a relationship between organic farming and conventional farming that is presented in the passage?

If the question gives you a line number, *go back and reread the sentences before and after the line(s)*. In fact, the line itself will frequently suggest something the opposite of the correct answer (they are tricky like that!).

Detail questions without line numbers are frequent subjects of evidence-based reasoning questions. If you have no idea where to go, the next question may give you some hints. If the question does not give a line number, you should **rely on your annotations and underlining** to get you to the right portion of the passage.

*Always* justify your answers to detail questions. Even if the next question is not an evidence question, detail questions come straight from the passage, so you should be able to answer them by citing textual evidence.

|  | Recognize (Question Type) | Restate (Core Questions) |
| --- | --- | --- |
| Specific | Line Numbers | • What do lines ## say? <br> • What does paragraph # say? |
| Specific | Open-ended | • What is [something]? <br> • What does the author/passage state about [something]? <br> • (Often followed by Evidence Question) |

### 13

According to the passage, Calcium perchlorate absorbs water molecules when

Restate _____

Recall _____

A) the relative humidity exceeds certain levels.
B) the temperature drops below freezing.
C) Martian streams and lakes form.
D) the soil dries.

Resolve  Ⓐ Ⓑ Ⓒ Ⓓ    Confidence ___/5

### 14

Which choice provides the best evidence for the answer to the previous question?

Restate _____

Recall _____

A) Lines 5-9 ("Calcium perchlorate ... water")
B) Lines 16-19 ("They indicate ... sunrise")
C) Lines 42-46 ("The air ... deliquescence")
D) Lines 57-60 ("Following ... life")

Resolve  Ⓐ Ⓑ Ⓒ Ⓓ    Confidence ___/5

### 15

Lines 5-9 ("Calcium ... water") indicate that the Curiosity mission

Restate _____

Recall _____

A) will eventually bring liquid brine from Mars back to Earth.
B) is the second mission to identify Calcium perchlorate in the Martian soil.
C) is unlikely to produce reliable data in cold and wet climates.
D) inserts liquid brine into the Martian surface.

Resolve  Ⓐ Ⓑ Ⓒ Ⓓ    Confidence ___/5

###

Write your own **line number detail** question (use the core question prompts on the previous page to help)

Restate _____

Prompt _____

Recall _____

Lesson 4: Mastering the Questions

## What If...? Inference Questions

**Inference** questions ask you to pull information out of the text, what the test makers call the "implicit meaning" of the text.

These questions ask you to draw an "if/then" conclusion. The "if" is something in the passage, and the "then" is the inference you should draw. For example, if I tell you that I grabbed an umbrella on the way out, you can infer that it might rain (or at least that I think it might rain). This would be an appropriate "inference or logical conclusion" from the data provided. A detail question would be "What did I grab on the way out?" The stock prompts typically include qualifying words to let you know that it's an inference question.

**5.13**

In Passage 1, Beecher implies that women's effect on public life is largely

**L.2**

The passage implies that Leibniz

There is a second kind of inference question, the "paired inference" question, that asks you how one author would respond to the other. We'll look at those shortly.

Many students struggle with inference questions because they make leaps in logic that extend beyond what the passage can support. Their "logical conclusions" can sometimes seem like they came from a totally different passage. I can offer three pieces of good news:

1. **Many inference questions have line numbers telling you where to look.** As with the detail questions, read before and after the lines in question to get the right answer.

2. Even if the question itself doesn't have line numbers, **inference questions are frequently paired with evidence questions.** This gives you four sections to read, *one of which contains the correct answer.*

3. **Your annotations and underlining can guide you.** Just because the passage doesn't explicitly state something doesn't mean that it's not in there, you just have to tease it out from the passage.

While inference questions can be a little harder than detail questions, the better your reading of the passage (*underline, annotate, identify*), the easier they become.

|  | Recognize (Question Type) | Restate (Core Questions) |
|---|---|---|
| Specific | Line Number | • What can you infer from lines ##? <br> • What do lines ## imply? |
| Specific | Open-Ended | • What does passage/paragraph # imply? <br> • What can be inferred about [topic/character/person]? <br> • (Often followed by Evidence Question) |

### 16

It is most likely that Gale Crater is

Restate _____

Recall _____

A) warmer than other sites of Calcium perchlorate.

B) home to microbial life.

C) a well-known deposit of Calcium perchlorates.

D) the result of a meteorite impact.

Resolve  Ⓐ Ⓑ Ⓒ Ⓓ     Confidence ___/5

### 17

Which choice provides the best evidence for the answer to the previous question?

Restate _____

Recall _____

A) Lines 46-49 ("Perchlorate salts…planet")

B) Lines 50-52 ("Gale Crater … shading")

C) Lines 57-60 ("Following … life")

D) Lines 60-63 ("Now … evolved")

Resolve  Ⓐ Ⓑ Ⓒ Ⓓ     Confidence ___/5

### 18

It can be inferred from the passage that Javier Martin-Torres is

Restate _____

Recall _____

A) expecting Curiosity to discover microbial life on Mars.

B) the first scientist to study Martian brine.

C) optimistic future expeditions could provide evidence of microbial life.

D) an expert on the formation of climates that support human habitation.

Resolve  Ⓐ Ⓑ Ⓒ Ⓓ     Confidence ___/5

---

Write your own **line number inference** question (use the core question prompts on the previous page to help)

Restate _____

Prompt _____

Recall _____

Lesson 4: Mastering the Questions

## What are the Numbers? Data Questions

Charts and graphs questions appear on two passages per test: one will be a science passage and one will be a social studies passage. There are typically a total of five or six data questions. (Note: We haven't seen any data questions in previous passages, so all the samples here come from the official practice tests).

**Data specific** questions ask focused questions about the charts or graphs. The prompt will point you to the data and ask you to analyze the data itself.

> **1.31**
> Which of the following claims is supported by figure 2?

> **1.28**
> Based on the table and passage, which choice gives the correct percentages of the purines in yeast DNA?

**Data synthesis** questions ask you to compare either (1) the data to the passage or (2) passage to the data.

> **1.21**
> The authors would likely attribute the differences in gift-giver and recipient mean appreciation as represented in the graph to

> **5.41**
> Data in the chart provide the most direct support for which idea in the passage?

When you were annotating the passage, you should have noted the caption, the axes, and the general trends in the data. Many of the questions can be resolved by looking at your annotations.

For our passage on the Curiosity rover, the chart indicates that there are large amounts of surface liquids at night and small amounts of subsurface liquids during the day. If you are asked for specific numbers in the data, simply read the chart and find the answer within. If you are looking for line numbers, you should treat the question like an evidence question, reading the lines and checking them against the passage. You can also practice the Khan Academy problem solving and data analysis questions.

|  | Recognize (Question Type) | Restate (Core Questions) |
|---|---|---|
| Specific | Data Specific | • What do the data say? |
| Synthesis | Data Synthesis | • Where do the passage and data agree? <br> • Where do the figures and tables agree or disagree with each other? <br> • What do the data support? |

### 19

The data in figure 1 most directly support which idea in the passage?

Restate _____

Recall _____

A) Previous studies have found brine beneath the surface.

B) Calcium perchlorate absorbs liquid quickly.

C) Higher latitudes have more liquid brine than lower latitudes.

D) Surface liquid brines evaporate during the day.

Resolve  Ⓐ Ⓑ Ⓒ Ⓓ        Confidence ___/5

### 20

Which lines provide information supported by the data?

Restate _____

Recall _____

A) Lines 9–13 ("This has ... conditions")

B) Lines 16-19 ("They indicate ... sunrise")

C) Lines 28-32 ("Conditions ... processes")

D) Lines 38-41 ("Curiosity ... nights)"

Resolve  Ⓐ Ⓑ Ⓒ Ⓓ        Confidence ___/5

### 21

What time of day had greatest the disparity between observations of surface and subsurface liquids?

Restate _____

Recall _____

A) Before dawn (2:30-5:00 Standard Martian Time)

B) Mid-morning (5:00-10:30 Standard Martian Time)

C) Mid-day (10:30-18:00 Standard Martian Time)

D) Night (22:00-02:30 Standard Martian Time)

Resolve  Ⓐ Ⓑ Ⓒ Ⓓ        Confidence ___/5

---

Write your own **data** question (use the core question prompts on the previous page to help)

Restate _____

Prompt _____

Recall _____

Lesson 4: Mastering the Questions

# Where Are the Authors Different? Paired Passage Questions

There is always one set of paired passages on the test. Though not exclusively, these passages are typically historical arguments. The paired passage questions are typically the final questions of the set, sometimes broken up with evidence-based reasoning questions.

The most common questions are **paired synthesis**. The stock prompts for paired passage all deal with either the relationship between the passages, details they do or do not share, and points of agreement and disagreement.

**1.49**
Which statement best describes the relationship between the passages?

**5.20**
Based on the passages, both authors would agree with which of the following claims?

Other questions are **paired specific** questions, asking you to infer what one author would say about a specific point in the other author's argument.

**1.50**
The author of Passage 2 would most likely respond to the discussion of the future of space mining in lines 18-28, Passage 1, by claiming that such a future

**5.21**
Beecher would most likely have reacted to lines 65-68 ("Now … woman") of Passage 2 with

You can actually start resolving these questions while you are reading the passage by noting where the authors agree and disagree. Sometimes, one of the passages will be a direct response written for that exact purpose or as part of a wider conversation in society.

Paired passages get to the essence of what an author is saying by giving you a direct foil for their position. This does not always mean that they are in opposition. After all, they must agree on the importance of the issue at hand, otherwise, they would not have bothered to write at all!

To help you practice, here is an abbreviated paired passage set. After reading the passages, try the four questions on the next pages. You'll then have the opportunity to write a few paired passage questions yourself. You can find my marked up passage and solutions for all the questions accompany the passage, including the **restate**, **recall**, and **resolve** steps on page S-23 in the solution manual.

|           | Recognize (Question Type) | Restate (Core Questions) |
|-----------|---------------------------|--------------------------|
| Specific  | Paired Inference          | • What would author 1 say about author 2?<br>• (Often followed by Evidence Question) |
| Synthesis | Paired Synthesis          | • Where do the passages agree?<br>• Where do the passages disagree?<br>• What is the relationship between the passages? |

# PRACTICE PASSAGE: HISTORY (PAIRED, ANTIQUATED ENGLISH)

Passage 1 is adapted from Abigail Adams's letter to her husband John Adams, March 31, 1776. Passage 2 is adapted from John Adams's response, April 14, 1776.

**Passage 1**

I long to hear that you have declared an independency. And, by the way, in the new code of laws which I suppose it will be necessary for you to
5 make, I desire you would remember the ladies and be more generous and favorable to them than your ancestors. Do not put such unlimited power into the hands of the husbands. Remember, all men would be tyrants if they could. If particular care and attention is
10 not paid to the ladies, we are determined to foment a rebellion, and will not hold ourselves bound by any laws in which we have no voice or representation.

That your sex are naturally tyrannical is a truth so thoroughly established as to admit of no dispute; but
15 such of you as wish to be happy willingly give up the harsh title of master for the more tender and endearing one of friend. Why, then, not put it out of the power of the vicious and the lawless to use us with cruelty and indignity with impunity? Men of sense in all ages
20 abhor those customs which treat us only as the vassals of your sex; regard us then as beings placed by Providence under your protection, and in imitation of the Supreme Being make use of that power only for our happiness.

**Passage 2**

25 As to Declarations of Independency, be patient ...
As to your extraordinary code of laws, I cannot but laugh. We have been told that our struggle has loosened the bands of government everywhere: that children and apprentices were disobedient; that
30 schools and colleges were grown turbulent; that Indians slighted their guardians and Negroes grew insolent to their masters.

But your letter was the first intimation that another tribe more numerous and powerful than all the rest
35 were grown discontented. This is rather too coarse a compliment but you are so saucy, I wont blot it out.

Depend upon it, we know better than to repeal our masculine systems. Although they are in full force, you know they are little more than theory. We dare not
40 exert our power in its full latitude. We are obliged to go fair, and softly, and in practice you know we are the subjects. We have only the name of masters, and rather than give up this, which would completely subject us to the despotism of the petticoat, I hope General
45 Washington, and all our brave heroes would fight. I am sure every good politician would plot, as long as he would against despotism, empire, monarchy, aristocracy, oligarchy, or ochlocracy[1] — a fine story

[1] Mob Rule

**1**

Both authors would likely agree that

Restate _____

Recall _____

A) if women are not given an equal vote, then they will revolt.
B) women have a greater capacity for generosity than men.
C) society is prone to disruption by despots.
D) only the most just rulers should have unlimited powers.

Resolve  Ⓐ Ⓑ Ⓒ Ⓓ      Confidence ___/5

**2**

Unlike Passage 1, Passage 2 discusses

Restate _____

Recall _____

A) international relations.
B) civil disturbances within the Colonies.
C) the rights of Native Americans and women.
D) early attempts to abolish slavery.

Resolve  Ⓐ Ⓑ Ⓒ Ⓓ      Confidence ___/5

Lesson 4: Mastering the Questions

### 3

It can reasonably be inferred that Abigail Adams would respond to lines 39-42 in Passage 2 ("We dare ... masters") by

Restate _____

Recall _____

A) rejecting John Adams's assessment of gender relations.

B) laughing at John Adams's playful banter.

C) accepting John Adams's portrayal of the legal system.

D) condemning John Adams as a tyrant.

Resolve  Ⓐ Ⓑ Ⓒ Ⓓ     Confidence ___/5

### 4

Which choice provides the best evidence for the answer to the previous question?

Restate _____

Recall _____

A) Lines 4-6 ("I desire ... ancestors")

B) Lines 9-10 ("If ... rebellion")

C) Lines 13-14 ("That ... dispute")

D) Lines 19-21 ("Men ... sex")

Resolve  Ⓐ Ⓑ Ⓒ Ⓓ     Confidence ___/5

---

Write your own **paired synthesis** question (use the core question prompts on the previous page to help)

Restate _____

Prompt _____

Recall _____

Write your own **paired specific** question (use the core question prompts on the previous page to help)

Restate _____

Prompt _____

Recall _____

# PRACTICE TEST: OFFICIAL TEST 6

You didn't wake up one day tying your shoes like a champ (or, at least, I've never met anyone who did). Why would you expect yourself to be magically great at answering standardized test questions?

Let's apply the skills you've learned in this lesson to a practice test. As you take the practice test, bolster your ability to understand the questions. Restate, recall, and resolve the questions using the three-step process:

1. **Restate:** What is it that the prompt is asking you?

2. **Recall:** How would you answer your paraphrased question?

3. **Resolve:** Which of the four answer choices gives the best answer to the prompt? What is your confidence?

As you work on understanding the questions, don't forget to be working on understanding the passages. **Underline**, **Annotate**, and **Identify** *every* passage on *every* test.

| Questions | General | Specific | Synthesis |
|---|---|---|---|
| Main Purpose | Purpose | Function | |
| Main Idea | Thesis | Topic | |
| Tone | Tone | Attitude | |
| Rhetoric | Structure | Argument | |
| Vocabulary | | Vocabulary | |
| Evidence | | Evidence | |
| Detail | | Detail | |
| Inference | | Inference | |
| Data | | Data Specific | Data Synthesis |
| Paired | | Paired Specific | Paired Synthesis |

Section 1 of Test 6 is on page 818 in the *Official SAT Study Guide*. You can find a free PDF on Khan Academy's website. There is a mirrored copy of the test as well at www.professorscompanion.com/sat.

Good luck, and don't forget to fill out the self-diagnostic on the next page!

## SELF-EVALUATION TEST 6

| | | | | | | |
|---|---|---|---|---|---|---|
| **Passage 1** | I felt confident during the first passage. | Strongly Agree | Somewhat Agree | No Opinion | Somewhat Disagree | Strongly Disagree |
| | Describe in two to three sentences how you felt on the first passage | | | | | |
| **Passage 2** | I felt confident during the second passage. | Strongly Agree | Somewhat Agree | No Opinion | Somewhat Disagree | Strongly Disagree |
| | Describe in two to three sentences how you felt on the second passage | | | | | |
| **Passage 3** | I felt confident during the third passage. | Strongly Agree | Somewhat Agree | No Opinion | Somewhat Disagree | Strongly Disagree |
| | Describe in two to three sentences how you felt on the third passage | | | | | |
| **Passage 4** | I felt confident during the fourth passage. | Strongly Agree | Somewhat Agree | No Opinion | Somewhat Disagree | Strongly Disagree |
| | Describe in two to three sentences how you felt on the fourth passage | | | | | |
| **Passage 5** | I felt confident during the fifth passage. | Strongly Agree | Somewhat Agree | No Opinion | Somewhat Disagree | Strongly Disagree |
| | Describe in two to three sentences how you felt on the fifth passage | | | | | |
| **Overall** | I felt confident during the reading section. | Strongly Agree | Somewhat Agree | No Opinion | Somewhat Disagree | Strongly Disagree |
| | I had enough time for the reading section. | Strongly Agree | Somewhat Agree | No Opinion | Somewhat Disagree | Strongly Disagree |
| | I cared about the passages I read. | Strongly Agree | Somewhat Agree | No Opinion | Somewhat Disagree | Strongly Disagree |
| | In three to four sentences, describe how you feel about the reading section | | | | | |

# LESSON 5: MASTERING THE ANSWERS

While understanding the question prompt is the first step, it is, of course, not how you get the points. Neither is recalling the answer to their question. They are important steps to getting you to the right answer, but you only get the points when you bubble in the correct letter. In other words, you get the points when you resolve the prompt and answer the question. *But how do you know what the correct answer is?*

After you restate and recall, there are essentially two outcomes you can plan for: when your recalled answer is in the answer bank and when your recalled answer isn't in the answer bank (or you don't have a recalled answer).

## WHEN YOUR RECALLED ANSWER IS IN THE ANSWER BANK

It's great when the answer you came up with during the recall step matches one of the answer choices. *You should tentatively give that answer with a 4/5 confidence*, then check to see if any of the other three options answers the question better, *just* in case. Every now and then, you'll have an answer that matches your recalled answer, but then you find something in the answer bank that you prefer. If you are a 5/5 confidence that answer is correct, you should switch your answer. Otherwise, go with your gut recalled answer.

## WHEN YOUR RECALLED ANSWER ISN'T IN THE ANSWER BANK

Even when you've restated and recalled the question, sometimes the answer you came up with *doesn't match any of the answers* the test creators had in mind. Or, even more distressing, *you don't have a recalled answer* to work with. Some students break out into a sweat. Some students just stare blankly at the passage. Others start jumping to answers that seem right even if they know that it's wrong. It's a pretty hopeless feeling.

All is not lost! The correct answer is one of the four answer choices in front of you. But which one is it? You can use the process of elimination to **resolve** the question.

There are two kinds of answer choices: **right answers** and **wrong answers**. The trick is to figure out which is which.

## Right Answer Types

The College Board describes the SAT as testing students' ability to support their reasoning with evidence. When you are looking for the right answer to bubble in, you're looking to support your answer with evidence.

- For **general questions**, the rights answer comes from the passage on the whole and your identification can be your evidence.

- For **specific questions with line numbers**, the sentences *before* and *after* the lines in question are the best places to look for evidence. For some questions, like the vocabulary-in-context questions, it's a matter of figuring out what the word means. Line-specific function and argument questions go back to the author's overarching purpose.

- For **specific questions without line numbers**, you should be able to point to lines that support your answer. You can almost pretend it will be followed with an evidence question: "How do you know that this the right answer?"

- For **evidence questions**, confirm your answer to the previous question. You'll frequently find the incorrect answers for the previous question are suitable words but wrong in these lines.

If the right answer doesn't jump out at you (5/5 confidence), you can increase your confidence by crossing out wrong answers. But how do you know if an answer is wrong?

## Wrong Answer Types

Three out of four answer choices is wrong. 75% of them are trying to lead you astray. If you succumb to their siren call, you will be denied the points your reading and question analysis has merited. *Wrong answers snatch defeat from the jaws of victory.*

So how do you avoid this trap? Keep your eyes open and look for what makes an answer wrong. There are patterns to wrong answer choices. Remember, **even if the right answer were eliminated, the wrong answers are still incorrect**. In other words, they are wrong for a reason, not just because there is a better answer.

The easiest to find are the answers that are **flatly false** and aren't supported by the passage.

Other wrong answers are somewhat harder to adjudicate, as they are **somewhat right**. They have a kernel of the right answer in there, but there is some fatal flaw. They may be too broad or too narrow. They could be an extreme version of the right answer. Here's the trick: *"Somewhat right" is entirely wrong.* The right answer isn't just partially correct, and so the somewhat right answers can be crossed out.

A different version of the somewhat correct are the answer choices that use **tempting words but don't answer the question** completely. They may be from the wrong part of the passage. They could use words from the passage, but they could be rearranged to give an incorrect interpretation. They could also be true, but irrelevant for the question at hand. These answer choices all lack *something*. **"Tempting words but" is a wrong answer.**

After you have read through the answer choices, the time comes to **resolve** the question. You can use the following table to help you judge between the wrong and right answers.

| If the answer choice is... | then it is... | and it should be... |
|---|---|---|
| right | correct | bubbled in. |
| flatly <u>false</u> | incorrect | crossed off. |
| somewhat right, but <u>too broad</u> | incorrect | crossed off. |
| somewhat right, but <u>too narrow</u> | incorrect | crossed off. |
| somewhat right, but <u>too extreme</u> | incorrect | crossed off. |
| tempting words, but <u>wrong part</u> | incorrect | crossed off. |
| tempting words, but <u>not true</u> | incorrect | crossed off. |
| tempting words, but <u>irrelevant</u> | incorrect | crossed off |
| mostly right | incorrect | crossed off... but bubbled in if it's the only answer left. |

Of these options, the hardest one to adjudicate is the "mostly right." These borderline cases can cause students a lot of grief, in part because you do not always have perfect knowledge of what is correct and incorrect. After you've eliminated all the very wrong answers, you can sometimes be left with two answer choices that you feel are mostly right. When this happens, *ask yourself which gives the better response to the core question.*

You can also flag the question to check your answer if you have time at the end of the passage (pacing!). Evidence-based questions can guide you to an answer. Alternatively, reviewing the passage when answering question 9 sometimes gives you a better idea of question 2. After reading the rest of the questions, if there's an answer to question 2 that you prefer, go with your preferred answer.

Again, the correct answer is right because it is supported by the passages. The incorrect answers are wrong, either because they are **false**, they are **only somewhat true** (but not completely), or use **tempting words but** do not answer the question correctly.

Lesson 5: Mastering the Answers

# WHEN SHOULD YOU SWITCH YOUR ANSWER?

While you can change your answer if reading the passage has changed your mind, I can't count the number of times a student says, "I had (C) bubbled and changed my answer to (D)." This is usually followed by a guttural "ugh," a soft sigh, or primeval "No!!!!" Changing a correct answer to an incorrect one is one of the most frustrating parts of taking standardized tests.

**When should you switch your answer?** When you can meet one of three criteria:

- You have 100% confidence another answer is right. *Switch!*

- You have 100% confidence your initial answer is wrong. *Switch!*

- You have 80% confidence your initial answer is wrong *and* 80% confidence another answer is right. *Switch!*

Changing your answer because you have reread the passage and have a new interpretation of what you previously read is fine, but don't go changing just because you aren't sure of what the answer is. This will waste time, and besides, your initial answer is more likely to be correct than the answer you settle on after a torturous deliberation and coin flip.

Don't put yourself through the pain and agony of switching off the correct answer. Trust your instincts and your confidence in your answers.

## WHAT SHOULD YOU DO IF YOU GET STREAKS OF THE SAME LETTER?

It can be a little unnerving to get a string of the same answers. Let's say that you have four C's in a row from questions 12-15. It's not likely, but it does happen. But now on question 16, you think the answer is C. You're pretty sure C is right, 80% confidence. But they wouldn't put five C's in row, would they?

First, they have **strings of three of the same letter all the time**. They can and do have **strings of four**; it's not common, but it does happen. If you think the fifth answer is C, then bubble in C!

Second, **the string could be an allusion because of an incorrect answer along the way.** You've bubbled in 12-15 as C, but then you get to 16 and you start to get in your head. So you bubble in D.

|    | Answers |
|----|---------|
| 12 | Ⓐ Ⓑ ● Ⓓ |
| 13 | Ⓐ Ⓑ ● Ⓓ |
| 14 | Ⓐ Ⓑ ● Ⓓ |
| 15 | Ⓐ Ⓑ ● Ⓓ |
| 16 | Ⓐ Ⓑ Ⓒ ● |

However, what if you were wrong on one of the answers that preceded it? Answer 16 is the one that got in your head, but you actually answered question 14 incorrectly.

|    | Your Answers | Correct Answers | Correct? |
|----|--------------|-----------------|----------|
| 12 | Ⓐ Ⓑ ● Ⓓ | Ⓐ Ⓑ ● Ⓓ | Yes |
| 13 | Ⓐ Ⓑ ● Ⓓ | Ⓐ Ⓑ ● Ⓓ | Yes |
| 14 | Ⓐ Ⓑ ● Ⓓ | Ⓐ ● Ⓒ Ⓓ | No |
| 15 | Ⓐ Ⓑ ● Ⓓ | Ⓐ Ⓑ ● Ⓓ | Yes |
| 16 | Ⓐ Ⓑ Ⓒ ● | Ⓐ Ⓑ ● Ⓓ | No |

If you worry about streaky answers, you let your mistake on question 14 count against you twice. If you have time at the end of the passage, you could check each of these questions, but don't hurry to go sniffing for a mistake—that kind of thinking can cost you the time you need to get questions 50, 51, and 52 right at the end of the section.

If you think 16 is C, then bubble in C. **Don't compound your mistakes!**

Lesson 5: Mastering the Answers

# GET THE POINTS YOU HAVE EARNED

Figuring out why wrong answers are incorrect and right answers are correct is a powerful tool for test takers, but only if you spend time practicing. So let's try a passage geared toward practicing this strategy.

Start, as always, with **underline**, **identify**, and **annotate**. *Don't forget to annotate the data.* Make sure you have a sketch for what the charts and graphs tell you before you jump to the questions. You may want to spend an additional 30 seconds looking over the passage as well, as the questions on this passage are tough.

Next, turn to the questions. For each of the questions on this passage, you should give the **question type**.

| Recognizes | General | Specific | Synthesis |
|---|---|---|---|
| Main Purpose | Purpose | Function | |
| Main Idea | Thesis | Topic | |
| Tone | Tone | Attitude | |
| Rhetoric | Structure | Argument | |
| Vocabulary | | Vocabulary | |
| Evidence | | Evidence | |
| Detail | | Detail | |
| Inference | | Inference | |
| Data | | Data Specific | Data Synthesis |
| Paired | | Paired Specific | Paired Synthesis |

Then, look at the answers and for A-D, give the **answer type**. If the answer is wrong, indicate why it is wrong. If it is right, give your evidence, including the line numbers or annotations that make the answer the correct choice. I've put a little cheat sheet at the end of the questions to help you remember.

| Answer Types | Reason |
|---|---|
| Wrong | Somewhat right, but too broad |
| Wrong | Somewhat right, but too narrow |
| Wrong | Somewhat right, but too extreme |
| Wrong | Tempting words, but wrong part |
| Wrong | Tempting words, but not true |
| Wrong | Tempting words, but irrelevant |
| Wrong | Flatly false |
| Right (general): | Give identify evidence |
| Right (specific): | Give line or annotation evidence |
| Right (synthesis): | Give identify evidence |

You can find my marked up passage and solutions for all the questions accompanying the passage, including my notes for **restate**, **recall**, and even **resolve**, on page S-26 in the solution manual.

# PRACTICE PASSAGE: SOCIAL STUDIES (WITH DATA)

The following passage is adapted from Derek Kan, "Roundtable on Data for Automated Vehicle Safety," published by the U.S. Department of Transportation, 2018.

Increasingly, personal cars and commercial trucks operate with varying degrees of computer assistance, which range from driver assistance to full automation. These Automated Driving Systems (ADS) use visual, positional, and radar data for safety and navigation.

For public transportation officials, vehicle manufacturing companies, and technological experts, they are also a goldmine of data. To mine this motherlode, the United States Department of Transportation (USDOT) established federal guidance for collection and dissemination of the data obtained from automated vehicles.

Industry experts believe that within and across all modes of transportation, data exchanges will be key to accelerating the safe deployment of automated vehicles in the United States. This includes the mutually beneficial exchange of data among private sector entities, infrastructure operators, and policy makers from various levels of government.

Planning and executing such exchanges can be difficult. Data are often siloed, but the USDOT can serve as a convener and facilitator to encourage collaboration in overcoming these challenges. By bringing together thought leaders in their respective areas of expertise, the federal government can collectively consider what voluntary data exchanges should look like and how they can be leveraged to accelerate the safe rollout of automated vehicles.

To act on this vision, the Department hosted the Roundtable on Data for Automated Vehicle Safety in December of 2017. This event brought together over sixty participants from federal, state, and local governments, the private sector (car manufacturers and software companies), transportation-based non-profit organizations, and research institutions to discuss the data exchanges that these participants believe are most critical to the safe deployment of automated vehicles. This roundtable was a key step toward developing a shared understanding of the data to be collected and exchanged, the purpose, and the federal government's unique role in facilitating voluntary data exchanges.

The Roundtable provided the USDOT with many diverse suggestions for next steps in facilitating near-term, voluntary automated vehicle data exchanges. The wide range of roundtable participants provided their initial feedback on core documents that the USDOT plans to refine and use to help organize this work and communicate priorities. Collectively, the various roundtable participants discussed five key areas that can be prioritized for voluntary data exchanges. And, finally, roundtable participants discussed overarching challenges and how the USDOT can help provide solutions.

Much of the day's discussions centered on new initiatives, new technical solutions, and the need for new data. This included not only increasing data collection and management through established channels, but also considering relatively novel approaches. For example, several breakout groups discussed the potential use of crowdsourcing for developing more detailed roadway inventories or real-time incident reporting.

At the same time, some participants noted that there is untapped value in existing data and data exchange models. Many mentioned improving current datasets as an immediate focus to advance emerging automated vehicle technologies. They also suggested studying existing initiatives that can serve as examples for further work by the government and private sector.

| ADS Available Options on Commercial Vehicles | Rank |
| --- | --- |
| Adaptive Cruise Control | 3.8 |
| Forward Collision Warnings | 2.7 |
| GPS Navigation Systems | 4.2 |
| Tire pressure monitoring systems | 4.5 |
| Vehicle-to-Vehicle Warnings | 1.8 |

Figure 1 – Desirability of five safety features according to a survey of commercial truck drivers (one was most preferred and five was least preferred). Adapted from the National Highway Traffic Safety Administration, 2016.

| Level | Name | Steering and Speed | Environmental Monitoring | Emergency Maneuvers | Driving Modes |
|---|---|---|---|---|---|
| 0 | No automation | 👤 | 👤 | 👤 | N/A |
| 1 | Driver Assistance | 👤🚗 | 👤 | 👤 | Some |
| 2 | Partial Automation | 🚗 | 👤 | 👤 | Some |
| 3 | Conditional Automation | 🚗 | 🚗 | 👤 | Some |
| 4 | High Automation | 🚗 | 🚗 | 👤🚗 | Some |
| 5 | Full Automation | 🚗 | 🚗 | 🚗 | All |

Figure 2 – "Levels of vehicle automation according to the Society of Automotive Engineers (SAE) International."

### 1

The passage is primarily concerned with

Recognize _____

A) the increasing automation of transportation in both public and private sectors.

Answer Type _____

B) the need to regulate automated vehicles and the collection of personal data.

Answer Type _____

C) how to collect and distribute new and existing data from automated vehicles.

Answer Type _____

D) the technical specifications automated vehicles use for navigation.

Answer Type _____

Resolve     Ⓐ Ⓑ Ⓒ Ⓓ     Confidence ___/5

### 2

The passage indicates that one potential source of real-time data collection could be

Recognize _____

A) government officials

Answer Type _____

B) state and local traffic cameras

Answer Type _____

C) everyday citizens

Answer Type _____

D) car manufacturing companies

Answer Type _____

Resolve     Ⓐ Ⓑ Ⓒ Ⓓ     Confidence ___/5

### 3

Which choice provides the best evidence for the answer to the previous question?

Recognize _____

A) Lines 31-33 ("This events … governments")

Answer Type _____

B) Lines 33-34 ("the private … companies")

Answer Type _____

C) Lines 49-54 ("Collectively … solutions")

Answer Type _____

D) Lines 60-63 ("several … reporting")

Answer Type _____

Resolve     Ⓐ Ⓑ Ⓒ Ⓓ     Confidence ___/5

## 4

In lines 16-19 ("this ... government") the author anticipates which of the following objections to the collection of ADS data?

Recognize _____

A) Sharing data will be detrimental to private companies.

Answer Type _____

B) Governmental control of transportation data is unnecessary.

Answer Type _____

C) Private industries cannot be responsible for ADS safety regulations.

Answer Type _____

D) Centralized collection of data slows innovation.

Answer Type _____

Resolve   Ⓐ Ⓑ Ⓒ Ⓓ   Confidence ___/5

## 5

As used in line 21, the word "siloed" most nearly means

Recognize _____

A) isolated.

Answer Type _____

B) archived.

Answer Type _____

C) compiled.

Answer Type _____

D) digitized.

Answer Type _____

Resolve   Ⓐ Ⓑ Ⓒ Ⓓ   Confidence ___/5

| Questions | General | Specific | Synthesis | Answers | Reason |
|---|---|---|---|---|---|
| Main Purpose | Purpose | Function | | Wrong | Somewhat right, but too broad |
| Main Idea | Thesis | Topic | | Wrong | Somewhat right, but too narrow |
| Tone | Tone | Attitude | | Wrong | Somewhat right, but too extreme |
| Rhetoric | Structure | Argument | | Wrong | Tempting words, but wrong part |
| Vocabulary | | Vocabulary | | Wrong | Tempting words, but not true |
| Evidence | | Evidence | | Wrong | Tempting words, but irrelevant |
| Detail | | Detail | | Wrong | Flatly false |
| Inference | | Inference | | Right (general): | Give identify evidence |
| Data | | Data Specific | Data Synthesis | Right (specific): | Give line or annotation evidence |
| Paired | | Paired Specific | Paired Synthesis | Right (synthesis): | Give identify evidence |

Lesson 5: Mastering the Answers

## 6

The main idea of the fourth paragraph (lines 20-28) is that

Recognize _____

A) the federal government is best suited to collect and disseminate ADS data.

Answer Type _____

B) the difficulties inherent in data collection can be reduced through market actions.

Answer Type _____

C) the Department of Transportation has an oversized role in the management of ADS data.

Answer Type _____

D) the current safety standards for ADS are insufficient.

Answer Type _____

Resolve  Ⓐ Ⓑ Ⓒ Ⓓ    Confidence ___/5

## 7

In line 59, the word "novel" most nearly means

Recognize _____

A) written

Answer Type _____

B) fresh

Answer Type _____

C) technical

Answer Type _____

D) narrative

Answer Type _____

Resolve  Ⓐ Ⓑ Ⓒ Ⓓ    Confidence ___/5

## 8

The main purpose of the final paragraph (lines 64-70) is to

Recognize _____

A) suggest methods of developing new automated vehicle prototypes.

Answer Type _____

B) argue that the existing data is insufficient.

Answer Type _____

C) outline plans to expand public/private partnerships.

Answer Type _____

D) stress the need to evaluate the current data repositories.

Answer Type _____

Resolve  Ⓐ Ⓑ Ⓒ Ⓓ    Confidence ___/5

## 9

Which statement from the passage is most consistent with figures 1 and 2?

Recognize _____

A) Lines 1-5 ("Cars … navigation")

Answer Type _____

B) Lines 13-16 ("Industry experts … United States")

Answer Type _____

C) Lines 49-51 ("Collectively … exchanges")

Answer Type _____

D) Lines 55-57 ("Much … data")

Answer Type _____

Resolve  Ⓐ Ⓑ Ⓒ Ⓓ    Confidence ___/5

**10**

According to figure 1, which features were most commonly preferred by survey respondents?

Recognize _____

A) Adaptive Cruise Control
Answer Type _____

B) GPS Navigation Systems
Answer Type _____

C) Tire Pressure Monitoring Systems
Answer Type _____

D) Vehicle-to-Vehicle Warnings
Answer Type _____

Resolve  Ⓐ Ⓑ Ⓒ Ⓓ   Confidence ___/5

**11**

According to figure 2, which levels of automation featured both human and machine control of the vehicle?

Recognize _____

A) Levels 0-2
Answer Type _____

B) Levels 1-4
Answer Type _____

C) Levels 3-5
Answer Type _____

D) Level 0 and level 5
Answer Type _____

Resolve  Ⓐ Ⓑ Ⓒ Ⓓ   Confidence ___/5

| Questions | General | Specific | Synthesis | Answers | Reason |
|---|---|---|---|---|---|
| Main Purpose | Purpose | Function | | Wrong | Somewhat right, but too broad |
| Main Idea | Thesis | Topic | | Wrong | Somewhat right, but too narrow |
| Tone | Tone | Attitude | | Wrong | Somewhat right, but too extreme |
| Rhetoric | Structure | Argument | | Wrong | Tempting words, but wrong part |
| Vocabulary | | Vocabulary | | Wrong | Tempting words, but not true |
| Evidence | | Evidence | | Wrong | Tempting words, but irrelevant |
| Detail | | Detail | | Wrong | Flatly false |
| Inference | | Inference | | Right (general): | Give identify evidence |
| Data | | Data Specific | Data Synthesis | Right (specific): | Give line or annotation evidence |
| Paired | | Paired Specific | Paired Synthesis | Right (synthesis): | Give identify evidence |

Trying to decode the wrong answers can be hard, so make sure you check out the solutions and my markup in the solution manual.

It's worth saying that you and I may not agree on all of the answer types. Classification can be more art than science, but these are the ways that I think about each of the wrong answers.

Lesson 5: Mastering the Answers

Let's give another passage a try. This time, you'll have the opportunity to be a little more creative. For each of the questions, you should identify the question type and then write your own answers. For each answer, give the answer type for the wrong answers (*somewhat right, but* and *tempting words, but*) and your evidence for the correct answer (*annotations*, *underlining*, or *identification*).

The central topic of the passage is

| | |
|---|---|
| Recognize | Thesis |
| Restate | What is the passage about? |
| Recall | Benjamin Bloom's taxonomy and its importance for teachers |
| Answer Ⓐ | The development of educational psychology as a tool for teachers |
| Answer Type | Somewhat right, but too narrow |
| Answer Ⓑ | Benjamin Bloom and the legacy of his taxonomy |
| Answer Type | Right (identify) |

For the first four questions, write two answers: one right and one wrong. For the next three, write one right answer and two wrong answers. For the final three questions, write one right answer and three wrong answers. This one's a **social studies without data** passage.

# PRACTICE PASSAGE: SOCIAL STUDIES (WITHOUT DATA)

The following passage is adapted from "Meaningful Learning," by Charles Fraatz. Benjamin Bloom (1913-1999) was an educational psychologist.

In 1956, Benjamin Bloom and a team of educational psychologists published *A Taxonomy of Educational Objectives*. This landmark study established the groundwork for how teachers develop their curricula, from creating learning goals to designing tests to evaluating student work. Bloom's most important innovation was a hierarchical taxonomy to classify learning objectives according to six levels of increasing complexity designed to make student learning meaningful.

In order to explain Bloom's taxonomy, we can engage in an extended hypothetical situation thousands of English teachers face every year. Imagine that you are an English teacher designing a series of assignments based on Shakespeare's *Hamlet*, the classic tale of Prince Hamlet's plot to avenge his father's murder. How might you apply Bloom's taxonomy to the creation of assignments for the Bard's great tragedy?

Bloom's first level is knowledge. This level pertains mostly to the retention of facts: "Who wrote *Hamlet*?" "Who are the main characters in *Hamlet*?" As Bloom defines it, knowledge is fundamental to more complex work. If a student cannot identify what soliloquy is (an extended aside to the audience), they cannot engage in higher-level thinking about Hamlet's monologues.

The second level of Bloom's taxonomy is comprehension. Comprehension requires students to understand the material in greater detail, perhaps interpreting facts or extrapolating information. For example, a quiz question about how Hamlet plans to reveal his uncle's treachery requires students to not only know who Hamlet is, but also to organize their knowledge about the play.

Bloom's third level is application. When students apply their knowledge to abstract situations, they have to comprehend the material and then make use of that information. If a student were asked "How might Ophelia react to Hamlet's madness if she knew his motivations?", their response would go beyond what happened to what might happen in a new context.

Bloom describes his fourth level, analysis, with regard to the organization of material and the understanding of the relationship(s) between the different elements within the material. A test question about how Hamlet's soliloquies disclose the prince's thoughts to the audience, for example, combines students' understanding of the relationship between the play's plot, the protagonist's motivations, and the meaning of his monologues; each is necessary to analyze how the soliloquies reveal Hamlet's thoughts.

The fifth level, synthesis, has elements of the second, third, and fourth levels, but it is more cohesive, widespread, and ultimately innovative than comprehension, application, and analysis. As Bloom describes it, an analysis essay may ask a student to describe the effect of Hamlet's madness upon his mother, but a synthesis asks the student to create their own hypothesis about Hamlet's madness; the student directs their own inquiry. This self-direction generates meaningful payoff for the student's long-term enjoyment of the material.

Bloom's final level, evaluation, should not be seen as the culmination of the five preceding levels, but it appears last because it is contingent upon the others. An essay on the ethical ramifications of Hamlet's actions, asking students to judge the prince's plot to avenge his father, requires a complexity of thought not found in the other levels. One cannot, according to Bloom, make judgments about Hamlet's vengeance without the cognitive ability to know its contents, comprehend the plot and characters, apply this comprehension to new or abstract situations, analyze its constituent parts, and finally synthesize one's thoughts cohesively. Similarly, students' evaluations of a scholar's interpretation require them to employ all the levels in the taxonomy.

Bloom's taxonomy was widely influential in both the US and abroad, having been translated into twenty languages. At the turn of the century, Bloom's student and co-author David Krathwohl and a new generation of educational psychologists revised Bloom's taxonomy. One change was to change the nouns to verbs to indicate the activity of education: students don't *have comprehension*, they *comprehend;* and they don't make analysis, they *analyze*. Krathwohl and his co-editors also condensed the fifth and sixth levels and added a new creative level. Creative learning, they argued, especially the acts of generating hypotheses, planning the tasks and subtasks necessary to test their hypotheses, and ultimately producing something, is the most complex learning objective. Fittingly, Bloom's heirs learned from their teacher and created something new of their own.

## 1

The overall purpose of the passage is to

Recognize _____

Restate _____
_____

Recall _____
_____

Answer Ⓐ _____
_____

Answer Type _____

Answer Ⓑ _____
_____

Answer Type _____

## 2

The author describes Bloom's work as

Recognize _____

Restate _____
_____

Recall _____
_____

Answer Ⓐ _____
_____

Answer Type _____

Answer Ⓑ _____
_____

Answer Type _____

## 3

Which choice provides the best evidence for the answer to the previous question?

Recognize _____

Restate _____
_____

Recall _____
_____

Answer Ⓐ _____
_____

Answer Type _____

Answer Ⓑ _____
_____

Answer Type _____

## 4

The word "designing" in line 6 most nearly means

Recognize _____

Restate _____
_____

Recall _____
_____

Answer Ⓐ _____
_____

Answer Type _____

Answer Ⓑ _____
_____

Answer Type _____

### 5

The hypothetical scenario described in lines 12-20 has the rhetorical effect of

Recognize _____

Restate _____
_____

Recall _____
_____

Answer Ⓐ _____
_____

Answer Type _____

Answer Ⓑ _____
_____

Answer Type _____

Answer Ⓒ _____
_____

Answer Type _____

### 6

Paragraph 7 (lines 56-66) predominantly serves to

Recognize _____

Restate _____
_____

Recall _____
_____

Answer Ⓐ _____
_____

Answer Type _____

Answer Ⓑ _____
_____

Answer Type _____

Answer Ⓒ _____
_____

Answer Type _____

| Questions | General | Specific | Synthesis | Answers | Reason |
|---|---|---|---|---|---|
| Main Purpose | Purpose | Function | | Wrong | Somewhat right, but too broad |
| Main Idea | Thesis | Topic | | Wrong | Somewhat right, but too narrow |
| Tone | Tone | Attitude | | Wrong | Somewhat right, but too extreme |
| Rhetoric | Structure | Argument | | Wrong | Tempting words, but wrong part |
| Vocabulary | | Vocabulary | | Wrong | Tempting words, but not true |
| Evidence | | Evidence | | Wrong | Tempting words, but irrelevant |
| Detail | | Detail | | Wrong | Flatly false |
| Inference | | Inference | | Right (general): | Give identify evidence |
| Data | | Data Specific | Data Synthesis | Right (specific): | Give line or annotation evidence |
| Paired | | Paired Specific | Paired Synthesis | Right (synthesis): | Give identify evidence |

Lesson 5: Mastering the Answers

### 7

As used in line 82, the word "employ" most nearly means

Recognize _____

Restate _____
_____

Recall _____
_____

Answer Ⓐ _____
_____

Answer Type _____

Answer Ⓑ _____
_____

Answer Type _____

Answer Ⓒ _____
_____

Answer Type _____

### 8

The passage implies that Krathwohl regarded Bloom's taxonomy with

Recognize _____

Restate _____
_____

Recall _____
_____

Answer Ⓐ _____
_____

Answer Type _____

Answer Ⓑ _____
_____

Answer Type _____

Answer Ⓒ _____
_____

Answer Type _____

Answer Ⓓ _____
_____

Answer Type _____

### 9

Which choice provides the best evidence for the answer to the previous question?

Recognize _____

Restate _____
_____

Recall _____
_____

Answer Ⓐ _____
_____

Answer Type _____

Answer Ⓑ _____
_____

Answer Type _____

Answer Ⓒ _____
_____

Answer Type _____

Answer Ⓓ _____
_____

Answer Type _____

### 10

The author's attitude toward Bloom is

Recognize _____

Restate _____
_____

Recall _____
_____

Answer Ⓐ _____
_____

Answer Type _____

Answer Ⓑ _____
_____

Answer Type _____

Answer Ⓒ _____
_____

Answer Type _____

Answer Ⓓ _____
_____

Answer Type _____

| Questions | General | Specific | Synthesis | Answers | Reason |
|---|---|---|---|---|---|
| Main Purpose | Purpose | Function | | Wrong | Somewhat right, but too broad |
| Main Idea | Thesis | Topic | | Wrong | Somewhat right, but too narrow |
| Tone | Tone | Attitude | | Wrong | Somewhat right, but too extreme |
| Rhetoric | Structure | Argument | | Wrong | Tempting words, but wrong part |
| Vocabulary | | Vocabulary | | Wrong | Tempting words, but not true |
| Evidence | | Evidence | | Wrong | Tempting words, but irrelevant |
| Detail | | Detail | | Wrong | Flatly false |
| Inference | | Inference | | Right (general): | Give identify evidence |
| Data | | Data Specific | Data Synthesis | Right (specific): | Give line or annotation evidence |
| Paired | | Paired Specific | Paired Synthesis | Right (synthesis): | Give identify evidence |

Lesson 5: Mastering the Answers

# PRACTICE TEST REVIEW: TEST 5 AND TEST 6

You've already taken these, but reviewing old tests is just as important as taking new ones. It doesn't do you any good to keep grinding through 65-minute sections if you aren't looking at what went right and what went wrong.

Athletes have film sessions to review games. It's part of what helps them excel at playing games. Steph Curry sells shoes by talking about game film.

> *Two kids wearing Under Armour clothing and escorted by a tour guide enter the film room. Steph is watching TV with his trainer.*

| | |
|---|---|
| Tour guide: | Oh hey, Steph Curry! Nobody works harder than this guy! |
| Kid 1: | Hey Steph. We got new Under Armour gear for the holidays. |
| Steph: | [Nods] Nice. Kids Foot Locker got you guys looking like pros. |
| Kid 2: | Whoa! You watch TV all day? |
| Steph: | No, no, this is game film. It's like homework. |
| Kid 1: | Is that a milkshake? |
| Steph: | No, it's a recovery shake. Guys, just 'cause this looks easy doesn't mean it's not hard work. |
| Trainer: | Hot tub's ready for you, Steph. |
| | *The kids look at each other.* |
| Steph: | [Smiles] Film sessions make my back tight. |

Steph Curry wants you to do two things: (1) Buy sweet Steph Curry merch at Kids' Foot Locker and (2) know that even the greats recognize that being great requires hard work *even after they become great*. Reviewing game film is like homework. Instead of taking another practice test, let's review some tests that you've already worked through.

For **every question you answered incorrectly**, indicate why your answer was wrong. Was your answer somewhat correct? Did you fall for their traps? What led you to choose an incorrect answer?

Now, **look at the correct answer.** What makes it right? What evidence supports this answer choice? Try to give line number evidence for specific questions and annotation/identification evidence for general or synthesis questions.

Your goal here is to comprehend how the SAT creates incorrect answer choices that are plausible enough to attract some students yet are wrong enough to convince other students to eliminate them. Obviously, the more questions you missed the longer this will take—give yourself time. It should take you between one and three minutes to review questions, maybe a little more at the beginning and a little less at the end. **The time you spend here will save you time on the test.**

Ready? *Let's go to the tape.*

## Test 5 Review: Recognize and Resolve

| Questions | General | Specific | Synthesis | Answers | Reason |
|---|---|---|---|---|---|
| Main Purpose | Purpose | Function | | Wrong | Somewhat right, but too broad |
| Main Idea | Thesis | Topic | | Wrong | Somewhat right, but too narrow |
| Tone | Tone | Attitude | | Wrong | Somewhat right, but too extreme |
| Rhetoric | Structure | Argument | | Wrong | Tempting words, but wrong part |
| Vocabulary | | Vocabulary | | Wrong | Tempting words, but not true |
| Evidence | | Evidence | | Wrong | Tempting words, but irrelevant |
| Detail | | Detail | | Wrong | Flatly false |
| Inference | | Inference | | Right (general): | Give identify evidence |
| Data | | Data Specific | Data Synthesis | Right (specific): | Give line or annotation evidence |
| Paired | | Paired Specific | Paired Synthesis | Right (synthesis): | Give identify evidence |

| | Recognize | Why My Incorrect Answer Is Wrong | Why the Correct Answer Is Right |
|---|---|---|---|
| 1 | | | |
| 2 | | | |
| 3 | | | |
| 4 | | | |
| 5 | | | |
| 6 | | | |
| 7 | | | |
| 8 | | | |
| 9 | | | |
| 10 | | | |
| 11 | | | |
| 12 | | | |
| 13 | | | |
| 14 | | | |
| 15 | | | |
| 16 | | | |
| 17 | | | |
| 18 | | | |
| 19 | | | |
| 20 | | | |
| 21 | | | |

Lesson 5: Mastering the Answers

| | Recognize | Why My Answer Is Wrong | Why the Correct Answer is Right |
|---|---|---|---|
| 22 | | | |
| 23 | | | |
| 24 | | | |
| 25 | | | |
| 26 | | | |
| 27 | | | |
| 28 | | | |
| 29 | | | |
| 30 | | | |
| 31 | | | |
| 32 | | | |
| 33 | | | |
| 34 | | | |
| 35 | | | |
| 36 | | | |
| 37 | | | |
| 38 | | | |
| 39 | | | |
| 40 | | | |
| 41 | | | |
| 42 | | | |
| 43 | | | |
| 44 | | | |
| 45 | | | |
| 46 | | | |
| 47 | | | |
| 48 | | | |
| 49 | | | |
| 50 | | | |
| 51 | | | |
| 52 | | | |

## Test 6 Review: Recognize and Resolve

| Questions | General | Specific | Synthesis | Answers | Reason |
|---|---|---|---|---|---|
| Main Purpose | Purpose | Function | | Wrong | Somewhat right, but too broad |
| Main Idea | Thesis | Topic | | Wrong | Somewhat right, but too narrow |
| Tone | Tone | Attitude | | Wrong | Somewhat right, but too extreme |
| Rhetoric | Structure | Argument | | Wrong | Tempting words, but wrong part |
| Vocabulary | | Vocabulary | | Wrong | Tempting words, but not true |
| Evidence | | Evidence | | Wrong | Tempting words, but irrelevant |
| Detail | | Detail | | Wrong | Flatly false |
| Inference | | Inference | | Right (general): | Give identify evidence |
| Data | | Data Specific | Data Synthesis | Right (specific): | Give line or annotation evidence |
| Paired | | Paired Specific | Paired Synthesis | Right (synthesis): | Give identify evidence |

| Recognize | Why My Answer Is Wrong | Why the Correct Answer is Right |
|---|---|---|
| 1 | | |
| 2 | | |
| 3 | | |
| 4 | | |
| 5 | | |
| 6 | | |
| 7 | | |
| 8 | | |
| 9 | | |
| 10 | | |
| 11 | | |
| 12 | | |
| 13 | | |
| 14 | | |
| 15 | | |
| 16 | | |
| 17 | | |
| 18 | | |
| 19 | | |
| 20 | | |
| 21 | | |

Lesson 5: Mastering the Answers

| | Recognize | Why My Answer Is Wrong | Why the Correct Answer is Right |
|---|---|---|---|
| 22 | | | |
| 23 | | | |
| 24 | | | |
| 25 | | | |
| 26 | | | |
| 27 | | | |
| 28 | | | |
| 29 | | | |
| 30 | | | |
| 31 | | | |
| 32 | | | |
| 33 | | | |
| 34 | | | |
| 35 | | | |
| 36 | | | |
| 37 | | | |
| 38 | | | |
| 39 | | | |
| 40 | | | |
| 41 | | | |
| 42 | | | |
| 43 | | | |
| 44 | | | |
| 45 | | | |
| 46 | | | |
| 47 | | | |
| 48 | | | |
| 49 | | | |
| 50 | | | |
| 51 | | | |
| 52 | | | |

This method of reviewing practice tests – looking at what went right and what went wrong – is one of the strongest ways to improve your test taking skills. This, like all things, comes with time, so you should **make sure you review questions and answers after every test**: What kind of question did you get wrong, why was your incorrect answer wrong, and why was the correct answer right?

You can find copies of tables above for all ten tests in Lesson 12.

# BONUS TIP! QUESTIONS AND ANSWER SERVICE

When you get your score from the College Board, you typically see the number of questions you answered correctly, incorrectly, and omitted. If you want to know which questions are which, you have to pay for the "Question-and-Answer Service" (QAS) or the less useful "Student Answer Service" (SAS).

- The **QAS** will give you a copy of the test, information about the type and difficulty of each question, and how you answered. It's very helpful when you're studying for a second shot at the test, and I recommend it to most students.

- The **SAS** gives you information in general about the questions you missed (type and difficulty) and the number of each question, but you won't have the question itself or the answers. I tend to recommend *not* getting the SAS.

While the College Board offers the SAS for most test dates and locations, they offer the QAS for the October test in North America and the May test in North America and globally. (If you have special accommodations for the test date, you may not be eligible for the October QAS).

See more information as www.sat.org.

# LESSON 6: UNDERSTANDING THE CLOCK

Pacing is important for doing well on standardized tests. There is, sadly, no substitute for pacing beside official practice tests. You cannot (and should not) try to match your pacing on digital passages with physical passages you print from the Khan Academy website or the official test book.

But simply taking practice tests doesn't necessarily improve your pacing. You need to take the test with the clock in the back of your brain. Don't obsess over it as you're reading the passage and answering the questions. You can keep track of your time in two ways.

## OPTION 1: THE TIME BANK

Pacing is a little more art than science. You have 65 minutes to answer the 52 questions on the 5 passages, or 13 minutes per passage. You can just divvy this up so that you have 13 minutes per passage, which is probably the easiest thing to do but may not be the best way to approach your pacing. You may find that the narrative fiction passages take a little longer than the science passages. You may find that the history passages take you longer than the science, or that the opposite is true. Some passages are shorter, some are longer, and some have tables that add a couple of minutes.

On the other hand, *it's better to be down two minutes than up fifteen*. Why? Because if you manage to answer all the questions on the test with that much time to spare, you either (1) read too quickly, giving you an imprecise understanding of the passage, or (2) answered the questions too quickly, leaving yourself open to simple mistakes. Worst of all is (3), a combination of reading too fast and answering without thinking things through. If you are two minutes short, it means that you had to guess on one or two questions on the final passage. If you are fifteen minutes fast, you have 52 possible errors on your answer sheet.

**Give yourself between 12 and 14 minutes per passage and stick to that timing**.

Let's use Test 6 as an example. When you start the first passage, stay on that passage and its questions for at least 12 minutes. If you finish "Nawabdin Electrician" two minutes early, *double- and triple-check your answers until the 12 minutes are up*. Recheck the evidence questions and the questions you were least confident in. Only after have the twelve minutes are finished should you move onto the next passage. You're up 60 seconds on the pace.

Ok, now you're on passage two. The author explains how the public's trust in the news has eroded. It's a little long (86 lines) and has a chart, so it takes a little longer than the first passage. You finish it a little over 13 minutes. Since you're within your ideal 12- to 14-minute window, move on to passage 3. You've eaten into the bank a little, but you're still up about a minute.

Passage three explains how plant smells affect bee pollination and beetle dung. It's not too bad, but question 27 is a doozy. And question 28 is an evidence question, leading you to double-check question 27 (which is a good thing). But you're starting to eat into the 60 seconds that you banked on the first passage and you have three questions left on this passage. Oh, and you still have two more passages to go, one of which is the antiquated English passage. You can't really afford to burn another two minutes on these questions. The first (question 30) is a complicated vocab question, so you spend 15 seconds picking your best answer. The second and third questions (question 31 and 32) are a detail question and its matching evidence question. To keep yourself moving, you give your best answer on 31 and find a matching evidence question. You're pretty sure 31 is B and its match is D, so you bubble in those letters.

You've got no time banked, but you don't owe any time to the next passages either. This is good since the fourth passage is a paired antiquated English passage: Abraham Lincoln and Henry David Thoreau on civil disobedience. In passage 1, Abraham Lincoln argues that we should follow unjust laws until they can be changed. Questions 33–37 deal with passage 1, so you answer those. In passage 2, Henry David Thoreau argues that some unjust laws can be followed until they are worn away, but others must be challenged more directly. There are only two questions on passage 2, so you answer 38 and 39. But these paired passages have taken time; you've used 11 minutes so far and you have three paired questions left to go. You have a good sense of where the authors agree and disagree, but when you hit the 13-minute mark you still have questions 40 and 41 to go. *This is ok.* You borrow one minute from the next passage and keep going. In the fourteenth minute, you answer 40 and 41, and you even have time to check question 41 (A). You're down 60 seconds, but that's fine.

You're on to the final passage with 12 minutes on the clock. It's a rather lengthy social studies passage with data, but the questions are pretty straightforward. You finish the final question with 20 seconds on the clock, double-check the data questions on 51 and 52, and get ready for your hard-earned break.

Notice how you can push and pull the pacing given the passages and your own strengths and weaknesses. You finished the first passage early, checked your answers, and then moved to the next passage with time banked. The fourth passage took a little longer, so you borrowed the time from the fifth passage to maximize your points.

If you are a student who values precision, you may find this method particularly effective. Students who have timed-test anxiety may also find this method reassuring since it lets you know when you should stay on the passage and when you should start wrapping up and move on to the rest of the test.

If you are going to use this method, you have to be firm.

- **Spend at least 12 minutes on each passage.** Make sure you get all the points, double checking your answers and your evidence.

- **Move on after 14 minutes.** You can't spend so long on the second passage that you don't have time to spend on the fourth and fifth passages.

It is possible that you have banked one minute on each of the three passages, such that you have 3:00 to allocate to the fourth and fifth passages. In these cases, you can spend a little extra time double-checking your answers.

One of the values in writing down your confidence in your answers (as you do in the resolve step) is that it lets you know where you should spend your extra time if you have it. If you had a confidence of 3 out of 5, that may be a good place to double-check your thinking. If you have confidences of 5 out of 5, there are probably other questions that deserve your attention.

## OPTION 2: GOING OLD-SCHOOL

It may be weird in the age of smartphones and speakers that can tell us the time whenever we ask, but an analog watch is the best tool for keeping track of the time on the test. **Before the reading section starts, set your watch to 10:55.** Since it's a 65-minute set, time will be up at 12:00.

By glancing at the watch, you can see exactly how much time is left without needing to do the math. The test proctor may be putting the time up on the board in the room, and there should be a clock visible. But bringing your own analog watch lets you avoid this internal monologue:

> We started the section at 8:22, which means that we end at/l ...9:27. (I think?) Ok. So it's 8:49. I have... 38 minutes left. And I'm starting passage three, so I have about 13 minutes per passage. Ugh. It's the 19th-century passage. Here we go!

With a watch, you know you've got 38 minutes left because... well, there are 38 minutes left.

If you are comfortable using the timer on a digital watch, you can use that (though they make noise). Smartwatches also have timers, but the test making companies give proctors the option to confiscate your smartwatch.

There is a wonderful simplicity to the analog watch method, as you don't have to fret about the precise time. You may have an internal time bank going, but you're not worrying over 45 seconds here or a half-minute there. You will want to practice pacing yourself repeatedly with this method, however, so that you have a better sense of how long it will take you to read the passages.

## EXTRA TIME?

The College Board's recognition that some students process information in different ways and speeds has increased the number of students receiving extended time on the SAT. Educators and parents have made strides to ensure the students who need extra time have it. "Extended time" is typically time and a half, meaning that students have **98 minutes to complete all five passages**, which averages out to about 19:30 per passage. Students may also receive a five-minute break in the middle of the section. This will likely split a passage in two, so it may be helpful to finish reading the third passage by the 49-minute mark.

For students with extended time, you should use a target of **about 18 to 21 minutes per passage**. However, because students with extended time may, for example, process the science passages slower than the literature, or the history passages slower than the social studies, I recommend a little more fluidity in your pacing. If you're done with the questions after 17 minutes, it's okay to move on to the next passage.

The more your practice, the better you'll **learn your individual strengths and weaknesses**. If you find the data passages confusing, give yourself a little bonus time for those passages. On the other hand, if you breeze through the literature, you can finish those up a little faster and bank that time.

Extended time students have to work harder and longer to reach their academic goals. Be patient with yourself and do your best. If you have friends who get extra time, be patient with them as they do their best. Test scores aren't about comparing yourself to your peers; they are about doing your best.

## RUNNING OUT OF TIME

Despite your practice, you may find yourself crunched for time on the final passage (less than 8 minutes or so). Even if you only have five minutes for the passage, you can still try to squeeze out some points before you guess on the remaining questions.

If (and only if) you find yourself with insufficient time to read the passage, *go straight to the questions* and cherry-pick the questions you can answer without reading the passage.

1. First options: Specific questions with line numbers

    - **Vocab-in-context questions:** Cross off the word, reread the sentences before and after the lines, and bubble in your best answer.

    - **Topic questions:** Read the paragraph, identify the topic, and bubble in your best answer.

    - **Detail questions with line numbers:** Read from the sentence before the lines in question through the sentence after the lines in question and bubble in your best answer.

    - **Data (detail) questions:** Look over the table or figure for the data pertaining to the question, check the units/numbers to make sure you're solving for the right thing, and bubble in your best answer.

2. Second options: General questions you can answer quickly

    - **Tone/Attitude questions:** Skim the passage looking for distinctive adjectives and unusual nouns and verbs, check the answer bank, and bubble in your best answer. (You can sometimes do this with attitude questions as well).

    - **Thesis questions:** Skim the passage looking for the author's argument on the whole, check the answer bank, and bubble in your best answer.

    - **Purpose questions:** Skim the passage looking for the reason the author wrote the passage on the whole, check the answer bank, and bubble in your best answer.

    - **Structure questions:** Skim the passage looking for the general structure, check the answer bank, and bubble in your best answer.

3. Final options: Complex specific questions, hard general questions, and all synthesis questions.

    - **Inference:** Even with line numbers, inference questions require more time than you probably have.

    - **Argument:** Without knowing the argument, it's hard to see how one part of the passage can affect the author's point.

    - **Function:** Every now and then, a function question can be answered quickly, but because they require you to integrate one part of the passage into the rest of it, they can also be time sucks.

    - **Evidence:** Reading four sets of lines to answer one question is too much time. Focus elsewhere.

    - **Synthesis:** Like with evidence questions, there's too much reading if you haven't read the passage.

4. **Bubble in your favorite letter for every question you don't know.** There is an approximately even distribution of answer choices (that is, C isn't more likely than B), and so by bubbling in the same letter, you increase the chances that you will get at least one or two questions right.

# PRACTICE TEST: OFFICIAL TEST 7

Let's work on pacing with a practice test. You may find that thinking about your pacing gives you another thing to worry about. *That's normal.* The SAT is a timed test; you're supposed to think about how long you're spending. Make sure that you practice with the pressure to relieve it on test day.

You should be feeling comfortable by now with the strategies for reading the passages and answer questions. **Underline, Annotate, and Identify** the passages. Students sometimes lose track of these basic reading strategies. They underline a little less, forget to make marginal notes. *Don't get lazy*! It can be tempting to let these things go. *Don't get lazy.* You might think it's taking you too long to get through the passages. It can take a little longer, but you may also find that it takes you less time to read the passage since the underlining and annotating will keep you moving. You're certainly going to answer the questions faster by understanding the passage better. *Don't get lazy!* The more effort you put into your test prep, the less likely you are to find yourself taking the test over and over again. You may take the test a second or third time. That's OK. But don't keep wasting Saturdays because you aren't putting in your best effort.

You should also be more comfortable with answering questions. **Restate, Recall, and Resolve** remains the best strategy for answering the questions. Hopefully, you can just jot down the **question type** as a proxy for Restate and Recall and you can find the right answer without going through all the wrong answer types. But this strategy really shines when you aren't sure what the answer is. Look at the answer choices, find the answers that are wrong, then pick the answer that is right.

Official Test 7 starts on page 692. You can find my annotations, underlining, and question type breakdown in lesson 11 (page 259).

Lesson 6: Understanding the Clock

# SELF-EVALUATION TEST 7

| | | | | | | |
|---|---|---|---|---|---|---|
| **Passage 1** | I felt confident during the first passage. | Strongly Agree | Somewhat Agree | No Opinion | Somewhat Disagree | Strongly Disagree |
| | Describe in two to three sentences how you felt on the first passage | | | | | |
| | Time spent | | | | | |
| **Passage 2** | I felt confident during the second passage. | Strongly Agree | Somewhat Agree | No Opinion | Somewhat Disagree | Strongly Disagree |
| | Describe in two to three sentences how you felt on the second passage | | | | | |
| | Time spent | | | | | |
| **Passage 3** | I felt confident during the third passage. | Strongly Agree | Somewhat Agree | No Opinion | Somewhat Disagree | Strongly Disagree |
| | Describe in two to three sentences how you felt on the third passage | | | | | |
| | Time spent | | | | | |
| **Passage 4** | I felt confident during the fourth passage. | Strongly Agree | Somewhat Agree | No Opinion | Somewhat Disagree | Strongly Disagree |
| | Describe in two to three sentences how you felt on the fourth passage | | | | | |
| | Time spent | | | | | |
| **Passage 5** | I felt confident during the fifth passage. | Strongly Agree | Somewhat Agree | No Opinion | Somewhat Disagree | Strongly Disagree |
| | Describe in two to three sentences how you felt on the fifth passage | | | | | |
| | Time spent | | | | | |
| **Overall** | I felt confident during the reading section. | Strongly Agree | Somewhat Agree | No Opinion | Somewhat Disagree | Strongly Disagree |
| | I had enough time for the reading section. | Strongly Agree | Somewhat Agree | No Opinion | Somewhat Disagree | Strongly Disagree |
| | I cared about the passages I read. | Strongly Agree | Somewhat Agree | No Opinion | Somewhat Disagree | Strongly Disagree |
| | In three to four sentences, describe how you feel about the reading section. | | | | | |
| | How was your timing? | | | | | |

# LESSON 7: MASTERING THE PASSAGES

Now that you've spent some time with the test, let's go back and get a bird's-eye view of the passages. You've taken a handful practice tests, so you should have a good idea of your strengths and weaknesses. The goal of this lesson is to help you target specific passage types and focus your energies there, rather than on the test overall.

There are two ways to divide up the passages: **passage type** (literature, science, and history/social studies) and **passage features** (passages with data, paired passages, and antiquated English passages).

## PASSAGE TOPICS: LITERATURE, HISTORY/SOCIAL STUDIES, AND SCIENCE PASSAGES

Way back in lesson 1, we looked at the different types of passages that appear on the SAT. As a refresher, there are three official passage types:

- Literature

- Science

- History/Social Studies

Let's look at each of the passage types with a little more detail.

## Literature

**The literature passage is always the first passage on the test.** The College Board describes the literature passages this way: "Literature selections come from classic and contemporary works by authors working in the United States and around the world." In practice, however, most of the authors have been American or British.

| Test | Literature | Origin |
| --- | --- | --- |
| 1 | Lydia Minatoya, *The Strangeness of Beauty* (1999) | Modern Japanese-American |
| 2 | Charlotte Brontë, *The Professor* (1857) | Victorian English |
| 3 | Saki, "The Schwartz-Metterklume Method" (1911) | Edwardian English |
| 4 | MacDonald Harris, *The Balloonist* (1976) | Mid-century American |
| 5 | William Maxwell, *The Folded Leaf* (1945) | Mid-century American |
| 6 | Daniyal Mueenuddin, "Nawabdin Electrician" (2009) | Modern Pakistani-American |
| 7 | George Eliot, *Silas Marner* (1861) | Victorian English |
| 8 | Carlos Ruiz Zafon, *The Angel's Game* (2008) | Modern Spanish (translated) |
| 9 | Amy Tan, *The Bonesetter's Daughter* (2001) | Modern Chinese-American |
| 10 | Mary Helen Stafaniak, *The Cailiffs of Baghdad, Georgia* (2010) | Modern American |

The literature passages are always prose, so you do not have to worry about reading poems or drama.

As noted, the literature passages often have attitude questions that ask you to **describe the conflict between characters**. You'll also find a fair number of structure questions that ask you to **describe the passage in generic terms** or to make inferences about a character's motivations.

The literature passages can be a bit of a mixed bag. If you like to read, you may find the passage and the accompanying questions relatively easy. If, on the other hand, you prefer the sciences to humanities, you may find it difficult to keep track of the characters and the reasons behind their actions. To help yourself, you may also want to identify the relationships between the characters as you read.

As we'll see later in this lesson, the literature passages are often written in antiquated English, which adds another wrinkle to your reading. The practice passages at the end of this lesson, "The Black Poodle," is one such passage.

## Science (with and without Data)

There are two science passages on every SAT. One of the two passages has data; the other does not. The science passage without data can be paired, as on practice tests 1 and 2. In general, however, the passage without data is a typical passage without any distinguishing features.

The College Board describes the science passages and their topics this way: "Science selections examine both foundational concepts and recent developments in the natural sciences, including Earth science, biology, chemistry, and physics (and their subfields)."

| Test | Science with Data | Science without Data |
|------|-------------------|----------------------|
| 1    | DNA               | Space Mining (Paired) |
| 2    | Undersea Waves    | Rewired Brains (Paired) |
| 3    | Honey Bees        | Bird Man |
| 4    | Medieval Volcano  | Goat Milk |
| 5    | Memory and MRI    | Organic Food |
| 6    | Solar Power       | Bees, Beetles, and Dung |
| 7    | Higgs-Boson       | Flying V |
| 8    | Nano-Salts        | Venus Fly Trap |
| 9    | Memory and Google | Antibiotics and Bacteria (Paired) |
| 10   | Weed Control      | Nerve Fibers |

It is important to note that the science passages do not require you to know any science material that does not appear in the passage. As the test writers put it, "Answers are derived from what is stated or implied in the passages and graphics rather than from prior knowledge of the topics." In other words, there is no reason that two-time Nobel Laureate Marie Skłodowska Curie would do any better on the SAT science passages than you would (apart from the fact that she was a genius and won two Nobel Prizes!)

That said, it may help you to think like a scientist would when you are reading the passage, as the test writers will ask questions about the details of the observations, hypotheses, and conclusions of scientific research. These can be detail questions (what was discovered?), inference questions (what can be inferred from the results of the study?), or data questions when the passage has data associated with it (what do the data show?). To make space for these questions, the science passages typically have one or even zero vocabulary questions.

Lesson 7: Mastering the Passages

# History and Social Studies

From a content perspective, the history and social studies passages have fairly **wide degree of variety.** The differences are significant enough that Khan Academy separates them into two categories. On one occasion, the College Board put two social studies and no history passages on the test, but you should prepare to have one of each.

As the College Board puts it, "History/social studies selections include portions of U.S.-based founding documents and texts in the Great Global Conversation—engaging often historically and culturally important works grappling with issues at the heart of civic and political life—and explorations of topics in the social sciences, including anthropology, communication studies, economics, education, human geography, law, linguistics, political science, psychology, and sociology (and their subfields)." This is an overly complicated sentence (probably one that they would insist be separated were it on the grammar test!), but a survey of the actual passages from the practice tests makes things clearer:

| Test | History | Paired? |
|---|---|---|
| 1 | Patriarchy and English Society | |
| 2 | Women's Suffrage | |
| 3 | Women's Education | Yes |
| 4 | Democracy and Revolution | Yes |
| 5 | Women and Abolitionism | Yes |
| 6 | Abolition and Unjust Laws | Yes |
| 7 | Gender and American Democracy | Yes |
| 8 | Lincoln-Douglas | Yes |
| 9 | Woman and Slavery | |
| 10 | American Imperialism | Yes |

**The history passages focus on the expansion of human rights.** Look at the topics included on the paired history passages: women's rights (tests 1, 2, 3, 5, and 7), abolition and the American Civil War (tests 5, 6, and 8), and democracy (test 4). Most of the history passages focus on America, though the passages on test 1 and 3 are about England and the passage on test 4 is about democracy in response to the French Revolution. The purpose of the history passage is typically to argue a position, and so you will often find function or rhetoric questions accompanying the passage.

**The passages do not rely on your outside knowledge.** While it may help you to have a sense of some of the major players in those debates, this could actually be detrimental in some cases. For example, the paired set from test 6 includes a passage from Abraham Lincoln talking about the dangers of the abolitionist movement. If you go into the passing saying to yourself "Lincoln freed the slaves; he is going to say slavery is bad and that we should end it," you'll get a handful of questions wrong. You also shouldn't approach the test with expecting to find woke 19th-century authors. It can be a little jarring to read an argument that women don't deserve the same education rights as men. Stick to what the passage says, not what you think the author should say.

**The social studies passages have more diverse topics**, though economics has been the focus about half of the time (tests 1, 2, 5, and 7). According to the SAT test specifications, one of the history/social studies passages has a graphic associated with them. *These have always been the social studies passages.* In addition, *none of the social studies passages are paired.* In theory, there could be a paired social studies passage or a history passage with data, but this would be unexpected.

| Test | Social Studies | Data? |
|---|---|---|
| 1 | Economics of Gift Giving | Yes |
| 2 | Ethical Economics | Yes |
| 3 | Public Transportation | Yes |
| 4 | The Great Inversion | Yes |
| 5 | Internet Reviews | Yes |
| 6 | Fake News | Yes |
| 7 | Employment and Technology | Yes |
| 8 | Null Hypotheses | Yes |
| 9 | Memory and Google | Yes |
| 10 | Traffic and the Environment | Yes |

Social studies passages tend to **explain some feature of the modern world**, be it economics or human geography or behavioral psychology. The passages may also have an argumentative side to them; the passage on public transportation on test 3, for example, explains that public transportation can be better than private car ownership, and thus argues that America could have a world-class transportation with proper investment in infrastructure.

# PASSAGE FEATURES: DATA, PAIRED, AND ANTIQUATED ENGLISH

The other way to think about the passages is by their distinctive features. There are three different features that the test writers include to trip up students:

- Passages with Data
- Paired Passages
- Antiquated English Passages

Each of these, in their own ways, can make understanding the passage a little more complicated.

## Passages with Data

Two passages per test have data that accompany them: one science passage and one social studies passage. In lesson 2, we looked at "reading" the data on SAT passages.

1. Start by looking for the **dependent and independent variables:** The independent variable is on the x-axis and the dependent variable on the y-axis.

2. Next, look for **trends in the data:** How does changing one variable affect the other variable(s)?

3. Finally, look for any **outliers in the data:** Do any data points not fit the overall trend?

In lesson 3, we looked at answering data questions. On the SAT, you will not be asked to make numerical calculations, but you will have to synthesize the data and the passage (where do the data and passage agree?) and identify details in the data. Data questions are always the last questions associated with any given passage.

**Numerical Tables** are the easiest way of presenting quantitative data. The leftmost column typically gives the independent variable tested (the thing that was varied) and the right columns give the dependent variable (the things that were measured). In the figure here, the independent variable is the date and the dependent variables are the high and low temperatures.

High and Low Temperatures for Chicago in February 2018

| Date (2018) | High (in °F) | Low (in °F) | Date (2018) | High (in °F) | Low (in °F) |
|---|---|---|---|---|---|
| 1-Feb | 36 | 9 | 15-Feb | 48 | 38 |
| 2-Feb | 22 | 5 | 16-Feb | 38 | 20 |
| 3-Feb | 42 | 22 | 17-Feb | 36 | 17 |
| 4-Feb | 35 | 7 | 18-Feb | 42 | 20 |
| 5-Feb | 12 | 0 | 19-Feb | 60 | 39 |
| 6-Feb | 22 | 6 | 20-Feb | 66 | 34 |
| 7-Feb | 21 | 12 | 21-Feb | 34 | 29 |
| 8-Feb | 22 | 9 | 22-Feb | 41 | 31 |
| 9-Feb | 29 | 22 | 23-Feb | 45 | 35 |
| 10-Feb | 26 | 17 | 24-Feb | 51 | 35 |
| 11-Feb | 24 | 13 | 25-Feb | 52 | 34 |
| 12-Feb | 29 | 4 | 26-Feb | 55 | 29 |
| 13-Feb | 36 | 17 | 27-Feb | 62 | 41 |
| 14-Feb | 46 | 28 | 28-Feb | 60 | 38 |

With a numerical table, it is relatively easy to identify particular data points, especially if the data is well organized (chronologically).

- What was the low temperature on February 5? (-1°F)

- What was the high temperature on February 15? (48°F)

The SAT may ask you to perform a second step and work backward. This may require you to look at more data to find the correct answer, but the answer is still on the page in front of you.

- Which day in February was the warmest? (February 20)

- For how many days in February was the high between 50 and 59°F? (Three)

Numerical tables are not, however, particularly effective at giving a quick overview of the trends in the data. Looking at a table of data, it's hard to see how the temperature fluctuated or how often it was "warm" and "cold." The SAT cares more about the *shape* of the data than individual data points.

- For what percentage of the days was the low temperature below 20 degrees?

- Was the high temperature above 40 degrees more often than it was below 30 degrees?

Fortunately, charts and graphs give information visually, making it easier to spot trends in the data and answer questions. You will, however, have to read the figures to get the answers. So let's work on that.

Lesson 7: Mastering the Passages

**Line graphs** can display multiple series of data on the same graphic. This chart gives the high and low temperatures using a solid line for the high temperatures and a dotted line for the low temperatures.

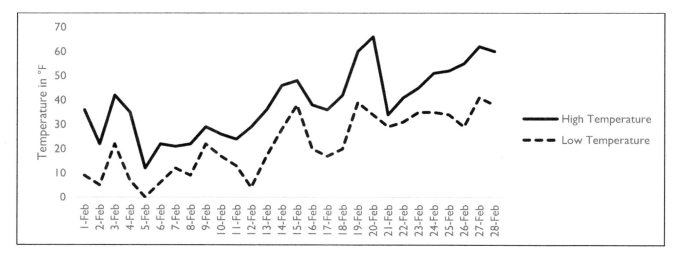

Finding answers on a line graph typically requires you to compare values on the horizontal and vertical axis.

- What was the low temperature on February 5? Look at the chart for February 5 (along the horizontal axis) and find the value on the vertical axis for low temperature: **about 0°F**

- What was the high temperature on February 15? Find February 15 on the horizontal axis, then go up to the high temperature line. The high temperature on February 15 was **about 50°F**.

- Which day in February was the warmest? Look for the highest point on the right line (is this the solid one or the dotted one?). When you've found the highest value on the vertical axis, find the corresponding value on the horizontal axis. The highest temperature was on **February 20**.

**Scatter plots**, like the one below, can be given a *line of best fit* or *trend line*, a linear (or exponential) equation that correlates the independent and dependent variables. From this equation, you can extrapolate unknown data points, like the most likely high temperature on March 1. Scatter plots haven't appeared on the verbal section of the test (yet), but one could appear on test day.

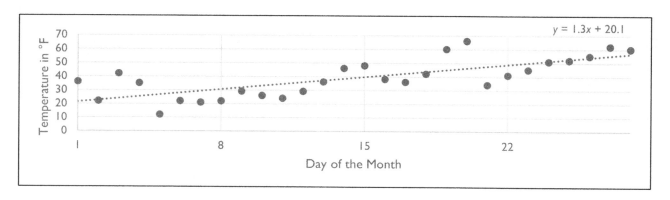

**Bar Graphs** (or **Bar Charts**) use rectangles to indicate quantities or frequencies. They do not always give the precision of the numerical table, but they make it much easier to see the trends in the data. The same data can be displayed with either horizontal bars or vertical columns, as with the examples below.

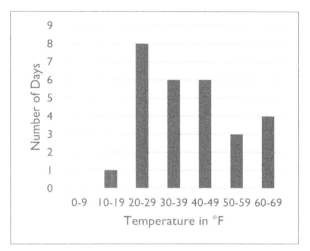
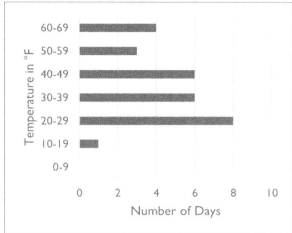

Bar charts lend themselves to displaying multiple sets of data in a single graphic. Notice that when you combine data, not all the temperature ranges have will necessarily have values: There were no days with a high between 0 and 9°F or days where the low was above 50°F.

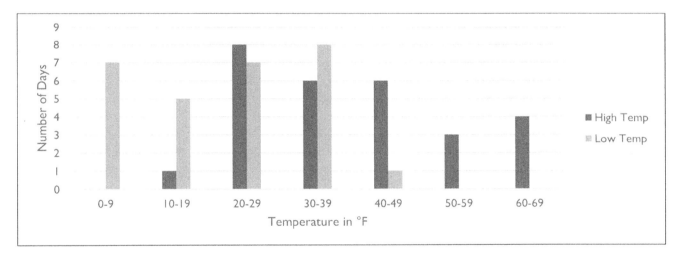

Bar charts make it easier to answer questions about the range of data or the frequency of events.

- For how many days in February was the high between 50 and 59°F? Look at the chart! There were three days with a high between 50 and 59 degrees, so the answer is three.

- Was the high temperature above 40 degrees more often than it was below 30 degrees? This is a little harder to tell on a bar chart, but it would appear that the sum of 40-49, 50-59, and 60-69 is greater than the sum of 10-19 and 20-29, even though 20-29 is the tallest column.

Maybe another chart type will be useful?

Lesson 7: Mastering the Passages

**Pie Charts** are best used to indicate percentages. The larger the slice of pie, the greater the percentage of the data points that fall into that category. You'll typically be given the boundaries of each category and the percentage of data points that fall into that category, here the temperature ranges.

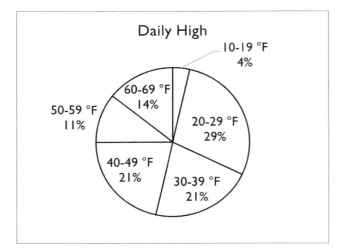
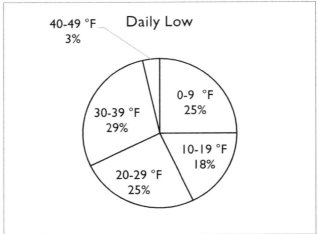

The **stacked bar chart** can be read like a vertical pie chart, with the percentage of the column representing the percentage of the circle. The data in two pie charts to the right, for example, could be presented with a stacked bar chart like the one below. They are particularly useful for comparing percentages, whether chronologically (changes over time) or a qualitative difference (changes between types of things). Stacked bar charts are not particularly common, but one did appear in SAT 8 comparing different types of scientific data, so it's worth knowing what they look like.

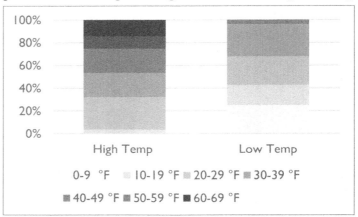

**Box and Whiskers plots** show the distribution and the range of a data set. The *box* in the middle gives the 25th percentile, the 50th percentile (the median), and the 75th percentile, sometimes called the first, second, and third quartiles because they contain a quarter of the data. For this set, the middle 50% of the highs were between 27 and 51°F with a median of 38°F, and the middle 50% of the lows were between 10 and 32°F. with a median of 21°F. The *whiskers* at the top and bottom give the highest and lowest values, sometimes called "outliers" because they lie outside the box. The distance between these points is the range. For this data set, the range is about 55°F for the highs and 41°F for the lows.

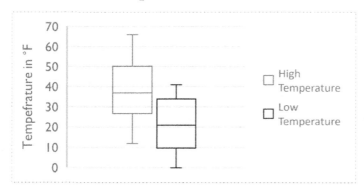

Finally, not all data can be displayed numerically. Compare these two charts on vehicle automation.

SOCIETY OF AUTOMOTIVE ENGINEERS (SAE) AUTOMATION LEVELS

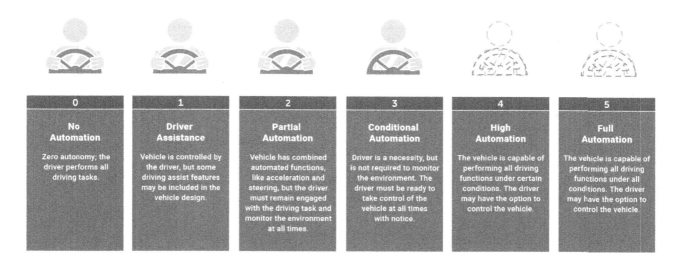

| Level | Name | Steering and Speed | Environmental Monitoring | Emergency Maneuvers | Driving Modes |
|---|---|---|---|---|---|
| 0 | No Automation | 👤 | 👤 | 👤 | N/A |
| 1 | Driver Assistance | 👤🚗 | 👤 | 👤 | Some |
| 2 | Partial Automation | 🚗 | 👤 | 👤 | Some |
| 3 | Conditional Automation | 🚗 | 🚗 | 👤 | Some |
| 4 | High Automation | 🚗 | 🚗 | 👤🚗 | Some |
| 5 | Full Automation | 🚗 | 🚗 | 🚗 | All |

They give roughly the same information (Level Number, Name, and Characteristics), as they are based on the same classification systems from the Society of Automotive Engineers. But the first figure gives the data graphically (note that the image in conditional automation the driver is using only one hand), while the second figure gives the data in a table. You'll need to be familiar with both kinds of data presentation on the test.

Khan Academy's non-SAT math practice materials give a helpful overview of the ways one can represent data. Just search for "reading and interpreting data" in the Khan Academy search bar or go to www.khanacademy.org/math/pre-algebra/pre-algebra-math-reasoning.

Lesson 7: Mastering the Passages

You can also check over the passages on the SAT. The table on the next page lists all the passages with data on each of the tests.

| Data Type | Test | Science | Social Studies |
|---|---|---|---|
| Numerical Tables | 1 | DNA | |
| | 3 | Honey Bees | |
| | 6 | | Fake News |
| | 10 | Weed Control | Traffic and the Environment |
| Line Graphs and Scatter Plots | 2 | | Ethical Economics |
| | 2 | Undersea Waves | |
| | 4 | Medieval Volcano | |
| | 5 | Organic Food | |
| | 6 | Solar Tech | |
| | 7 | | Jobs and Tech |
| | 8 | Nano Salts | |
| Bar Chart | 1 | | Gift Giving |
| | 4 | | Great Inversion |
| | 6 | Solar Tech | |
| | 7 | | Jobs and Tech |
| | 8 | | Null Results |
| | 9 | Guppies and Evolution | Memory and Google |
| | 10 | | Traffic and the Environment |
| Pie Chart | 3 | | Public Transportation |
| | 4 | | Great Inversion |
| Box and Whiskers | 5 | | Internet Comments |

You'll notice that (in general), the sciences passages have more tables and line graphs and the social studies have more bar charts, pie charts, and the only box and whiskers.

# Paired Passages

There is one paired passage per test. These passages tend to fall under the "history" category, but they can also be science or social studies. Before 2015, there were paired literature passages, though there are no examples from the revised SAT.

As a reminder, there are typically three or four paired passage questions that ask you to synthesize your reading from the two passages. The core questions ask you about how the passages relate to each other or one how one author may respond to the other.

- What is the relationship between Passage 1 and Passage 2?

- Unlike Passage 1, Passage 2 discusses

- The author of Passage 1 would likely respond to Passage 2 by

The paired passages, like the data passages, give the synthesis questions at the end of the question set. There is, however, another pattern in the questions: The questions for Passage 1 always precede the questions from Passage 2. This means that the questions will be in roughly the following order:

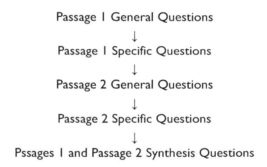

This means that you should start by reading Passage 1 and answering the questions about Passage 1 *before you move on* and read Passage 2. Then, read Passage 2 *looking for where the passages agree and disagree*. After you answer the questions for Passage 2, answer the synthesis questions considering both passages.

Beyond that, the paired passages are no different from other passages, except for the fact that they are prone to be history passages. And when they are history passages, they have antiquated English. That's another difficulty altogether.

In addition to the passage here, look for bonus antiquated English passages and other readings at www.professorscompanion.com. You can never have too much reading!

## Antiquated English Passages

Students often struggle with the dense prose of antiquated English passages. Every test, however, includes at least one if not two passages that were written a century or more ago. **Getting used to the style and vocabulary of these passages can be tough.**

To date, all of the antiquated English passages have been literature or history passages. Moreover, five of the six administered tests (tests 5-10) have had a paired antiquated English history passage.

| Test | Literature | History |
| --- | --- | --- |
| 1 | Lydia Minatoya, *The Strangeness of Beauty* (1999, set in 1920) | Virginia Woolf, "Three Guineas" (1938) |
| 2 | Charlotte Brontë, *The Professor* (1857) | Elizabeth Cody Stanton, address to the 1869 Women's Suffrage Convention (1869) |
| 3 | Saki, "The Schwartz-Metterklume Method" (1911) | Talleyrand et al., *Report on Public Instruction* (1791) and Mary Wollstonecraft, *A Vindication of the Rights of Women* (1792), (Paired) |
| 4 | MacDonald Harris, *The Balloonist* (1976, set in 1897) | Edmund Burke, "Reflections on the Revolution in France" (1790) and Thomas Paine, *Rights of Man* (1791 |
| 5 | William Maxwell, *The Folded Leaf* (1945) | Catherine Beecher, *Essays on Slavery and Abolitionism* (1837) and Angelina E. Grimké, *Letters to Catherine Beecher* (1838), (Paired) |
| 6 | | Abraham Lincoln, "Address to the Young Men's Lyceum of Springfield, Illinois" (1838) and Henry David Thoreau, "Resistance to Civil Government" (1848), (Paired) |
| 7 | George Eliot, *Silas Marner* (1861) | Alexis de Tocqueville, *Democracy in America* (1840) and Harriet Taylor Mill, "Enfranchisement of Women" (1851), (Paired) |
| 8 | Carlos Ruiz Zafon, *The Angel's Game* (2008, set in early twentieth-century Barcelona) | Abraham Lincoln and Stephen Douglas, *The Lincoln-Douglas Debates* (1858), (Paired) |
| 9 | | Sara T. Smith, Speech to the Second Anti-Slavery Convention of American Women (1838) |
| 10 | | Albert J. Beveridge, "March of the Flag" (1898) and William Jennings Bryan, "Imperialism" (1900), (Paired) |

To improve on the antiquated English passages, your best strategy is to read antiquated English. Anything assigned for school should be good, but I am partial to reading short stories. The mysteries of Sherlock Holmes take about 35 minutes to read (the length of a grammar section) and make for a good read. Fans of *Stranger Things* should check out Edgar Allan Poe and H.P. Lovecraft. Some of the best satire is from the 19th century, like that of Mark Twain, George Eliot, and Oscar Wilde. As always, reading regularly will make these (and other) passages easier.

# PRACTICE PASSAGE: LITERATURE (ANTIQUATED ENGLISH)

The following passage is from the short story "The Black Poodle" by F. Anstey. The setting is late 19th-century Britain.

I have set myself the task of relating in the course of this story, without suppressing or altering a single detail, the most painful and humiliating episode in my life. I do this, not because it will give me the least pleasure, but simply because it affords me an opportunity of extenuating myself which has hitherto been wholly denied to me.

As a general rule I am quite aware that to publish a lengthy explanation of one's conduct in any questionable transaction is not the best means of recovering a lost reputation; but in my own case there is one to whom I shall never more be permitted to justify myself by word of mouth—even if I found myself able to attempt it. And as she could not possibly think worse of me than she does at present, I write this, knowing it can do me no harm, and faintly hoping that it may come to her notice and suggest a doubt whether I am quite so unscrupulous a villain, so consummate a hypocrite, as I have been forced to appear in her eyes. The bare chance of such a result makes me perfectly indifferent to all else: I cheerfully expose to the derision of the whole reading world the story of my weakness and my shame, since by doing so I may possibly rehabilitate myself somewhat in the good opinion of one person. Having said so much, I will begin my confession without further delay:

My name is Algernon Weatherhead, and I may add that I am in one of the Government departments; that I am an only son, and live at home with my mother.

We had had a house at Hammersmith until just before the period covered by this history, when, our lease expiring, my mother decided that my health required country air at the close of the day, and so we took a 'desirable villa residence' on one of the many new building estates which have lately sprung up in such profusion in the home counties.

We have called it 'Wistaria Villa.' It is a pretty little place, the last of a row of detached villas, each with its tiny rustic carriage gate and gravel sweep in front, and lawn enough for a tennis court behind, which lines the road leading over the hill to the railway station. It is a pleasant house, and I can now almost forgive the landlord for what I shall always consider an act of gross selfishness on his part.

In the country, even so near town, a next-door neighbor is something more than a mere numeral; he is a possible acquaintance, who will at least consider a new-comer as worth the experiment of a call. I soon knew that 'Shuturgarden,' the next house to our own, was occupied by a Colonel Currie, a retired Indian officer; and often, as across the low boundary wall I caught a glimpse of a graceful girlish figure flitting about amongst the rose-bushes in the neighboring garden, I would lose myself in pleasant anticipations of a time not far distant when the wall which separated us would be (metaphorically) levelled.

I remember—ah, how vividly!—the thrill of excitement with which I heard from my mother on returning from town one evening that the Curries had called, and seemed disposed to be all that was neighborly and kind. I remember, too, the Sunday afternoon on which I returned their call — alone, as my mother had already done so during the week. I was standing on the steps of the Colonel's villa waiting for the door to open when I was startled by a furious snarling and yapping behind, and, looking round, discovered a large poodle in the act of making for my legs.

He was a coal-black poodle, with half of his right ear gone, and absurd little thick moustaches at the end of his nose; he was shaved in the sham-lion fashion, which is considered, for some mysterious reason, to improve a poodle, but the barber had left sundry little tufts of hair which studded his haunches capriciously.

He made me intensely uncomfortable, for I am of a slightly nervous temperament, with a constitutional horror of dogs and a liability to attacks of diffidence on performing the ordinary social rites under the most favorable conditions, and certainly the consciousness that a strange and apparently savage dog was engaged in worrying the heels of my boots was the reverse of reassuring.

Lesson 7: Mastering the Passages

### 1

The primary purpose of the first paragraph (lines 1-7) is to passage is to

A) establish Algernon's attitude toward the events that follow.
B) provide insight into Algernon's actions prior to his encounter with the Curries.
C) describe Algernon's failed attempts to apologize.
D) explore the psychological effects of moving to the country.

### 2

Which choice best describes the developmental pattern of the passage?

A) A man describes the origins of a conflict between his mother and her acquaintances.
B) A notorious villain harasses his neighbors and is then confronted by their dog.
C) An intruder provokes and then attacks the family pet.
D) A man asks for understanding for an embarrassing event and then describes it.

### 3

The word "bare" in line 21 most nearly means

A) devoid.
B) slight.
C) empty.
D) grizzly.

### 4

It can be inferred from lines 32-38 (We had … counties") that

A) Algernon's mother was in poor health.
B) Algernon had an interest in studying history.
C) Algernon and his mother had recently moved.
D) Algernon and his mother were foreigners.

### 5

The main function of the fourth paragraph (lines 32-38) is to

A) condemn the greedy landlord who leased the house to Algernon and his mother.
B) explain why Algernon left Hammersmith.
C) introduce the relationship between Algernon and the Curries.
D) describe Algernon's new surroundings.

### 6

Algernon responds to the appearance of the black poodle with

A) disdain and terror.
B) empathy and awe.
C) joy and affection.
D) rage and violence.

**7**

As used in line 81, the word "constitutional" most nearly means

A) legal
B) innate
C) communal
D) learned

**8**

Algernon imagines that unnamed girl's attitude toward him is one of

A) pity.
B) disgust.
C) infatuation.
D) delight.

**9**

Which choice provides the best evidence for the answer to the previous question?

A) Lines 1-7 ("I have … me")
B) Lines 14-19 ("And as … eyes")
C) Lines 27-29 ("My name … mother")
D) Lines 54-56 ("and often … garden")

**10**

The tone of the passage overall is

A) embittered.
B) delighted.
C) pleading
D) hopeful.

When tackling these kinds of antiquated English passages, make sure you have a good grasp of the author's purpose and tone. A lot of these questions can be tough if you don't recognize that Algernon is trying to explain his actions, actions that somehow have made the unnamed girl think the worst of him.

### Online Bonus Content
One of the best ways to practice antiquated English passages is to read a lot of older English. Many of the books you read in school fall into this category, but it can also be helpful to read short stories. They don't take a ton of time and tend to move more quickly than novels. If you want to read more about the black poodle and why Algernon believes the unnamed girl despises him, check out the full story at www.professorscompanion.com/reading.

Lesson 7: Mastering the Passages

# PASSAGE TYPE AND FEATURES: EXTRA PASSAGES

Understanding both the content and features of the passages will help you read the passage and answer the questions better. The content can help you focus on the author's purpose and the kinds of questions to expect. The special features can help orient your reading strategies, whether this means annotating the data, reading the paired passages individually, or working through complicated sentences structures.

| Content | Features | Purpose | Recognizes |
|---|---|---|---|
| Literature | • Antiquated English (frequently) | • To describe literary characters | • Attitude<br>• Structure |
| Science | • Data (always one with and one without)<br>• Paired (sometimes) | • To explain scientific phenomena | • Detail<br>• Data |
| History | • Antiquated English (always)<br>• Paired (frequently) | • To argue a position | • Argument<br>• Function<br>• Paired |
| Social Studies | • Data (always with) | • To explain modern society | • Argument<br>• Data |

The best way to improve is to target the passages types you most struggle with. I like to **work through the passage features, bouncing from test to test.** So if you need to practice your data passages, you have ten practice passages ready to go. If you want to work on paired passages, go read about brain training, women's education, or American Imperialism. If you're struggling with the antiquated English, spending some extra time here can help. While you can pace yourself on these, it's important that you are working on how to read the passages and answer the kinds of questions that you'll be asked. You should certainly spend at least 12 minutes on each passage and questions, but if you went up to 15 minutes because you were focusing, that's fine too.

| Feature | Test 2 | Test 3 | Test 4 | Test 9 | Test 10 |
|---|---|---|---|---|---|
| Data Passages | • Ethical Economics<br>• Undersea Waves | • Public Transportation<br>• Honey Bees | • Medieval Volcano<br>• The Great Inversion | • Guppies and Evolution<br>• Memory and Google | • Weed Control<br>• Traffic and the Environment |
| Paired Passages | • Brain Training | • Women's Education | • Democracy and Revolution | • Antibiotics and Bacteria | • American Imperialism |
| Antiquated English Passages | • The Professor<br>• Women's Suffrage | • The Schwartz-Metterklume Method<br>• Women's Education | • Democracy and Revolution | • Women and Slavery | • American Imperialism |

# DATA PASSAGES SELF-DIAGNOSTIC

| | | | | | | |
|---|---|---|---|---|---|---|
| **Test 2** | I felt confident with the data in the Ethical Economics passage. | Strongly Agree | Somewhat Agree | No Opinion | Somewhat Disagree | Strongly Disagree |
| | What variables (independent and dependent) do the data display? | | | | | |
| | I felt confident with the data in the Undersea Waves passage. | Strongly Agree | Somewhat Agree | No Opinion | Somewhat Disagree | Strongly Disagree |
| | What variables (independent and dependent) do the data display? | | | | | |
| **Test 3** | I felt confident with the data in the Public Transportation passage. | Strongly Agree | Somewhat Agree | No Opinion | Somewhat Disagree | Strongly Disagree |
| | What variables (independent and dependent) do the data display? | | | | | |
| | I felt confident with the data in the Honey Bees passage. | Strongly Agree | Somewhat Agree | No Opinion | Somewhat Disagree | Strongly Disagree |
| | What variables (independent and dependent) do the data display? | | | | | |
| **Test 4** | I felt confident with the data in the Great Inversion passage. | Strongly Agree | Somewhat Agree | No Opinion | Somewhat Disagree | Strongly Disagree |
| | What variables (independent and dependent) do the data display? | | | | | |
| | I felt confident with the data in the Medieval Volcano passage. | Strongly Agree | Somewhat Agree | No Opinion | Somewhat Disagree | Strongly Disagree |
| | What variables (independent and dependent) do the data display? | | | | | |
| **Test 9** | I felt confident with the data in the Guppies and Evolution passage. | Strongly Agree | Somewhat Agree | No Opinion | Somewhat Disagree | Strongly Disagree |
| | What variables (independent and dependent) do the data display? | | | | | |
| | I felt confident with the data in the Memory and Google passage. | Strongly Agree | Somewhat Agree | No Opinion | Somewhat Disagree | Strongly Disagree |
| | What variables (independent and dependent) do the data display? | | | | | |
| **Test 10** | I felt confident with the data in the Weed Control passage. | Strongly Agree | Somewhat Agree | No Opinion | Somewhat Disagree | Strongly Disagree |
| | What variables (independent and dependent) do the data display? | | | | | |
| | I felt confident with the data in the Traffic and the Environment passage. | Strongly Agree | Somewhat Agree | No Opinion | Somewhat Disagree | Strongly Disagree |
| | What variables (independent and dependent) do the data display? | | | | | |

Lesson 7: Mastering the Passages

# PAIRED PASSAGES SELF-DIAGNOSTIC

| | | | | | | |
|---|---|---|---|---|---|---|
| Test 2 | I understood the argument in Passage 1 on Brain Training. | Strongly Agree | Somewhat Agree | No Opinion | Somewhat Disagree | Strongly Disagree |
| | I understood the argument in Passage 2 on Brain Training. | Strongly Agree | Somewhat Agree | No Opinion | Somewhat Disagree | Strongly Disagree |
| | I understand the places of agreement and disagreement between the passages. | Strongly Agree | Somewhat Agree | No Opinion | Somewhat Disagree | Strongly Disagree |
| | What is the relationship between Passage 1 and Passage 2? How do you know? | | | | | |
| Test 3 | I understood the argument in Passage 1 on Women's Education. | Strongly Agree | Somewhat Agree | No Opinion | Somewhat Disagree | Strongly Disagree |
| | I understood the argument in Passage 2 on Women's Education. | Strongly Agree | Somewhat Agree | No Opinion | Somewhat Disagree | Strongly Disagree |
| | I understand the places of agreement and disagreement between the passages. | Strongly Agree | Somewhat Agree | No Opinion | Somewhat Disagree | Strongly Disagree |
| | What is the relationship between Passage 1 and Passage 2? How do you know? | | | | | |
| Test 4 | I understood the argument in Passage 1 on Democracy and Revolution. | Strongly Agree | Somewhat Agree | No Opinion | Somewhat Disagree | Strongly Disagree |
| | I understood the argument in Passage 2 on Democracy and Revolution. | Strongly Agree | Somewhat Agree | No Opinion | Somewhat Disagree | Strongly Disagree |
| | I understand the places of agreement and disagreement between the passages. | Strongly Agree | Somewhat Agree | No Opinion | Somewhat Disagree | Strongly Disagree |
| | What is the relationship between Passage 1 and Passage 2? How do you know? | | | | | |
| Test 9 | I understood the argument in Passage 1 on Antibiotics and Bacteria. | Strongly Agree | Somewhat Agree | No Opinion | Somewhat Disagree | Strongly Disagree |
| | I understood the argument in Passage 2 on Antibiotics and Bacteria. | Strongly Agree | Somewhat Agree | No Opinion | Somewhat Disagree | Strongly Disagree |
| | I understand the places of agreement and disagreement between the passages. | Strongly Agree | Somewhat Agree | No Opinion | Somewhat Disagree | Strongly Disagree |
| | What is the relationship between Passage 1 and Passage 2? How do you know? | | | | | |
| Test 10 | I understood the argument in Passage 1 on American Imperialism. | Strongly Agree | Somewhat Agree | No Opinion | Somewhat Disagree | Strongly Disagree |
| | I understood the argument in Passage 2 on American Imperialism. | Strongly Agree | Somewhat Agree | No Opinion | Somewhat Disagree | Strongly Disagree |
| | I understand the places of agreement and disagreement between the passages. | Strongly Agree | Somewhat Agree | No Opinion | Somewhat Disagree | Strongly Disagree |
| | What is the relationship between Passage 1 and Passage 2? How do you know? | | | | | |

## ANTIQUATED ENGLISH PASSAGES SELF-DIAGNOSTIC

| | | | | | | |
|---|---|---|---|---|---|---|
| **Test 2** | I felt confident with the sentences in *The Professor*. | Strongly Agree | Somewhat Agree | No Opinion | Somewhat Disagree | Strongly Disagree |
| | I felt confident with the vocabulary in *The Professor*. | Strongly Agree | Somewhat Agree | No Opinion | Somewhat Disagree | Strongly Disagree |
| | After re-reading the passage, does it make more sense? Why or why not? | | | | | |
| | I felt confident with the sentences in the Women's Suffrage passage. | Strongly Agree | Somewhat Agree | No Opinion | Somewhat Disagree | Strongly Disagree |
| | I felt confident with the vocabulary in the Women's Suffrage passage. | Strongly Agree | Somewhat Agree | No Opinion | Somewhat Disagree | Strongly Disagree |
| | After re-reading the passages, do they make more sense? Why or why not? | | | | | |
| **Test 3** | I felt confident with the sentences in "The Schwartz-Metterklume Method." | Strongly Agree | Somewhat Agree | No Opinion | Somewhat Disagree | Strongly Disagree |
| | I felt confident with the vocabulary in "The Schwartz-Metterklume Method." | Strongly Agree | Somewhat Agree | No Opinion | Somewhat Disagree | Strongly Disagree |
| | After re-reading the passage, does it make more sense? Why or why not? | | | | | |
| | I felt confident with the sentences in the Women's Education passage. | Strongly Agree | Somewhat Agree | No Opinion | Somewhat Disagree | Strongly Disagree |
| | I felt confident with the vocabulary in the Women's Education passage. | Strongly Agree | Somewhat Agree | No Opinion | Somewhat Disagree | Strongly Disagree |
| | After re-reading the passage, does it make more sense? Why or why not? | | | | | |
| **Test 4** | I felt confident with the sentences in the Democracy and Revolution passage. | Strongly Agree | Somewhat Agree | No Opinion | Somewhat Disagree | Strongly Disagree |
| | I felt confident with the vocabulary in the Democracy and Revolution passage. | Strongly Agree | Somewhat Agree | No Opinion | Somewhat Disagree | Strongly Disagree |
| | After re-reading the passage, does it make more sense? Why or why not? | | | | | |
| **Test 5** | I felt confident with the sentences in the Women and Slavery passage. | Strongly Agree | Somewhat Agree | No Opinion | Somewhat Disagree | Strongly Disagree |
| | I felt confident with the vocabulary in the Women and Slavery passage. | Strongly Agree | Somewhat Agree | No Opinion | Somewhat Disagree | Strongly Disagree |
| | After re-reading the passage, does it make more sense? Why or why not? | | | | | |
| **Test 10** | I felt confident with the sentences in the American Imperialism passage. | Strongly Agree | Somewhat Agree | No Opinion | Somewhat Disagree | Strongly Disagree |
| | I felt confident with the vocabulary in the American Imperialism passage. | Strongly Agree | Somewhat Agree | No Opinion | Somewhat Disagree | Strongly Disagree |
| | After re-reading the passage, does it make more sense? Why or why not? | | | | | |

Lesson 7: Mastering the Passages

As always, remember to **review the passages, the questions, and the answers** when you are done. Lesson 11 includes my **annotations** and **identifications** along with a breakdown of **question type recognition**. You'll also find **review tables** for all the practice tests. To do your best, put in the extra time to anchor down the lessons you've just learned.

# LESSON 8: MASTERING THE CLOCK

The passages on the SAT are not necessarily "fun" to read. They have strange topics, or at least topics that you are unlikely to read in your spare time. On a good test, you'll find two passages you like, two you can tolerate, and one that you just don't care about.

You know what? *You're going to miss the most questions on the passages you don't care about.* You probably knew this intuitively; when you don't care about something, it's harder to put the effort into the passage and questions. So to learn to focus, you need to learn to care.

## LEARNING TO FOCUS 13 MINUTES AT A TIME

Here's the bargain you need to make with yourself. "I will care about this passage for thirteen minutes." You don't need to commit anything beyond those thirteen minutes. You don't have to care after the test. You don't have to care after the section. You don't even need to care after the passage. **Just care for 13 minutes**. You can do that, right?

To help you practice your focusing skills, here are some passages to practice. They have been edited so they should take you around thirteen minutes to read at the benchmark reading speeds for high school students (between 200 and 250 words per minute). You'll notice that they are longer than the real SAT passages. That's because they don't have the typical SAT questions that you need to answer. They do have short questions so you can practice your reading comprehension skills.

# The Bet (Anton Chekhov)

*This passage is adapted from Anton Chekhov, "The Bet." Originally published in Russian in 1901 and translated into English in 1915.*

It was a dark autumn night. The old banker was pacing from corner to corner of his study, recalling to his mind the party he gave in the autumn fifteen years ago. There were many clever people at the party and much interesting conversation. They talked among other things of capital punishment. The guests, among them not a few scholars and journalists, for the most part disapproved of capital punishment. They found it obsolete as a means of punishment, unfitted to a Christian State and immoral. Some of them thought that capital punishment should be replaced universally by life-imprisonment.

"I don't agree with you," said the host. "I myself have experienced neither capital punishment nor life-imprisonment, but if one may judge a priori, then in my opinion capital punishment is more moral and more humane than imprisonment. Execution kills instantly, life-imprisonment kills by degrees. Who is the more humane executioner, one who kills you in a few seconds or one who draws the life out of you incessantly, for years?"

"They're both equally immoral," remarked one of the guests, "because their purpose is the same, to take away life. The State is not God. It has no right to take away that which it cannot give back, if it should so desire."

Among the company was a lawyer, a young man of about twenty-five. On being asked his opinion, he said:" Capital punishment and life-imprisonment are equally immoral; but if I were offered the choice between them, I would certainly choose the second. It's better to live somehow than not to live at all."

There ensued a lively discussion. The banker who was then younger and more nervous suddenly lost his temper, banged his fist on the table, and turning to the young lawyer, cried out:

"It's a lie. I bet you two millions you wouldn't stick in a cell even for five years."

"If that's serious," replied the lawyer, "then I bet I'll stay not five but fifteen."

"Fifteen! Done!" cried the banker. "Gentlemen, I stake two millions."

"Agreed. You stake two millions, I my freedom," said the lawyer.

So this wild, ridiculous bet came to pass. The banker, who at that time had too many millions to count, spoiled and capricious, was beside himself with rapture. During supper he said to the lawyer jokingly:

"Come to your senses, young man, before it's too late. Two millions are nothing to me, but you stand to lose three or four of the best years of your life. I say three or four, because you'll never stick it out any longer. Don't forget either, you unhappy man, that voluntary is much heavier than enforced imprisonment. The idea that you have the right to free yourself at any moment will poison the whole of your life in the cell. I pity you."

And now the banker pacing from corner to corner, recalled all this and asked himself:

"Why did I make this bet? What's the good? The lawyer loses fifteen years of his life and I throw away two millions. Will it convince people that capital punishment is worse or better than imprisonment for life? No, No! all stuff and rubbish. On my part, it was the caprice of a well-fed man; on the lawyer's, pure greed of gold."

He recollected further what happened after the evening party. It was decided that the lawyer must undergo his imprisonment under the strictest observation, in a garden-wing of the banker's house. It was agreed that during the period he would be deprived of the right to cross the threshold, to see living people, to hear human voices, and to receive letters and newspapers. He was permitted to have a musical instrument, to read books, to write letters, to drink wine and smoke tobacco. By the agreement he could communicate, but only in silence, with the outside world through a little window specially constructed for this purpose. Everything necessary, books, music, wine, he could receive in any quantity by sending a note through the window. The agreement provided for all the minutest details, which made the confinement strictly solitary, and it obliged the lawyer to remain exactly fifteen years from twelve o'clock of November 14th 1870 to twelve o'clock of November 14th 1885. The least attempt on his part to violate the conditions, to escape if only for two minutes before the time freed the banker from the obligation to pay him the two millions.

During the first year of imprisonment, the lawyer, as far as it was possible to judge from his short notes, suffered terribly from loneliness and boredom. From his wing day and night came the sound of the piano. He rejected wine and tobacco. "Wine," he wrote, "excites desires, and desires are the chief foes of a prisoner; besides, nothing is more boring than to drink good wine alone," and tobacco spoils the air in his room. During the first year the lawyer was sent books of a light character; novels with a complicated love interest, stories of crime and fantasy, comedies, and so on.

In the second year the piano was heard no longer and the lawyer asked only for classics. In the fifth year, music was heard again, and the prisoner asked for wine. Those who watched him said that during the whole of that year he was only eating, drinking, and lying on his bed. He yawned often and talked angrily to himself. Books he did not read. Sometimes at nights he would sit down to write. He would write for a long time and tear it all up in the morning. More than once he was heard to weep.

In the second half of the sixth year, the prisoner began zealously to study languages, philosophy, and history. He fell on these subjects so hungrily that the banker hardly had time to get books enough for him. In the space of four years about six hundred volumes were bought at his request. It was while that passion lasted that the banker received the following letter from the prisoner: "My dear jailer, I am writing these lines in six languages. Show them to experts. Let them read them. If they do not find one single mistake, I beg you to give orders to have a gun fired off in the garden. By the noise I shall know that my efforts have not been in vain. The geniuses of all ages and countries speak in different languages; but in them all burns the same flame. Oh, if you knew my heavenly happiness now that I can understand them!" The prisoner's desire was fulfilled. Two shots were fired in the garden by the banker's order.

Later on, after the tenth year, the lawyer sat immovable before his table and read only the New Testament. The banker found it strange that a man who in four years had mastered six hundred erudite volumes, should have spent nearly a year in reading one book, easy to understand and by no means thick. The New Testament was then replaced by the history of religions and theology.

During the last two years of his confinement the prisoner read an extraordinary amount, quite haphazard. Now he would apply himself to the natural sciences, then would read Byron or Shakespeare. Notes used to come from him in which he asked to be sent at the same time a book on chemistry, a text-book of medicine, a novel, and some treatise on philosophy or theology. He read as though he were swimming in the sea among the broken pieces of wreckage, and in his desire to save his life was eagerly grasping one piece after another.

****

The banker recalled all this, and thought:

"Tomorrow at twelve o'clock he receives his freedom. Under the agreement, I shall have to pay him two millions. If I pay, it's all over with me. I am ruined forever…"

Fifteen years before he had too many millions to count, but now he was afraid to ask himself which he had more of, money or debts. Gambling on the Stock-Exchange, risky speculation, and the recklessness of which he could not rid himself even in old age, had gradually brought his business to decay; and the fearless, self-confident, proud man of business had become an ordinary banker, trembling at every rise and fall in the market.

"That cursed bet," murmured the old man clutching his head in despair… "Why didn't the man die? He's only forty years old. He will take away my last farthing, marry, enjoy life, gamble on the Exchange, and I will look on like an envious beggar and hear the same words from him every day: 'I'm obliged to you for the happiness of my life. Let me help you.' No, it's too much! The only escape from bankruptcy and disgrace — is that the man should die."

The clock had just struck three. The banker was listening. In Ike house everyone was asleep, and one could hear only the frozen trees whining outside the windows. Trying to make no sound, he took out of his safe the key of the door which had not been opened for fifteen years, put on his overcoat, and went out of the house. The garden was dark and cold. It was raining. A keen damp wind hovered howling over all the garden and gave the trees no rest. Though he strained his eyes, the banker could see neither the ground, nor the white statues, nor the garden-wing, nor the trees. Approaching the place where the garden wing stood, he called the watchman twice. There was no answer. Evidently the watchman had taken shelter from the bad weather and was now asleep somewhere in the kitchen or the greenhouse.

"If I have the courage to fulfil my intention," thought the old man, "the suspicion will fall on the watchman first of all."

In the darkness he groped for the stairs and the door and entered the hall of the gardenwing, then poked his way into a narrow passage and struck a match. Not a soul was there. Someone's bed, with no bedclothes on it, stood there, and an iron stove was dark in the corner. The seals on the door that led into the prisoner's room were unbroken.

When the match went out, the old man, trembling from agitation, peeped into the little window.

In the prisoner's room a candle was burning dim. The prisoner himself sat by the table. Only his back, the hair on his head and his hands were visible. On the table, the two chairs, the carpet by the table open books were strewn.

Five minutes passed and the prisoner never once stirred. Fifteen years confinement had taught him to sit motionless. The banker tapped on the window with his finger, but the prisoner gave no movement in reply. Then the banker cautiously tore the seals from the door and put the key into the lock. The rusty lock gave a hoarse groan and the door creaked. The banker expected instantly to hear a cry of surprise and the sound of steps. Three minutes passed and it was as quiet behind the door as it had been before. He made up his mind to enter. Before the table sat a man, unlike an ordinary human being. It was a skeleton, with tight-drawn skin, with a woman's long curly hair, and a shaggy beard. The color of his face was yellow, of an earthy shade; the cheeks were sunken, the back long and narrow, and the hand upon which he leaned his hairy head was so lean and skinny that it was painful to look upon. His hair was already silvering with grey, and no one who glanced at the senile emaciation of the face would have believed that he was only forty years old. On the table, before his bended head, lay a sheet of paper on which something was written in a tiny hand.

"Poor devil," thought the banker, "he's asleep and probably seeing millions in his dreams. I have only to take and throw this half-dead thing on the bed, smother him a moment with the pillow, and the most careful examination will find no trace of unnatural death. But, first, let us read what he has written here."

The banker took the sheet from the table and read:

"Tomorrow at twelve o'clock midnight, I shall obtain my freedom and the right to mix with people. But before I leave this room and see the sun I think it necessary to say a few words to you. On my own clear conscience and before God who sees me I declare to you that I despise freedom, life, health, and all that your books call the blessings of the world.

"For fifteen years I have diligently studied earthly life. True, I saw neither the earth nor the people, but in your books I drank fragrant wine, sang songs, hunted deer and wild boar in the forests, loved women... And beautiful women, like clouds ethereal, created by the magic of your poets' genius, visited me by night and whispered me wonderful tales, which made my head drunken. In your books I climbed the summits of Elbruz and Mont Blanc and saw from thence how the sun rose in the morning, and in the evening overflowed the sky, the ocean and the mountain ridges with a purple gold. I saw from thence how above me lightning glimmered cleaving the clouds; I saw green forests, fields, rivers, lakes, cities; I heard sirens singing, and the playing of the pipes of Pan; I touched the wings of beautiful devils who came flying to me to speak of God... In your books I cast myself into bottomless abysses, worked miracles, burned cities to the ground, preached new religions, conquered whole countries...

"Your books gave me wisdom. All that unwearying human thought created in the centuries is compressed to a little lump in my skull. I know that I am more clever than you all.

"And I despise your books, despise all worldly blessings and wisdom. Everything is void, frail, visionary and delusive like a mirage. Though you be proud and wise and beautiful, yet will death wipe you from the face of the earth like the mice underground; and your posterity, your history, and the immortality of your men of genius will be as frozen slag, burnt down together with the terrestrial globe.

"You are mad, and gone the wrong way. You take lie for truth and ugliness for beauty. You would marvel if by certain conditions there should suddenly grow on apple and orange trees, instead of fruit, frogs and lizards, and if roses should begin to breathe the odor of a sweating horse. So do I marvel at you, who have bartered heaven for earth. I do not want to understand you.

"That I may show you in deed my contempt for that by which you live, I waive the two millions of which I once dreamed as of paradise, and which I now despise. That I may deprive myself of my right to them, I shall come out from here five minutes before the stipulated term, and thus shall violate the agreement."

When he had read, the banker put the sheet on the table, kissed the head of the strange man, and began to weep. He went out of the wing. Never at any other time, not even after his terrible losses on the Exchange, had he felt such contempt for himself as now. Coming home, he lay down on his bed, but agitation and tears kept him long from sleep...

The next morning the poor watchman came running to him and told him that they had seen the man who lived in the wing climbing through the window into the garden. He had gone to the gate and disappeared. Together with his servants the banker went instantly to the wing and established the escape of his prisoner. To avoid unnecessary rumors he took the paper with the renunciation from the table and, on his return, locked it in his safe.

1. How would you describe this story to somebody who had never read it?

2. What part of the story did you find most engaging?

3. What adjectives would you use to describe the banker, without saying what role he plays in the story?

4. What adjectives would you use to describe the lawyer, without saying what role he plays in the story?

5. Who was right?

# Blood Groups and Red Cell Antigens (Laura Dean)

This passage is adapted from Laura Dean, *Blood Groups and Red Cell Antigens*. It was published by National Center for Biotechnology Information (NCBI), National Library of Medicine, and the National Institutes of Health in 2005.

The average human adult has more than 5 liters (6 quarts) of blood in his or her body. Blood carries oxygen and nutrients to living cells and takes away their waste products. It also delivers immune cells to
5  fight infections and contains platelets that can form a plug in a damaged blood vessel to prevent blood loss.

Through the circulatory system, blood adapts to the body's needs. When you are exercising, your heart pumps harder and faster to provide more blood and
10 hence oxygen to your muscles. During an infection, the blood delivers more immune cells to the site of infection, where they accumulate to ward off harmful invaders.

All of these functions make blood a precious fluid.
15 Each year in the USA, 30 million units of blood components are transfused to patients who need them. Blood is deemed so precious that is also called "red gold" because the cells and proteins it contains can be sold for more than the cost of the same weight in gold.
20 If a test tube of blood is left to stand for half an hour, the blood separates into three layers as the denser components sink to the bottom of the tube and fluid remains at the top.

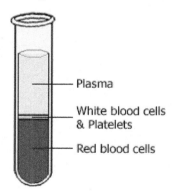

The straw-colored fluid that forms the top layer is
25 called plasma and forms about 60% of blood. The middle white layer is composed of white blood cells (WBCs) and platelets, and the bottom red layer is the red blood cells (RBCs). These bottom two layers of cells form about 40% of the blood. Plasma is mainly
30 water, but it also contains many important substances such as proteins (albumin, clotting factors, antibodies, enzymes, and hormones), sugars (glucose), and fat particles.

All of the cells found in the blood come from bone
35 marrow. They begin their life as stem cells, and they mature into three main types of cells — RBCs, WBCs, and platelets. In turn, there are three types of WBC — lymphocytes, monocytes, and granulocytes — and three main types of granulocytes (neutrophils,
40 eosinophils, and basophils).

A sample of blood can be further separated into its individual components by spinning the sample in a centrifuge. The force of the spinning causes denser elements to sink, and further processing enables the
45 isolation of a particular protein or the isolation of a particular type of blood cell. With the use of this method, antibodies and clotting factors can be harvested from the plasma to treat immune deficiencies and bleeding disorders, respectively.
50 Likewise, RBCs can be harvested for blood transfusion.

Every second, 2-3 million RBCs are produced in the bone marrow and released into the circulation. Also known as erythrocytes, RBCs are the most common type of cell found in the blood, with each
55 cubic millimeter of blood containing 4-6 million cells. With a diameter of only 6 μm, RBCs are small enough to squeeze through the smallest blood vessels. They circulate around the body for up to 120 days, at which point the old or damaged RBCs are removed from the
60 circulation by specialized cells (macrophages) in the spleen and liver.

In humans, as in all mammals, the mature RBC lacks a nucleus. This allows the cell more room to store hemoglobin, the oxygen-binding protein, enabling the
65 RBC to transport more oxygen. RBCs are also biconcave in shape; this shape increases their surface area for the diffusion of oxygen across their surfaces. In non-mammalian vertebrates such as birds and fish, mature RBCs do have a nucleus.

70 If a patient has a low level of hemoglobin, a condition called anemia, they may appear pale because hemoglobin gives RBCs, and hence blood, their red color. They may also tire easily and feel short of breath because of the essential role of hemoglobin in
75 transporting oxygen from the lungs to wherever it is needed around the body.

WBCs come in many different shapes and sizes. Some cells have nuclei with multiple lobes, whereas others contain one large, round nucleus. Some contain packets of granules in their cytoplasm and so are known as granulocytes.

Despite their differences in appearance, all of the various types of WBCs have a role in the immune response. They circulate in the blood until they receive a signal that a part of the body is damaged. Signals include interleukin 1 (IL-1), a molecule secreted by macrophages that contributes to the fever of infections, and histamine, which is released by circulating basophils and tissue mast cells, and contributes to allergic reactions. In response to these signals, the WBCs leave the blood vessel by squeezing through holes in the blood vessel wall. They migrate to the source of the signal and help begin the healing process.

Individuals who have low levels of WBCs may have more and worse infections. Depending upon which WBCs are missing, the patient is at risk for different types of infection. For example, macrophages are especially good at swallowing bacteria, and a deficiency in macrophages leads to recurrent bacterial infections. In contrast, T cells are particularly skilled in fighting viral infections, and a loss of their function results in an increased susceptibility to viral infections.

Neutrophils are also known as polymorphonuclear cells because they contain a nucleus whose shape (morph) is irregular and contains many (poly) lobes. They also belong to a group of WBCs known as granulocytes because their cytoplasm is dotted with granules that contain enzymes that helps them digest pathogens.

Monocytes are young WBCs that circulate in the blood. They develop into macrophages after they have left the blood and migrated into tissue. There they provide an immediate defense because they can engulf (phagocytose) and digest pathogens before other types of WBCs reach the area.

In the liver, tissue macrophages are called Kupffer cells, and they specialize in removing harmful agents from blood that has left the gut. Alveolar macrophages are in the lungs and remove harmful agents that may have been inhaled. Macrophages in the spleen remove old or damaged red blood cells and platelets from the circulation.

Macrophages are also "antigen-presenting cells", presenting the foreign proteins (antigens) to other immune cells, triggering an immune response.

Lymphocytes are round cells that contain a single, large round nucleus. There are two main classes of cells, the B cells that mature in the bone marrow, and the T cells that mature in the thymus gland.

Once activated, the B cells and T cells trigger different types of immune response. The activated B cells, also known as plasma cells, produce highly specific antibodies that bind to the agent that triggered the immune response. T cells, called helper T cells, secrete chemicals that recruit other immune cells and help coordinate their attack. Another group, called cytotoxic T cells, attacks virally infected cells.

Platelets are irregularly shaped fragments of cells that circulate in the blood until they are either activated to form a blood clot or are removed by the spleen. Thrombocytopenia is a condition of low levels of platelets and carries an increased risk of bleeding. Conversely, a high level of platelets (thrombocythemia) carries an increased risk of forming inappropriate blood clots. These could deprive essential organs such as the heart and brain, of their blood supply, causing heart attacks and strokes, respectively.

As with all the cells in the blood, platelets originate from stem cells in the bone marrow. The stem cells develop into platelet precursors (called megakaryocytes) that "shed" platelets into the bloodstream. There, platelets circulate for about 9 days. If they encounter damaged blood vessel walls during this time, they stick to the damaged area and are activated to form a blood clot. This plugs the hole. Otherwise, at the end of their life span they are removed from the circulation by the spleen. In a diverse number of diseases where the spleen is overactive, e.g. rheumatoid arthritis and leukemia, the spleen removes too many platelets, leading to increased bleeding.

A complete blood count (CBC) is a simple blood test that is commonly ordered as part of a routine medical assessment. As the name suggests, it is a count of the different types of cells found in the blood. The test can diagnose and monitor many different diseases, such as anemia, infection, inflammatory diseases, and malignancy. The CBC also includes information about RBCs that is calculated from the other measurements, e.g., the amount (MCH) and concentration (MCHC) of hemoglobin in RBCs.

| Blood component | Abbreviation used | Reference range |
|---|---|---|
| White blood cells | WBC | 4500-11,000/mm$^3$ |
| Red blood cells | RBC | Male: 4.3-5.9 million/mm$^3$<br>Female: 3.5-5.5 million/mm$^3$ |
| Hemoglobin | HGB | Male: 13.5-17.5 g/dL<br>Female: 12.0-16.0 g/dL |
| Hematocrit | HT | Male: 41%-53%<br>Female: 36%-46% |
| Mean corpuscular volume | MCV | 80-100 μm$^3$ |
| Mean corpuscular hemoglobin | MCH | 25.4-34.6 pg/cell |
| Mean corpuscular hemoglobin concentration | MCHC | 31%-36% HGB/cell |
| Platelets | Platelets | 150,000-400,000/mm$^3$ |

The number of RBCs and the amount of hemoglobin in the blood are lower in women than in men. This is because of the menstrual loss of blood each month. Below a certain level of hemoglobin, a patient is said to be anemic, suggesting a clinically significant drop in oxygen carrying capacity. Anemia is not a diagnosis but a symptom of an underlying disease that has to be investigated.

A clue to the cause of anemia is the average size of RBC (mean corpuscular volume, MCV). Causes of a high MCV include a deficiency of $B_{12}$ or folate vitamins in the diet. $B_{12}$ is found in red meat therefore, a deficiency of $B_{12}$ is especially common in vegetarians and vegans. Conversely, folate is plentiful in fresh leafy green vegetables, therefore, a deficiency of folate is common in the elderly, who may have a poor diet.

Low MCV anemia is common and may be a result of hereditary blood disorders, such as thalassemia, but is most often caused by a deficiency of iron. For example, women of reproductive age may lose too much iron through heavy menstrual bleeding and are prone to this form of anemia, known as iron-deficiency anemia.

The hematocrit measures the fraction of the blood that is made up of RBCs. It reflects the combination of the total number of RBCs, and the volume that they occupy.

One of the changes seen in pregnancy is a drop in hematocrit. This occurs because although the production of RBCs does not change greatly, the plasma volume increases, i.e., the RBCs are "diluted". Alternatively, a low hematocrit can reflect a drop in RBC production by the bone marrow. This may be attributable to bone marrow disease (damage by toxins or cancer) or due to a decrease in erythropoietin, a hormone secreted by the kidney that stimulates RBC production. Decreased RBCs may also be the result of a reduced life span of the RBCs (e.g., chronic bleeding).

A high hematocrit value may truly reflect an increase in the fraction of RBCs (e.g., increased erythropoietin attributable to a tumor of RBCs called polycythemia rubra vera), or it may reflect a drop in the plasma component of the blood (e.g., fluid loss in burn victims).

The WBC count is a count of the number of WBCs found in one cubic millimeter of blood. An increased number of WBCs is most commonly caused by infections, such as a urinary tract infection or pneumonia. It may also be caused by WBC tumors, such as leukemia. A decreased number of WBCs is caused by the bone marrow failing to produce WBCs or by an increased removal of WBCs from the circulation by a diseased liver or an overactive spleen. Bone marrow failure may be caused by toxins or by the normal bone marrow cells being replaced by tumor cells.

The WBC differential part of the CBC breaks down the WBCs into five different types: neutrophils, lymphocytes, monocytes, eosinophils, and basophils. Finding out the count of each type of WBC gives more information about the underlying problem. For example, in the early stages of an infection, most of the increase in WBCs is attributable to the increase in neutrophils. As the infection continues, lymphocytes increase. Worm infections can trigger an increase in eosinophils, whereas allergic conditions, such as hay fever, trigger an increase in basophils.

Normally, one cubic millimeter of blood contains between 150,000 and 400,000 platelets. If the number drops below this range, uncontrolled bleeding becomes a risk, whereas a rise above the upper limit of this range indicates a risk of uncontrolled blood clotting.

Hemoglobin is the oxygen-carrying protein that is found within all RBCs. It picks up oxygen where it is abundant (the lungs) and drops off oxygen where it is needed around the body. Hemoglobin is also the pigment that gives RBCs their red color.

As its name suggests, hemoglobin is composed of "heme" groups (iron-containing rings) and "globins" (proteins). In fact, hemoglobin is composed of four globin proteins — two alpha chains and two beta chains — each with a heme group. The heme group contains one iron atom, and this can bind one molecule of oxygen. Because each molecule of hemoglobin contains four globins, it can carry up to four molecules of oxygen.

In the lungs, a hemoglobin molecule is surrounded by a high concentration of oxygen, therefore, it binds oxygen. In active tissues, the oxygen concentration is lower, so hemoglobin releases its oxygen.

This behavior is much more effective because the hemoglobin––oxygen binding is "co-operative". This means that the binding of one molecule of oxygen makes it easier for the binding of subsequent oxygen molecules. Likewise, the unbinding of oxygen makes it easier for other oxygen molecules to be released. This means that the response of hemoglobin to the oxygen needs of active tissues is much quicker.

Aside from the oxygen saturation of hemoglobin, other factors that influence how readily hemoglobin binds oxygen include plasma pH, plasma bicarbonate levels, and the pressure of oxygen in the air (high altitudes in particular).

The molecule 2,3-diphosphoglycerate (2,3-DPG) binds to hemoglobin and lowers its affinity for oxygen, thus promoting oxygen release. In individuals who have become acclimatized to living at high altitudes, the level of 2,3-DPG in the blood increases, allowing the delivery of more oxygen to tissues under low oxygen tension.

Fetal hemoglobin differs from adult hemoglobin in that it contains two gamma chains instead of two beta chains. Fetal hemoglobin binds oxygen with a much greater affinity than adult hemoglobin; this is an advantage in the womb because it allows fetal blood to extract oxygen from maternal blood, despite its low concentration of oxygen. Normally, all fetal hemoglobin is replaced by adult hemoglobin by the time of birth.

Old or damaged RBCs are removed from the circulation by macrophages in the spleen and liver, and the hemoglobin they contain is broken down into heme and globin. The globin protein may be recycled, or broken down further to its constituent amino acids, which may be recycled or metabolized. The heme contains precious iron that is conserved and reused in the synthesis of new hemoglobin molecules.

During its metabolism, heme is converted to bilirubin, a yellow pigment that can discolor the skin and sclera of the eye if it accumulates in the blood, a condition known as jaundice. Instead, the plasma protein albumin binds to bilirubin and carries it to the liver, where it is secreted in bile and also contributes to the color of feces.

Jaundice is one of the complications of an incompatible blood transfusion. This occurs when the recipient's immune system attacks the donor RBCs as being foreign. The rate of RBC destruction and subsequent bilirubin production can exceed the capacity of the liver to metabolize the bilirubin produced.

Hemoglobinopathies form a group of inherited diseases that are caused by mutations in the globin chains of hemoglobin. Sickle cell anemia is the most common of these and is attributable to a mutation that changes one of the amino acids in the hemoglobin beta chain, producing hemoglobin that is "fragile". When the oxygen concentration is low, RBCs tend to become distorted and "sickle" shaped. These deformed cells can block small blood vessels and damage the organs they are supplying. This can be very painful, and if not treated, a sickle cell crisis can be fatal.

Another inherited anemia that particularly affects individuals of Mediterranean descent is thalassemia. A fault in the production of either alpha or beta globin chains causes a range of symptoms, depending on how many copies of the alpha and beta genes are affected. Some individuals may be carriers of the disease and have no symptoms, whereas if all copies of the genes are lost, the disease is fatal.

The porphyria are a group of inherited disorders in which the synthesis of heme is disrupted. Depending upon the stage at which the disruption occurs, there are a range of neurological and gastrointestinal side effects. King George III of England ("the madness of King George") was one of the most famous individuals who suffered from porphyria.

1. How would you describe this passage to somebody who had never read it?

2. How are the different types of blood cells separated?

3. What information does table 1 provide?

4. What information can a blood test provide?

5. Why study blood?

## Jane Eyre (Charlotte Bronte)

This passage is adapted from Charlotte Bronte, *Jane Eyre: An Autobiography*. Originally published in 1847.

I resisted all the way: a new thing for me, and a circumstance which greatly strengthened the bad opinion Bessie and Miss Abbot were disposed to entertain of me. The fact is, I was a trifle beside myself;
[5] or rather *out* of myself, as the French would say: I was conscious that a moment's mutiny had already rendered me liable to strange penalties, and, like any other rebel slave, I felt resolved, in my desperation, to go all lengths.
[10] "Hold her arms, Miss Abbot: she's like a mad cat."
"For shame! for shame!" cried the lady's-maid. "What shocking conduct, Miss Eyre, to strike a young gentleman, your benefactress's son! Your young master."
[15] "Master! How is he my master? Am I a servant?"
"No; you are less than a servant, for you do nothing for your keep. There, sit down, and think over your wickedness."
They had got me by this time into the apartment
[20] indicated by Mrs. Reed, and had thrust me upon a stool: my impulse was to rise from it like a spring; their two pair of hands arrested me instantly.
"If you don't sit still, you must be tied down," said Bessie. "Miss Abbot, lend me your garters; she would
[25] break mine directly."
Miss Abbot turned to divest a stout leg of the necessary ligature. This preparation for bonds, and the additional ignominy it inferred, took a little of the excitement out of me.
[30] "Don't take them off," I cried; "I will not stir." In guarantee whereof, I attached myself to my seat by my hands.
"Mind you don't," said Bessie; and when she had ascertained that I was really subsiding, she loosened
[35] her hold of me; then she and Miss Abbot stood with folded arms, looking darkly and doubtfully on my face, as incredulous of my sanity.
"She never did so before," at last said Bessie, turning to the Abigail.
[40] "But it was always in her," was the reply. "I've told Missis often my opinion about the child, and Missis agreed with me. She's an underhand little thing: I never saw a girl of her age with so much cover."
Bessie answered not; but ere long, addressing me,
[45] she said — "You ought to be aware, Miss, that you are under obligations to Mrs. Reed: she keeps you: if she were to turn you off, you would have to go to the poorhouse."
I had nothing to say to these words: they were not
[50] new to me: my very first recollections of existence included hints of the same kind. This reproach of my dependence had become a vague sing-song in my ear: very painful and crushing, but only half intelligible. Miss Abbot joined in —
[55] "And you ought not to think yourself on an equality with the Misses Reed and Master Reed, because Missis kindly allows you to be brought up with them. They will have a great deal of money, and you will have none: it is your place to be humble, and to try
[60] to make yourself agreeable to them."
"What we tell you is for your good," added Bessie, in no harsh voice, "you should try to be useful and pleasant, then, perhaps, you would have a home here; but if you become passionate and rude, Missis will
[65] send you away, I am sure."
"Besides," said Miss Abbot, "God will punish her: He might strike her dead in the midst of her tantrums, and then where would she go? Come, Bessie, we will leave her: I wouldn't have her heart for anything. Say
[70] your prayers, Miss Eyre, when you are by yourself; for if you don't repent, something bad might be permitted to come down the chimney and fetch you away."
They went, shutting the door, and locking it behind them.
[75] The red-room was a square chamber, very seldom slept in, I might say never, indeed, unless when a chance influx of visitors at Gateshead Hall rendered it necessary to turn to account all the accommodation it contained: yet it was one of the largest and stateliest
[80] chambers in the mansion. A bed supported on massive pillars of mahogany, hung with curtains of deep red damask, stood out like a tabernacle in the center; the two large windows, with their blinds always drawn down, were
[85] half shrouded in festoons and falls of similar drapery; the carpet was red; the table at the foot of the bed was covered with a crimson cloth; the walls were a soft fawn color with a blush of pink in it; the wardrobe, the toilet-table, the chairs were of darkly polished old
[90] mahogany. Out of these deep surrounding shades rose high, and glared white, the piled-up mattresses and pillows of the bed, spread with a snowy Marseilles counterpane. Scarcely less prominent was an ample cushioned easy-chair near the head of the bed, also

white, with a footstool before it; and looking, as I thought, like a pale throne.

This room was chill, because it seldom had a fire; it was silent, because remote from the nursery and kitchen; solemn, because it was known to be so seldom entered. The house-maid alone came here on Saturdays, to wipe from the mirrors and the furniture a week's quiet dust: and Mrs. Reed herself, at far intervals, visited it to review the contents of a certain secret drawer in the wardrobe, where were stored divers parchments, her jewel-casket, and a miniature of her deceased husband; and in those last words lies the secret of the red-room — the spell which kept it so lonely in spite of its grandeur.

Mr. Reed had been dead nine years: it was in this chamber he breathed his last; here he lay in state; hence his coffin was borne by the undertaker's men; and, since that day, a sense of dreary consecration had guarded it from frequent intrusion.

My seat, to which Bessie and the bitter Miss Abbot had left me riveted, was a low ottoman near the marble chimney-piece; the bed rose before me; to my right hand there was the high, dark wardrobe, with subdued, broken reflections varying the gloss of its panels; to my left were the muffled windows; a great looking-glass between them repeated the vacant majesty of the bed and room. I was not quite sure whether they had locked the door; and when I dared move, I got up and went to see. Alas! yes: no jail was ever more secure. Returning, I had to cross before the looking-glass; my fascinated glance involuntarily explored the depth it revealed. All looked colder and darker in that visionary hollow than in reality: and the strange little figure there gazing at me, with a white face and arms specking the gloom, and glittering eyes of fear moving where all else was still, had the effect of a real spirit: I thought it like one of the tiny phantoms, half fairy, half imp, Bessie's evening stories represented as coming out of lone, ferny dells in moors, and appearing before the eyes of belated travelers. I returned to my stool.

Superstition was with me at that moment; but it was not yet her hour for complete victory: my blood was still warm; the mood of the revolted slave was still bracing me with its bitter vigor; I had to stem a rapid rush of retrospective thought before I quailed to the dismal present.

All John Reed's violent tyrannies, all his sisters' proud indifference, all his mother's aversion, all the servants' partiality, turned up in my disturbed mind like a dark deposit in a turbid well. Why was I always suffering, always browbeaten, always accused, forever condemned? Why could I never please? Why was it useless to try to win any one's favor? Eliza, who was headstrong and selfish, was respected. Georgiana, who had a spoiled temper, a very acrid spite, a captious and insolent carriage, was universally indulged. Her beauty, her pink cheeks and golden curls, seemed to give delight to all who looked at her, and to purchase indemnity for every fault. John no one thwarted, much less punished; though he twisted the necks of the pigeons, killed the little pea-chicks, set the dogs at the sheep, stripped the hothouse vines of their fruit, and broke the buds off the choicest plants in the conservatory: he called his mother "old girl," too; sometimes reviled her for her dark skin, similar to his own; bluntly disregarded her wishes; not unfrequently tore and spoiled her silk attire; and he was still "her own darling." I dared commit no fault: I strove to fulfil every duty; and I was termed naughty and tiresome, sullen and sneaking, from morning to noon, and from noon to night.

My head still ached and bled with the blow and fall I had received: no one had reproved John for wantonly striking me; and because I had turned against him to avert farther irrational violence, I was loaded with general opprobrium.

"Unjust! — unjust!" said my reason, forced by the agonizing stimulus into precocious though transitory power: and Resolve, equally wrought up, instigated some strange expedient to achieve escape from insupportable oppression — as running away, or, if that could not be effected, never eating or drinking more, and letting myself die.

What a consternation of soul was mine that dreary afternoon! How all my brain was in tumult, and all my heart in insurrection! Yet in what darkness, what dense ignorance, was the mental battle fought! I could not answer the ceaseless inward question — *why* I thus suffered; now, at the distance of — I will not say how many years, I see it clearly. I was a discord in Gateshead Hall: I was like nobody there; I had nothing in harmony with Mrs. Reed or her children, or her chosen vassalage. If they did not love me, in fact, as little did I love them. They were not bound to regard with affection a thing that could not sympathize with one amongst them; a heterogeneous thing, opposed to them in temperament, in capacity, in propensities; a useless thing, incapable of serving their interest, or adding to their pleasure; a noxious thing, cherishing the germs of indignation at their treatment, of contempt of their judgment. I know that had I been a sanguine, brilliant, careless, exacting, handsome, romping child — though equally dependent and friendless — Mrs. Reed would have endured my presence more complacently; her children would have entertained for me more of the cordiality of fellow-feeling; the servants would have been less prone to make me the scapegoat of the nursery.

Daylight began to forsake the red-room; it was past four o'clock, and the beclouded afternoon was tending to drear twilight. I heard the rain still beating continuously on the staircase window, and the wind howling in the grove behind the hall; I grew by degrees cold as a stone, and then my courage sank. My habitual mood of humiliation, self-doubt, forlorn depression, fell damp on the embers of my decaying ire. All said I was wicked, and perhaps I might be so; what thought had I been but just conceiving of starving myself to death? That certainly was a crime: and was I fit to die? Or was the vault under the chancel of Gateshead Church an inviting bourne? In such vault I had been told did Mr. Reed lie buried; and led by this thought to recall his idea, I dwelt on it with gathering dread. I could not remember him; but I knew that he was my own uncle — my mother's brother — that he had taken me when a parentless infant to his house; and that in his last moments he had required a promise of Mrs. Reed that she would rear and maintain me as one of her own children. Mrs. Reed probably considered she had kept this promise; and so she had, I dare say, as well as her nature would permit her; but how could she really like an interloper not of her race, and unconnected with her, after her husband's death, by any tie? It must have been most irksome to find herself bound by a hard-wrung pledge to stand in the stead of a parent to a strange child she could not love, and to see an uncongenial alien permanently intruded on her own family group.

A singular notion dawned upon me. I doubted not — never doubted — that if Mr. Reed had been alive he would have treated me kindly; and now, as I sat looking at the white bed and overshadowed walls — occasionally also turning a fascinated eye towards the dimly gleaning mirror — I began to recall what I had heard of dead men, troubled in their graves by the violation of their last wishes, revisiting the earth to punish the perjured and avenge the oppressed; and I thought Mr. Reed's spirit, harassed by the wrongs of his sister's child, might quit its abode — whether in the church vault or in the unknown world of the departed — and rise before me in this chamber. I wiped my tears and hushed my sobs, fearful lest any sign of violent grief might waken a preternatural voice to comfort me, or elicit from the gloom some haloed face, bending over me with strange pity. This idea, consolatory in theory, I felt would be terrible if realized: with all my might I endeavored to stifle it — I endeavored to be firm. Shaking my hair from my eyes, I lifted my head and tried to look boldly round the dark room; at this moment a light gleamed on the wall. Was it, I asked myself, a ray from the moon penetrating some aperture in the blind? No; moonlight was still, and this stirred; while I gazed, it glided up to the ceiling and quivered over my head. I can now conjecture readily that this streak of light was, in all likelihood, a gleam from a lantern carried by someone across the lawn: but then, prepared as my mind was for horror, shaken as my nerves were by agitation, I thought the swift darting beam was a herald of some coming vision from another world. My heart beat thick, my head grew hot; a sound filled my ears, which I deemed the rushing of wings; something seemed near me; I was oppressed, suffocated: endurance broke down; I rushed to the door and shook the lock in desperate effort.

Steps came running along the outer passage; the key turned, Bessie and Abbot entered.

"Miss Eyre, are you ill?" said Bessie.

"What a dreadful noise! it went quite through me!" exclaimed Abbot.

"Take me out! Let me go into the nursery!" was my cry.

"What for? Are you hurt? Have you seen something?" again demanded Bessie.

"Oh! I saw a light, and I thought a ghost would come." I had now got hold of Bessie's hand, and she did not snatch it from me.

"She has screamed out on purpose," declared Abbot, in some disgust. "And what a scream! If she had been in great pain one would have excused it, but she only wanted to bring us all here: I know her naughty tricks."

"What is all this?" demanded another voice peremptorily; and Mrs. Reed came along the corridor, her cap flying wide, her gown rustling stormily. "Abbot and Bessie, I believe I gave orders that Jane Eyre should be left in the red-room till I came to her myself."

"Miss Jane screamed so loud, ma'am," pleaded Bessie.

"Let her go," was the only answer. "Loose Bessie's hand, child: you cannot succeed in getting out by these means, be assured. I abhor artifice, particularly in children; it is my duty to show you that tricks will not answer: you will now stay here an hour longer, and it is only on condition of perfect submission and stillness that I shall liberate you then."

"O aunt! have pity! Forgive me! I cannot endure it — let me be punished some other way! I shall be killed if — "

"Silence! This violence is all most repulsive:" and so, no doubt, she felt it. I was a precocious actress in her eyes; she sincerely looked on me as a compound of virulent passions, mean spirit, and dangerous duplicity.

Bessie and Abbot having retreated, Mrs. Reed, impatient of my now frantic anguish and wild sobs, abruptly thrust me back and locked me in, without farther parley. I heard her sweeping away; and soon after she was gone, I suppose I had a species of fit: unconsciousness closed the scene.

1. How would you describe this passage to somebody who had never read it?

2. What part of the story did you find most engaging?

3. How does Jane view her family members?

4. How do Jane's family members view her?

5. Does Jane have allies?

# Love of God, Love of Man, Love of Country (Frederick Douglass)

This passage is adapted from Frederick Douglass, "Love of God, Love of Man, Love of Country." Douglass delivered this speech in New York City in October of 1847.

    For a long time when I was a slave, I was led to think from hearing such passages as "servants obey, etc." that if I dared to escape, the wrath of God would follow me. All are willing to acknowledge my right to be free; but after this acknowledgement, the good man goes to the Bible and says "after all I see some difficulty about this thing. You know, after the deluge, there was Shem, Ham, and Japhet; and you know that Ham was black and had a curse put upon him; and I know not but it would be an attempt to thwart the purposes of Jehovah if these men were set at liberty." It is this kind of religion I wish to have you laugh at — it breaks the charm there is about it. If I could have the men at this meeting who hold such sentiments and could hold up the mirror to let them see themselves as others see them, we should soon make head against this pro-slavery religion.

    I dwell mostly upon the religious aspect, because I believe it is the religious people who are to be relied on in this Anti-Slavery movement. Do not misunderstand my railing — do not class me with those who despise religion — do not identify me with the infidel. I love the religion of Christianity — which cometh from above — which is pure, peaceable, gentle, easy to be entreated, full of good fruits, and without hypocrisy. I love that religion which sends its votaries to bind up the wounds of those who have fallen among thieves. By all the love I bear to such a Christianity as this, I hate that of the Priest and Levite, that with long-faced Phariseeism goes up to Jerusalem and worships, and leaves the bruised and wounded to die. I despise that religion that can carry Bibles to the heathen on the other side of the globe and withhold them from [the] heathen on this side — which can talk about human rights yonder and traffic in human flesh here. I love that which makes its votaries do to others as they would that others should do to them. I hope to see a revival of it — thank God it is revived. I see revivals of it in the absence of the other sort of revivals. I believe it to be confessed now, that there has not been a sensible man converted after the old sort of way, in the last five years. Le Roy Sunderland, the mesmerizer, has explained all this away, so that Knapp and others who have converted men after that sort have failed.

    There is another religion. It is that which takes off fetters instead of binding them on — that breaks every yoke — that lifts up the bowed down. The Anti-Slavery platform is based on this kind of religion. It spreads its table to the lame, the halt, and the blind. It goes down after a long neglected race. It passes, link by link till it finds the lowest link in humanity's chain — humanity's most degraded form in the most abject condition. It reaches down its arm and tells them to stand up. This is Anti-Slavery — this is Christianity. It is reviving gloriously among the various denominations. It is threatening to supercede those old forms of religion having all of the love of God and none of man in it. (Applause.) I now leave this aspect of the subject and proceed to inquire into that which probably must be the inquiry of every honest mind present. I trust I do not misjudge the character of my audience when I say they are anxious to know in what way they're contributing to uphold Slavery.

    The question may be answered in various ways. I leave the outworks of political parties and social arrangements, and come at once to the Constitution, to which I believe all present are devotedly attached I will not say all, for I believe I know some, who, however they may be disposed to admire some of the beautiful truths set forth in that instrument, recognize its pro-slavery features, and are ready to form a republic in which there shall be neither tyrant nor slave. The Constitution I hold to be radically and essentially slave-holding, in that it gives the physical and numerical power of the nation to keep the slave in his chains, by promising that that power shall in any emergency be brought to bear upon the slave, to crush him in obedience to his master. The language of the Constitution is you shall be a slave or die. We know it is such, and knowing it we are not disposed to have part nor lot with that Constitution. For my part I had rather that my right hand should wither by my side than cast a ballot under the Constitution of the United States.

    Then, again, in the clause concerning fugitives — in this you are implicated. Your whole country is one vast hunting ground from Texas to Maine. Ours is a glorious land; and from across the Atlantic we welcome those who are stricken by the storms of despotism. Yet the damning facts remain, there is not a rood of earth under the stars and the eagle of your flag, where a man of my complexion can stand free. There is no mountain so high, no plain so extensive, no spot so sacred, that it can secure to me the right of liberty. Wherever waves the star-spangled banner there the bondman may be arrested and hurried back to the jaws of Slavery. This is your "land of the free," your "home of the brave." From Lexington, from Ticonderoga, from Bunker Hill, where rises that grand shaft with its capstone in the clouds, asks, in the name of the first blood that spurted in behalf of freedom, to protect the slave from the infernal clutches of his master. That petition would be denied, and he bid go back to the tyrant.

I never knew what freedom was till I got beyond the limits of the American eagle. When I first rested my head on a British Island I felt that the eagle might scream, but from its talons and beak I was free, at least for a time. No slave-holder can clutch me on British soil. There I could gaze the tyrant in the face and with the indignation of a tyrant in my look, wither him before me. But republican, Christian America will aid the tyrant in catching his victim.

I know this kind of talk is not agreeable to what are called patriots. Indeed, some have called me a traitor. That profanely religious Journal "The Olive Branch," edited by the Rev. Mr. Norris, recommended that I be hung as a traitor. Two things are necessary to make a traitor. One is, he shall have a country. I believe if I had a country, I should be a patriot. I think I have all the feelings necessary — all the moral material, to say nothing about the intellectual. I do not know that I ever felt the emotion, but sometimes thought I had a glimpse of it. When I have been delighted with the little brook that passes by the cottage in which I was born — with the woods and the fertile fields — I felt a sort of glow which I suspect resembles a little what they call patriotism. I can look with some admiration on your wide lakes, your fertile fields, your enterprise, your industry, your many lovely institutions. I can read with pleasure your Constitution to establish justice, and secure the blessings of liberty to posterity. Those are precious sayings to my mind. But when I remember that the blood of four sisters and one brother, is making fat the soil of Maryland and Virginia; when I remember that an aged grandmother who has reared twelve children for the Southern market, and these one after another as they arrived at the most interesting age, were torn from her bosom; when I remember that when she became too much racked for toil, she was turned out by a professed Christian master to grope her way in the darkness of old age, literally to die with none to help her, and the institutions of this country sanctioning and sanctifying this crime, I have no words of eulogy, I have no patriotism. How can I love a country where the blood of my own blood, the flesh of my own flesh, is now toiling under the lash? America's soil reddened by the stain from woman's shrinking flesh.

No, I make no pretension to patriotism. So long as my voice can be heard on this or the other side of the Atlantic, I will hold up America to the lightning scorn of moral indignation. In doing this, I shall feel myself discharging the duty of a true patriot; for he is a lover of his country who rebukes and does not excuse its sins. It is righteousness that exalteth a nation while sin is a reproach to any people. But to the idea of what you at the North have to do with Slavery. You furnish the bulwark of protection, and promise to put the slaves in bondage. As the American Anti-Slavery Society says, "if you will go on branding, scourging, sundering family ties, trampling in the dust your down trodden victims, you must do it at your own peril." But if you say, "we of the North will render you no assistance: if you still continue to trample on the slave, you must take the consequences," I tell you the matter will soon be settled.

I have been taunted frequently with the want of valor: so has my race, because we have not risen upon our masters. It is adding insult to injury to say this. You belong to 17,000,000, with arms, with means of locomotion, with telegraphs. We are kept in ignorance three millions to seventeen. You taunt us with not being able to rescue ourselves from your clutch. Shame on you! Stand aside — give us fair play — leave us with the tyrants, and then if we do not take care of ourselves, you may taunt us. I do not mean by this to advocate war and bloodshed. I am not a man of war. The time was when I was. I was then a slave: I had dreams, horrid dreams of freedom through a sea of blood. But when I heard of the Anti-Slavery movement, light broke in upon my dark mind. Bloody visions fled away, and I saw the star of liberty peering above the horizon. Hope then took the place of desperation, and I was led to repose in the arms of Slavery. I said, I would suffer rather than do any act of violence — rather than that the glorious day of liberty might be postponed.

Since the light of God's truth beamed upon my mind, I have become a friend of that religion which teaches us to pray for our enemies — which, instead of shooting balls into their hearts, loves them. I would not hurt a hair of a slaveholder's head. I will tell you what else I would not do. I would not stand around the slave

195 with my bayonet pointed at his breast, in order to keep him in the power of the slaveholder.

I am aware that there are many who think the slaves are very well off, and that they are very well treated, as if it were possible that such a thing could be.
200 A man happy in chains! Even the eagle loves liberty.

As with the eagle, so with man. No amount of attention or finery, no dainty dishes can be a substitute for liberty. Slaveholders know this, and knowing it, they exclaim — "The South are surrounded by a
205 dangerous population, degraded, stupid savages, and if they could but entertain the idea that immediate, unconditional death would not be their portion, they would rise at once and enact the St. Domingo tragedy. But they are held in subordination by the
210 consciousness that the whole nation would rise and crush them." Thus they live in constant dread from day to day.

Friends, Slavery must be abolished, and that can only be done by enforcing the great principles of
215 justice. Vainly you talk about voting it down. When you have cast your millions of ballots, you have not reached the evil. It has fastened its root deep into the heart of the nation, and nothing but God's truth and love can cleanse the land. We must change the moral
220 sentiment. Hence, we ask you to support the Anti-Slavery Society. It is not an organization to build up political parties, or churches, nor to pull them down, but to stamp the image of Anti-Slavery truth upon the community. Here we may all do something.

1. How would you describe this speech to somebody who had never read it?

2. What part of the speech did you find most engaging?

3. How would you describe this speech to somebody who had never read it?

4. What evidence does Frederick Douglass use to support his claims?

5. What is Douglass advocating for?

Lesson 8: Mastering the Clock

# Remarks at Pearl Harbor (Japanese Prime Minister Abe and President Obama)

The following speeches commemorating the 75th anniversary of the bombing of Pearl Harbor were given by Japanese Prime Minister Shinzo Abe and President Barack Obama on December 27, 2016.

## Passage 1

President Obama, Commander Harris, ladies and gentlemen, and all American citizens: I stand here at Pearl Harbor as the Prime Minister of Japan.

If we listen closely, we can make out the sound of restless waves breaking and then retreating again. The calm inlet of brilliant blue is radiant with the gentle sparkle of the warm sun. Behind me, a striking white form atop the azure, is the USS Arizona Memorial.

Together, with President Obama, I paid a visit to that memorial, the resting place for many souls. It's a place which brought utter silence to me. Inscribed there are the names of the servicemen who lost their lives. Sailors and Marines hailing from California and New York, Michigan and Texas, and various other places, serving to uphold their noble duty of protecting the homeland they loved, lost their lives amidst searing flames that day, when aerial bombing tore the USS Arizona in two.

Even 75 years later, the USS Arizona, now at rest atop the seabed, is the final resting place for a tremendous number of sailors and Marines. Listening again as I focus my senses, alongside the song of the breeze and the rumble of the rolling waves, I can almost discern the voices of those crewmen. Voices of lively conversation, upbeat and at ease, on that day, on a Sunday morning. Voices of young servicemen talking to each other about their future and dreams; voices calling out names of loved ones in their very final moments; voices praying for the happiness of children still unborn. And every one of those servicemen had a mother and a father anxious about his safety. Many had wives and girlfriends they loved, and many must have had children they would have loved watch grow up. All of that was brought to an end. When I contemplate that solemn reality, I am rendered entirely speechless.

"Rest in peace, precious souls of the fallen." With that overwhelming sentiment, I cast flowers, on behalf of Japanese people, upon the waters where those sailors and Marines sleep.

President Obama, the people of the United States of America, and the people around the world, as the Prime Minister of Japan, I offer my sincere and everlasting condolences to the souls of those who lost their lives here, as well as to the spirits of all the brave men and women whose lives were taken by a war that commenced in this very place, and also to the souls of the countless innocent people who became the victims of the war.

We must never repeat the horrors of war again. This is the solemn vow we, the people of Japan, have taken. Since the war, we have created a free and democratic country that values the rule of law, and has resolutely upheld our vow never again to wage war. We, the people of Japan, will continue to uphold this unwavering principle while harboring quiet pride in the path we have walked as a peace-loving nation over these 70 years since the war ended.

To the souls of the servicemen who lie in eternal rest aboard the USS Arizona, to the American people, and to all peoples around the world, I pledge that unwavering vow here as the Prime Minister of Japan.

Yesterday, at the Marine Corps Base Hawaii in Kaneohe Bay, I visited the memorial marker for an Imperial Japanese Navy officer. He was a fighter pilot by the name of Commander Fusata Iida, who was hit during the attack on Pearl Harbor, and gave up on returning to his aircraft carrier. He went back instead, and died. It was not Japanese who erected a marker at the site that Iida's fighter plane crashed; it was U.S. servicemen who had been on the receiving end of his attack. Applauding the bravery of the dead pilot, they erected this stone marker.

On the marker, his rank at that time is inscribed: Lieutenant, Imperial Japanese Navy — showing the respect to a serviceman who gave his life for his country. "The brave respect the brave." So wrote Ambrose Bierce in a famous poem. Showing respect even to an enemy they fought against, trying to understand even an enemy that they hated. Therein lies the spirit of tolerance embraced by the American people.

When the war ended, and Japan was a nation in burnt-out ruins as far as the eye could see, suffering under abject poverty, it was the United States and its good people that unstintingly sent us food to eat and clothes to wear. The Japanese people managed to survive and make their way toward the future, thanks to the sweaters and milk sent by the American people. And it was the United States that opened up the path for Japan to return to the international community once more after the war.

Under the leadership of the United States, Japan, as a member of the free world, was able to enjoy peace and prosperity. The goodwill and assistance you extended to us Japanese — the enemy you had fought so furiously — together with the tremendous spirit of tolerance, were etched deeply into the hearts and minds of our grandfathers and mothers. We also remember them. Our children and grandchildren will also continue to pass these memories down and never forget what you did for us.

The words pass through my mind — those words described on the wall at the Lincoln Memorial in Washington, D.C., where I visited with President Obama: "With malice toward none, with charity for all, let us strive on to do all which may achieve and cherish a lasting peace among ourselves and with all nations." These are the words of Abraham Lincoln.

On behalf of the Japanese people, I hereby wish to express once again my heartfelt gratitude to the United States and to the world for the tolerance extended to Japan.

It has now been 75 years since that Pearl Harbor. Japan and the United States, which fought a fierce war that will go down in the annals of human history, have become allies, with deep and strong ties rarely found anywhere in history. We are allies that will tackle together to an even greater degree than ever before the many challenges covering the globe. Ours is an alliance of hope that will lead us to the future.

What has binded us together is the hope of reconciliation made possible through the spirit, the tolerance. What I want to appeal to the people of the world here at Pearl Harbor, together with President Obama, is this power of reconciliation. Even today, the horrors of war have not been eradicated from the surface of the world. There is no end to the spiral where hatred creates hatred. The world needs the spirit of tolerance and the power of reconciliation now, and especially now.

Japan and the United States, which have eradicated hatred and cultivated friendship and trust on the basis of common values, are now — and especially now — taking responsibility for appealing to the world about the importance of tolerance and the power of reconciliation. That is precisely why the Japan-U.S. alliance is an alliance of hope.

The inlet gazing at us is tranquil as far as the eye can see. Pearl Harbor. It is precisely this inlet, flowing like shimmering pearls, that is a symbol of tolerance and reconciliation. It is my wish that our Japanese children and — President Obama, your American children, and, indeed, their children and grandchildren — and people all around the world will continue to remember Pearl Harbor as a symbol of reconciliation.

We will spare no efforts to continue our endeavors to make that wish a reality. Together with President Obama, I hereby make my steadfast pledge. Thank you very much.

**Passage 2**
Prime Minister Abe, on behalf of the American people, thank you for your gracious words. Thank you for your presence here today — an historic gesture that speaks to the power of reconciliation and the alliance between the American and Japanese peoples; a reminder that even the deepest wounds of war can give way to friendship and lasting peace.

Distinguished guests, members of our armed forces — and most of all, survivors of Pearl Harbor and their loved ones — aloha.

To Americans — especially to those of us who call Hawaii home — this harbor is a sacred place. As we lay a wreath or toss flowers into waters that still weep, we think of the more than 2,400 American patriots — fathers and husbands, wives and daughters — manning Heaven's rails for all eternity. We salute the defenders of Oahu who pull themselves a little straighter every December 7th, and we reflect on the heroism that shone here 75 years ago.

As dawn broke that December day, paradise never seemed so sweet. The water was warm and impossibly blue. Sailors ate in the mess hall, or readied themselves for church, dressed in crisp white shorts and t-shirts. In the harbor, ships at anchor floated in neat rows: the California, the Maryland and the Oklahoma, the Tennessee, the West Virginia and the Nevada. On the deck of the Arizona, the Navy band was tuning up.

That morning, the ranks on men's shoulders defined them less than the courage in their hearts. Across the island, Americans defended themselves however they could — firing training shells, working old bolt-action rifles. An African-American mess steward, who would typically be confined to cleaning duties, carried his commander to safety, and then fired an anti-aircraft gun until he ran out of ammo.

We honor Americans like Jim Downing — a gunner's mate first class on the West Virginia. Before he raced to the harbor, his new bride pressed into his hand a verse of Scripture: "The eternal God is thy refuge, and underneath are the everlasting arms." As Jim fought to save his ship, he simultaneously gathered the names of the fallen so that he could give closure to their families. He said, "It was just something you do."

We remember Americans like Harry Pang — a fireman from Honolulu who, in the face of withering fire, worked to douse burning planes until he gave his last full measure of devotion — one of the only civilian firefighters ever to receive the Purple Heart.

We salute Americans like Chief Petty Officer John Finn, who manned a .50-caliber machine gun for more than two hours and was wounded more than 20 times, earning him our nation's highest military decoration, the Medal of Honor.

And it is here that we reflect on how war tests our most enduring values — how, even as Japanese Americans were deprived of their own liberty during the war, one of the most decorated military units in the history of the United States was the 442nd Infantry Regiment and its 100th Infantry Battalion — the Japanese-American Nisei. In that 442nd served my friend and proud Hawaiian, Daniel Inouye — a man who was a senator from Hawaii for most of my life and with whom I would find myself proud to serve in the Senate chamber; a man who was not only a recipient of the Medal of Honor and the Presidential Medal of Freedom, but was one of the most distinguished statesmen of his generation as well.

Here at Pearl Harbor, America's first battle of the Second World War roused a nation. Here, in so many ways, America came of age. A generation of Americans — including my grandparents — the Greatest Generation — they did not seek war, but they refused to shrink from it. And they all did their part on fronts and in factories. And while, 75 years later, the proud ranks of Pearl Harbor survivors have thinned with time, the bravery we recall here is forever etched in our national heart. I would ask all our Pearl Harbor and World War II veterans who are able to, to please stand or raise your hands — because a grateful nation thanks you.

The character of nations is tested in war, but it is defined in peace. After one of the most horrific chapters in human history — one that took not tens of thousands, but tens of millions of lives — with ferocious fighting across this ocean — the United States and Japan chose friendship and peace. Over the decades, our alliance has made both of our nations more successful. It has helped underwrite an international order that has prevented another World War and that has lifted more than a billion people out of extreme poverty. And today, the alliance between the United States and Japan — bound not only by shared interests, but also rooted in common values — stands as the cornerstone of peace and stability in the Asia Pacific and a force for progress around the globe. Our alliance has never been stronger.

In good times and in bad, we are there for each other. Recall five years ago, when a wall of water bore down on Japan and reactors in Fukushima melted, America's men and women in uniform were there to help our Japanese friends. Across the globe, the United States and Japan work shoulder-to-shoulder to strengthen the security of the Asia Pacific and the world — turning back piracy, combating disease, slowing the spread of nuclear weapons, keeping the peace in war-torn lands.

In this sense, our presence here today — the connections not just between our governments, but between our people, the presence of Prime Minister Abe here today — remind us of what is possible between nations and between peoples. Wars can end. The most bitter of adversaries can become the strongest of allies. The fruits of peace always outweigh the plunder of war. This is the enduring truth of this hallowed harbor.

It is here that we remember that even when hatred burns hottest, even when the tug of tribalism is at its most primal, we must resist the urge to turn inward. We must resist the urge to demonize those who are different. The sacrifice made here, the anguish of war, reminds us to seek the divine spark that is common to all humanity. It insists that we strive to be what our Japanese friends call *otagai no tame ni* — "with and for each other."

That's the lesson of Captain William Callaghan of the Missouri. Even after an attack on his ship, he ordered that the Japanese pilot be laid to rest with military honors, wrapped in a Japanese flag sewn by American sailors. It's the lesson, in turn, of the Japanese pilot who, years later, returned to this harbor, befriended an old Marine bugler and asked him to play taps and lay two roses at this memorial every month — one for America's fallen and one for Japan's.

It's a lesson our two peoples learn every day, in the most ordinary of ways — whether it's Americans studying in Tokyo, young Japanese studying across America; scientists from our two nations together unraveling the mysteries of cancer, or combating climate change, exploring the stars. It's a baseball player like Ichiro lighting up a stadium in Miami, buoyed by the shared pride of two peoples, both American and Japanese, united in peace and friendship.

As nations, and as people, we cannot choose the history that we inherit. But we can choose what lessons to draw from it, and use those lessons to chart our own futures.

Prime Minister Abe, I welcome you here in the spirit of friendship, as the people of Japan have always 300 welcomed me. I hope that together, we send a message to the world that there is more to be won in peace than in war; that reconciliation carries more rewards than retribution.

Here in this quiet harbor, we honor those we lost, 305 and we give thanks for all that our two nations have won — together, as friends.

May God hold the fallen in His everlasting arms. May He watch over our veterans and all who stand guard on our behalf. May God bless us all.

1. How would you describe passage 1 to somebody who had never read it?

2. How would you describe passage 2 to somebody who had never read it?

3. According to the speakers, what makes Pearl Harbor special?

4. What are the differences between Prime Minster Abe's and President Obama's portrayal of the events of Pearl Harbor?

5. What are the similarities between Prime Minster Abe's and President Obama's portrayal of the events of Pearl Harbor?

Lesson 8: Mastering the Clock

# TEN BOOKS TO READ FOR FUN

Here are ten of my favorite books for high school students to read. Not all of them are *literature* as such (though some are), but they are all *fun*. They are also all classics, readily available at your public or school library, online, or at your local bookstore. I recommend reading books that match your interests. So, for example, if you like satire you might like *The Princess Bride* and if you like *Game of Thrones* you might like *All the President's Men*.

| If you like... | ...try reading |
|---|---|
| The Handmaid's Tale | • A Room of One's Own |
| | • Dragonflight & Dragonsong |
| Stranger Things | • One Hundred Years of Solitude |
| The outdoors | • Silent Spring |
| Satire | • The Princess Bride |
| Math and science | • Cosmos |
| | • Pale Blue Dot |
| | • Silent Spring |
| Parks and Recreation | • Silent Spring |
| Hamilton | • Souls of Black Folk |
| Science fiction and dystopian literature | • Dragonflight & Dragonsong |
| | • One Hundred Years of Solitude |
| Game of Thrones | • All the President's Men |
| | • Dragonflight & Dragonsong |
| Literature | • A Room of One's Own |
| African American history | • Souls of Black Folk |
| The Cold War | • All the President's Men |
| Philosophy | • One Hundred Years of Solitude |

This is a partial list, one that I am constantly revising as student interests change. There are more suggestions in the online bonus content (www.professorscompanion.com/reading). Do you have suggestions for your peers? Send me an email at tom@professorscompanion.com and you may find your suggestion featured on the website, in a newsletter, or in a future edition of this book!

You can also check out a collection of 50 essays, short stories, and speeches I have curated as part of my SAT and ACT standardized reading list. These range in length from standard passages (4-5 minutes plus questions) to section-long passages (35 and 65 minutes).

*All the President's Men* by Carl Bernstein and Bob Woodward

In 1972, five operatives from CREEP, the Committee to Re-Elect the President (Richard Nixon), broke into the Democratic National Committee's headquarters at the Watergate office complex. A cover-up, orchestrated from the White House, brought down the president. *All the President's Men*, written by two of the *Washington Post* journalists who uncovered the conspiracy, chronicles the tumultuous Watergate years and the end of the Nixon presidency.

> June 17, 1972. Nine o'clock Saturday morning. Early for the telephone. Woodward fumbled for the receiver and snapped awake. The city editor of the *Washington Post* was on the line. Five men had been arrested earlier that morning in a burglary at Democratic headquarters, carrying photographic equipment and electronic gear.

*Silent Spring* by Rachel Carson

Probably the most influential environmental science book, Rachel Carson's *Silent Spring* investigated the harmful effects of pesticides and is credited with bringing the environmentalist movement to popular consciousness.

> As crude a weapon as the cave man's club, the chemical barrage has been hurled against the fabric of life—a fabric on the one hand delicate and destructible, on the other miraculously tough and resilient, and capable of striking back in unexpected ways. These extraordinary capacities of life have been ignored by the practitioners of chemical control who have brought to their task no 'high-minded orientation', no humility before the vast forces with which they tamper. The 'control of nature' is a phrase conceived in arrogance, born of the Neanderthal age of biology and philosophy, when it was supposed that nature exists for the convenience of man. The concepts and practices of applied entomology for the most part date from that Stone Age of science. It is our alarming misfortune that so primitive a science has armed itself with the most modern and terrible weapons, and that in turning them against the insects it has also turned them against the earth.

*The Souls of Black Folk* by W. E. B. Du Bois

W. E. B. Du Bois's 1903 anthology *The Souls of Black Folk* is a landmark of African American literature and the field of sociology. One of the Modern Library's 100 best works of non-fiction, *The Souls of Black Folk* describes the "double-consciousness" of African American identity, the idea that African Americans have dual yet distinct identities (a concept that is related to today's concept of "intersectional" identities).

> After the Egyptian and Indian, the Greek and Roman, the Teuton and Mongolian, the Negro is a sort of seventh son, born with a veil, and gifted with second-sight in this American world—a world which yields him no true self-consciousness, but only lets him see himself through the revelation of the other world. It is a peculiar sensation, this double-consciousness, this sense of always looking at one's self through the eyes of others, of measuring one's soul by the tape of a world that looks on in amused contempt and pity. One ever feels his two-ness—an American, a Negro; two souls, two thoughts, two unreconciled strivings; two warring ideals in one dark body, whose dogged strength alone keeps it from being torn asunder.

*The Princess Bride: S. Morgenstern's Classic Tale of True Love and High Adventure* by William Goldman

Beloved as a movie, *The Princess Bride* is the "abridgment" of a fictitious Renaissance history of Guilder and Florin by S. Morgenstern. Its author, William Goldman, was also the Academy Award–winning screenwriter of *Butch Cassidy and the Sundance Kid* and *All the President's Men.*

> What happens when the most beautiful girl in the world marries the handsomest prince of all time and he turns out to be…well…a lot less than the man of her dreams? As a boy, William Goldman claims, he loved to hear his father read the "S. Morgenstern classic, The Princess Bride. But as a grown-up he discovered that the boring parts were left out of good old Dad's recitation, and only the "good parts" reached his ears. Now Goldman does Dad one better. He's reconstructed the "Good Parts Version" to delight wise kids and wide-eyed grownups everywhere. What's it about? Fencing. Fighting. True Love. Strong Hate. Harsh Revenge. A Few Giants. Lots of Bad Men. Lots of Good Men. Five or Six Beautiful Women. Beasties Monstrous and Gentle. Some Swell Escapes and Captures. Death, Lies, Truth, Miracles, and a Little Sex. In short, it's about everything.

*Dragonflight* and *Dragonsong* by Anne McCaffrey

The Dragonriders of Pern is a long-running series of books and anthologies created by Anne McCaffrey, the first woman to win the Hugo and Nebula awards for science fiction and fantasy writing. The series chronicles the world of Pern, a planet settled by humans and plagued by deadly spores that fall from rogue planet every 500 years. *Dragonflight*, the first book of the series, tells of Lessa, a young girl who has sworn revenge against the man who murdered her father, an oath that Lessa must balance with her responsibilities to Pern. *Dragonsong* tells a different tale, the tale of a young fisherman's girl who longs to sing and write music, despite the fact that the profession of "harper" was closed to women.

> When is a legend a legend? Why is a myth a myth? How old and disused must a fact be for it to be relegated to the category "Fairy-tale"? And why do certain facts remain incontrovertible while others lose their validity to assume a shabby, unsuitable character?

*One Hundred Years of Solitude* by Gabriel Garcia Marquez

The magnum opus of Colombian author and Nobel Prize for Literature laureate Gabriel Garcia Marquez, *One Hundred Years of Solitude* is perhaps the best-known example of magical realism. Readers willing to press on through the quixotic tale of the town of Macondo and the Buendía family are rewarded with a complex tale of history and politics, economic and technological advancement, and mystery.

> Many years later, as he faced the firing squad, Colonel Aureliano Buendía was to remember that distant afternoon when his father took him to discover ice.

*Cosmos* and *Pale Blue Dot: A Vision of the Human Future in Space* by Carl Sagan

Carl Sagan, the public intellectual and astronomer, brought the sheer size of the universe to millions of bookshelves in America and around the world. *Cosmos* was a New York Times best seller in 1980, and in 1994, Sagan wrote *Pale Blue Dot* after reflecting on the Voyager One satellite's photograph of the planet Earth from 4 billion miles away.

> Look again at that dot. That's here. That's home. That's us. On it everyone you love, everyone you know, everyone you ever heard of, every human being who ever was, lived out their lives. The aggregate of our joy and suffering, thousands of confident religions, ideologies, and economic doctrines, every hunter and forager, every hero and coward, every creator and destroyer of civilization, every king and peasant, every young couple in love, every mother and father, hopeful child, inventor and explorer, every teacher of morals, every corrupt politician, every "superstar," every "supreme leader," every saint and sinner in the history of our species lived there-on a mote of dust suspended in a sunbeam.

*A Room of One's Own* by Virginia Woolf

Virginia Woolf was a proto-feminist English author. *A Room of One's Own* advocates for women authors to have their own literal space and metaphorical freedom (through financial independence). In addition to her oft-quoted maxim, "One cannot think well, love well, sleep well, if one has not dined well," and the titular, "A woman must have money and a room of her own if she is to write fiction," *A Room of One's Own* concludes by encouraging women to write.

> "Therefore I would ask you to write all kinds of books, hesitating at no subject however trivial or however vast. By hook or by crook, I hope that you will possess yourselves of money enough to travel and to idle, to contemplate the future or the past of the world, to dream over books and loiter at street corners and let the line of thought dip deep into the stream."

## PRACTICE TEST: OFFICIAL TEST 8

In order to master your time, you need to keep yourself engaged with the passages, not getting too far ahead and not getting too far behind.

Let's try practice test 8 (official guide page 553). As you take the test, keep track of your time like we did in lesson 6, making sure that you never get more than 2 minutes ahead or 2 minutes behind. If, after lessons 6 and 7, you know you want more time on one type of passage (antiquated English, data, paired, etc.), feel free to take that time. Just don't get *too* far behind.

Oh, and remember to care, even if it's only for 13 minutes.

# SELF-EVALUATION TEST 8

| | | | | | | |
|---|---|---|---|---|---|---|
| **Passage 1** | I felt confident during the first passage. | Strongly Agree | Somewhat Agree | No Opinion | Somewhat Disagree | Strongly Disagree |
| | Describe in two to three sentences how you felt on the first passage | | | | | |
| | Time spent | | | | | |
| **Passage 2** | I felt confident during the second passage. | Strongly Agree | Somewhat Agree | No Opinion | Somewhat Disagree | Strongly Disagree |
| | Describe in two to three sentences how you felt on the second passage | | | | | |
| | Time spent | | | | | |
| **Passage 3** | I felt confident during the third passage. | Strongly Agree | Somewhat Agree | No Opinion | Somewhat Disagree | Strongly Disagree |
| | Describe in two to three sentences how you felt on the third passage | | | | | |
| | Time spent | | | | | |
| **Passage 4** | I felt confident during the fourth passage. | Strongly Agree | Somewhat Agree | No Opinion | Somewhat Disagree | Strongly Disagree |
| | Describe in two to three sentences how you felt on the fourth passage | | | | | |
| | Time spent | | | | | |
| **Passage 5** | I felt confident during the fifth passage. | Strongly Agree | Somewhat Agree | No Opinion | Somewhat Disagree | Strongly Disagree |
| | Describe in two to three sentences how you felt on the fifth passage | | | | | |
| | Time spent | | | | | |
| **Overall** | I felt confident during the reading section. | Strongly Agree | Somewhat Agree | No Opinion | Somewhat Disagree | Strongly Disagree |
| | I had enough time for the reading section. | Strongly Agree | Somewhat Agree | No Opinion | Somewhat Disagree | Strongly Disagree |
| | I cared about the passages I read. | Strongly Agree | Somewhat Agree | No Opinion | Somewhat Disagree | Strongly Disagree |
| | In three to four sentences, describe how you feel about the reading section. | | | | | |
| | How was your timing? | | | | | |

# LESSON 9: MASTERING KHAN ACADEMY

Khan Academy has a ton of free materials, but they are not always easy to use. They are presented on a computer (or phone/tablet), but you take the test on paper. The reading materials, however, give you ample practice to work on the passage reading and question answering skills.

## KHAN ACADEMY WORKSHEETS

Before you start, write down the passage name, your starting skill level, and the date. You'll give your number correct when you finish the passage. These might not seem critical now, but when you want to review a passage at a later date, this information will be crucial.

**Passage Name:** Human Carrying Capacity          **Skill Level:** 3/4          **Date:** 7/1          **Correct:** _____

### Part 1: Underline, Annotate, and Identify

In order to take advantage of Khan Academy's materials, you have to treat the passage like would treat a printed passage. This means you have to *simulate* a printed passage as you read.

Remember, there are three steps to reading each passage:

1. **Underline** anything that you think might possibly be relevant.

2. **Annotate** the passage.

3. **Identify** the author's purpose.

Khan Academy has a useful highlighting tool that works like **underlining** on the printed page. You can highlight the passage by selecting the text and clicking "add highlight."

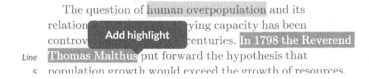

It is more complicated to **annotate** the Khan Academy passages. This is where the worksheets become helpful. As you read, jot down your annotations on the worksheets. Remember to keep your annotations brief (2-4 words) and frequent (1-2 annotations per paragraph).

When you are done with the annotations, **identify** the author's purpose, their thesis or topic, and their tone. You should also identify the relationships present in the data.

| Line | | | |
|---|---|---|---|
| | Overpopulation | Purpose | To explain how populations grow faster than resources (food) develop |
| 10 | Thomas Malthus's fears | | |
| | Didn't happen | Topic/Thesis | Fears overpopulation have worried people with for reasons |
| 20 | Population bomb | | |
| | 1960 - US responses to famine | Tone | Points out both sides |
| 30 | | | |
| | Increase of food production | (Data) | Exponential growth (14+ Bil), but lower fertility decreases population |
| 40 | | | |
| | Increased average life expectancy | | |
| 50 | Population still growing | | |
| 60 | Three decades of breathing space | | |
| 70 | | | |
| 80 | | | |

## Part 2: Restate, Recall, and Resolve

Next, turn to the questions. As a reminder, there are three steps to answering every test question:

1. **Restate**: What question is it that the prompt is asking you?

2. **Recall**: How would you answer the question?

3. **Resolve**: Which of the choices in the answer bank gives the best answer?

For the worksheets, it can help to include the question type. Give the question type, and then **restate** (your paraphrase of the prompt), **recall** (your answer to the question), and **resolve** (your best answer).

When resolving, indicate if each of the choices is either right or wrong. If it is wrong, indicate why (too broad, irrelevant, etc.) If it's correct, give your annotation or line number evidence (you'll get a cheat sheet). Finally, give your confidence 1-5.

**1**

| | | | |
|---|---|---|---|
| Recognize | Main purpose | Answer Type | Flatly false |
| Restate | What is the author's primary purpose? | Answer Type | Somewhat correct but too narrow |
| | | Answer Type | Identification |
| Recall | To explain how populations grow faster than resources (food) develop | Answer Type | Somewhat correct but too extreme |
| | | Resolve | Ⓐ Ⓑ ● Ⓓ    Confidence 4/5 |

**2**

| | | | |
|---|---|---|---|
| Recognize | Detail | Answer Type | Right words but not true |
| Restate | Why was Thomas Malthus important? | Answer Type | Mostly correct |
| | | Answer Type | Lines 3-6 |
| Recall | He introduced the idea that food will not grow as fast as population | Answer Type | Somewhat correct, but too extreme |
| | | | Ⓐ Ⓑ ● Ⓓ    Confidence 3/5 |

You can find a synopsis of question types and answer types at the end of the worksheet.

| Questions | General | Specific | Synthesis |
|---|---|---|---|
| Main Purpose | Purpose | Function | |
| Main Idea | Thesis | Topic | |
| Tone | Tone | Attitude | |
| Rhetoric | Structure | Argument | |
| Vocabulary | | Vocabulary | |
| Evidence | | Evidence | |
| Detail | | Detail | |
| Inference | | Inference | |
| Data | | Data Specific | Data Synthesis |
| Paired | | Paired Specific | Paired Synthesis |

| Answers | Reason |
|---|---|
| Wrong | somewhat right but too broad |
| Wrong | somewhat right but too narrow |
| Wrong | somewhat right but too extreme |
| Wrong | tempting words, but wrong part |
| Wrong | tempting words, but not true |
| Wrong | tempting words, but irrelevant |
| Wrong | not true |
| Right (general) | Give identify evidence |
| Right (specific) | Give line or annotation evidence |
| Right (synthesis) | Give identify evidence |

After you have finished filling out the worksheet, submit your answers and Khan Academy will score the passage for you.

## Part 3: Review

Just because you've finished the passage and questions doesn't mean you are finished. You should review the questions, not just the question you answered incorrectly, but the questions you answered correctly but were not as confident as you would have liked. Start by submitting your answers and seeing how things went:

Lesson 9: Mastering Khan Academy

Reading: Social science

Skill level 4

Jump to a question: ✓ ✗ ✗ ✓ ✓ ✓ ✓ ✓ ✓    [Exit this practice]  [Review your answers]

We got 9 out of 11. Not bad! Write this number down at the start of the worksheet so you can find this later.

**Passage Name:** Human Carrying Capacity    **Skill Level:** 4/4    **Date:** 7/1    **Correct:** 9-2

Now, let's look at what happened. We weren't super confident during question 2, just a 3/5. Sometimes, you narrow it down to a 50/50 shot and you guess the wrong one. In this case, B was the correct answer, not C. We got doubly unlucky too since question 3 was an evidence question paired with question 2's inference question.

After you browse through the questions, consider the following four questions:

1. What questions did you find hardest (lowest confidence level)? What made them hard?

2. What questions did you find easiest (highest confidence level)? What made them easy?

3. Are there patterns to the question types you find harder than others?

4. Look at the questions you answered incorrectly. Why was your answer wrong? What makes the correct answer right?

One important thing to note on pacing: These Khan Academy worksheets take longer to complete than you have for the passages. *Practice your pacing on full tests*, not on Khan. Use Khan Academy to *practice your test day strategies*: **Underline, Annotate, and Identify** and **Restate, Recall, and Resolve**. The better you get now, the better you'll be when it matters.

# FIVE WORKSHEETS

Here are five practice worksheets for you, one in each of the four categories (science, literature, history, and social studies) and one paired passage. If you want more worksheets than what you find here, you can download more at www.professorscompanion.com.

One final note: Your scores on Khan Academy's practice passages will not reflect your performance on test days as accurately as full practice tests do. Online materials are good, but the real thing is better. Even more importantly, the passages on Khan have not undergone the same rigorous testing that the College Board puts into the official tests. Khan Academy is an excellent resource, however, to expand your skills and reinforce the strategies you have developed.

Ready for some practice passages?

## Passage Type: Science

Passage Name: _____    Skill Level: _____   Date: _____   Correct: _____

### Underline, Annotate, and Identify

Line

10

20

30

40

50

60

70

80

Purpose _____
_____

Topic/Thesis _____
_____

Tone _____
_____

(Data) _____
_____

## Restate, Recall, and Resolve

### 1

Recognize _____  Answer Type _____

Restate _____  Answer Type _____

_____  Answer Type _____

Recall _____  Answer Type _____

_____  Resolve  Ⓐ Ⓑ Ⓒ Ⓓ   Confidence ___/5

### 2

Recognize _____  Answer Type _____

Restate _____  Answer Type _____

_____  Answer Type _____

Recall _____  Answer Type _____

_____  Resolve  Ⓐ Ⓑ Ⓒ Ⓓ   Confidence ___/5

### 3

Recognize _____  Answer Type _____

Restate _____  Answer Type _____

_____  Answer Type _____

Recall _____  Answer Type _____

_____  Resolve  Ⓐ Ⓑ Ⓒ Ⓓ   Confidence ___/5

### 4

Recognize _____  Answer Type _____

Restate _____  Answer Type _____

_____  Answer Type _____

Recall _____  Answer Type _____

_____  Resolve  Ⓐ Ⓑ Ⓒ Ⓓ   Confidence ___/5

## 5

Recognize _____    Answer Type _____

Restate _____    Answer Type _____

_____    Answer Type _____

Recall _____    Answer Type _____

_____    Resolve   Ⓐ Ⓑ Ⓒ Ⓓ      Confidence ___/5

## 6

Recognize _____    Answer Type _____

Restate _____    Answer Type _____

_____    Answer Type _____

Recall _____    Answer Type _____

_____    Resolve   Ⓐ Ⓑ Ⓒ Ⓓ      Confidence ___/5

## 7

Recognize _____    Answer Type _____

Restate _____    Answer Type _____

_____    Answer Type _____

Recall _____    Answer Type _____

_____    Resolve   Ⓐ Ⓑ Ⓒ Ⓓ      Confidence ___/5

## 8

Recognize _____    Answer Type _____

Restate _____    Answer Type _____

_____    Answer Type _____

Recall _____    Answer Type _____

_____    Resolve   Ⓐ Ⓑ Ⓒ Ⓓ      Confidence ___/5

## 9

| | | | |
|---|---|---|---|
| Recognize | _____ | Answer Type | _____ |
| Restate | _____ | Answer Type | _____ |
| | _____ | Answer Type | _____ |
| Recall | _____ | Answer Type | _____ |
| | _____ | Resolve Ⓐ Ⓑ Ⓒ Ⓓ | Confidence ___/5 |

## 10

| | | | |
|---|---|---|---|
| Recognize | _____ | Answer Type | _____ |
| Restate | _____ | Answer Type | _____ |
| | _____ | Answer Type | _____ |
| Recall | _____ | Answer Type | _____ |
| | _____ | Resolve Ⓐ Ⓑ Ⓒ Ⓓ | Confidence ___/5 |

## 11

| | | | |
|---|---|---|---|
| Recognize | _____ | Answer Type | _____ |
| Restate | _____ | Answer Type | _____ |
| | _____ | Answer Type | _____ |
| Recall | _____ | Answer Type | _____ |
| | _____ | Resolve Ⓐ Ⓑ Ⓒ Ⓓ | Confidence ___/5 |

| Questions | General | Specific | Synthesis | Answers | Reason |
|---|---|---|---|---|---|
| Main Purpose | Purpose | Function | | Wrong | Somewhat right, but too broad |
| Main Idea | Thesis | Topic | | Wrong | Somewhat right, but too narrow |
| Tone | Tone | Attitude | | Wrong | Somewhat right, but too extreme |
| Rhetoric | Structure | Argument | | Wrong | Tempting words, but wrong part |
| Vocabulary | | Vocabulary | | Wrong | Tempting words, but not true |
| Evidence | | Evidence | | Wrong | Tempting words, but irrelevant |
| Detail | | Detail | | Wrong | Flatly false |
| Inference | | Inference | | Right (general) | Give identify evidence |
| Data | | Data Specific | Data Synthesis | Right (specific) | Give line or annotation evidence |
| Paired | | Paired Specific | Paired Synthesis | Right (synthesis) | Give identify evidence |

Lesson 9: Mastering Khan Academy

## Review

1. What was the purpose of the passage? What was the author's central claim? Which questions were related to that claim?

2. If there were charts and graphs, how did they support the author's claims?

3. What questions did you find hardest? What made them hard (e.g., the question itself, the answers, the passage, something else)?

4. What questions did you find easiest? What made them easy (e.g., the question itself, the answers, the passage, something else)?

5. Are there patterns to the question types you find harder than others? For example, did you find that general or specific are harder? What about individual question types (e.g., detail, inference, vocabulary)?

6. Look at each of the questions you answered incorrectly. Why was your answer wrong? What makes the correct answer right?

## Passage Type: Literature

Passage Name: _____ Skill Level: _____ Date: _____ Correct: _____

### Underline, Annotate, and Identify

*Line*

10

20

30

40

50

60

70

80

Purpose _____
_____

Topic/Thesis _____
_____

Tone _____
_____

(Data) _____
_____

Lesson 9: Mastering Khan Academy

## Restate, Recall, and Resolve

**1**

Recognize _____  Answer Type _____

Restate _____  Answer Type _____

_____  Answer Type _____

Recall _____  Answer Type _____

_____  Resolve  Ⓐ Ⓑ Ⓒ Ⓓ   Confidence ___/5

**2**

Recognize _____  Answer Type _____

Restate _____  Answer Type _____

_____  Answer Type _____

Recall _____  Answer Type _____

_____  Resolve  Ⓐ Ⓑ Ⓒ Ⓓ   Confidence ___/5

**3**

Recognize _____  Answer Type _____

Restate _____  Answer Type _____

_____  Answer Type _____

Recall _____  Answer Type _____

_____  Resolve  Ⓐ Ⓑ Ⓒ Ⓓ   Confidence ___/5

**4**

Recognize _____  Answer Type _____

Restate _____  Answer Type _____

_____  Answer Type _____

Recall _____  Answer Type _____

_____  Resolve  Ⓐ Ⓑ Ⓒ Ⓓ   Confidence ___/5

### 5

Recognize

Restate

Recall

Answer Type

Answer Type

Answer Type

Answer Type

Resolve    Ⓐ Ⓑ Ⓒ Ⓓ    Confidence ___/5

### 6

Recognize

Restate

Recall

Answer Type

Answer Type

Answer Type

Answer Type

Resolve    Ⓐ Ⓑ Ⓒ Ⓓ    Confidence ___/5

### 7

Recognize

Restate

Recall

Answer Type

Answer Type

Answer Type

Answer Type

Resolve    Ⓐ Ⓑ Ⓒ Ⓓ    Confidence ___/5

### 8

Recognize

Restate

Recall

Answer Type

Answer Type

Answer Type

Answer Type

Resolve    Ⓐ Ⓑ Ⓒ Ⓓ    Confidence ___/5

## 9

Recognize _____

Restate _____

_____

Recall _____

_____

Answer Type _____

Answer Type _____

Answer Type _____

Answer Type _____

Resolve Ⓐ Ⓑ Ⓒ Ⓓ    Confidence ___/5

## 10

Recognize _____

Restate _____

_____

Recall _____

_____

Answer Type _____

Answer Type _____

Answer Type _____

Answer Type _____

Resolve Ⓐ Ⓑ Ⓒ Ⓓ    Confidence ___/5

## 11

Recognize _____

Restate _____

_____

Recall _____

_____

Answer Type _____

Answer Type _____

Answer Type _____

Answer Type _____

Resolve Ⓐ Ⓑ Ⓒ Ⓓ    Confidence ___/5

| Questions | General | Specific | Synthesis | Answers | Reason |
|---|---|---|---|---|---|
| Main Purpose | Purpose | Function | | Wrong | Somewhat right, but too broad |
| Main Idea | Thesis | Topic | | Wrong | Somewhat right, but too narrow |
| Tone | Tone | Attitude | | Wrong | Somewhat right, but too extreme |
| Rhetoric | Structure | Argument | | Wrong | Tempting words, but wrong part |
| Vocabulary | | Vocabulary | | Wrong | Tempting words, but not true |
| Evidence | | Evidence | | Wrong | Tempting words, but irrelevant |
| Detail | | Detail | | Wrong | Flatly false |
| Inference | | Inference | | Right (general) | Give identify evidence |
| Data | | Data Specific | Data Synthesis | Right (specific) | Give line or annotation evidence |
| Paired | | Paired Specific | Paired Synthesis | Right (synthesis) | Give identify evidence |

## Review

1. What is the relationship between the characters? Which questions were related to this relationship?

2. How would you describe the passage in generic terms (e.g., a stranger comes to town)?

3. What questions did you find hardest? What made them hard (e.g., the question itself, the answers, the passage, something else)?

4. What questions did you find easiest)? What made them easy (e.g., the question itself, the answers, the passage, something else)?

5. Are there patterns to the question types you find harder than others? For example, did you find that general or specific are harder? What about individual question types (e.g., detail, inference, vocabulary)?

6. Look at each of the questions you answered incorrectly. Why was your answer wrong? What makes the correct answer right?

## Passage Type: History

Passage Name: _____ Skill Level: _____ Date: _____ Correct: _____

## Underline, Annotate, and Identify

Line

10

20

30

40

50

60

70

80

Purpose _____

_____

Thesis _____

_____

Tone _____

_____

_____

_____

www.professorscompanion.com

## Restate, Recall, and Resolve

**1**

Recognize _____    Answer Type _____
Restate   _____    Answer Type _____
          _____    Answer Type _____
Recall    _____    Answer Type _____
          _____    Resolve  Ⓐ Ⓑ Ⓒ Ⓓ    Confidence ___/5

**2**

Recognize _____    Answer Type _____
Restate   _____    Answer Type _____
          _____    Answer Type _____
Recall    _____    Answer Type _____
          _____    Resolve  Ⓐ Ⓑ Ⓒ Ⓓ    Confidence ___/5

**3**

Recognize _____    Answer Type _____
Restate   _____    Answer Type _____
          _____    Answer Type _____
Recall    _____    Answer Type _____
          _____    Resolve  Ⓐ Ⓑ Ⓒ Ⓓ    Confidence ___/5

**4**

Recognize _____    Answer Type _____
Restate   _____    Answer Type _____
          _____    Answer Type _____
Recall    _____    Answer Type _____
          _____    Resolve  Ⓐ Ⓑ Ⓒ Ⓓ    Confidence ___/5

Lesson 9: Mastering Khan Academy

## 5

Recognize _____   Answer Type _____
Restate   _____   Answer Type _____
          _____   Answer Type _____
Recall    _____   Answer Type _____
          _____   Resolve  Ⓐ Ⓑ Ⓒ Ⓓ     Confidence ___/5

## 6

Recognize _____   Answer Type _____
Restate   _____   Answer Type _____
          _____   Answer Type _____
Recall    _____   Answer Type _____
          _____   Resolve  Ⓐ Ⓑ Ⓒ Ⓓ     Confidence ___/5

## 7

Recognize _____   Answer Type _____
Restate   _____   Answer Type _____
          _____   Answer Type _____
Recall    _____   Answer Type _____
          _____   Resolve  Ⓐ Ⓑ Ⓒ Ⓓ     Confidence ___/5

## 8

Recognize _____   Answer Type _____
Restate   _____   Answer Type _____
          _____   Answer Type _____
Recall    _____   Answer Type _____
          _____   Resolve  Ⓐ Ⓑ Ⓒ Ⓓ     Confidence ___/5

## 9

Recognize _____  Answer Type _____
Restate    _____  Answer Type _____
           _____  Answer Type _____
Recall     _____  Answer Type _____
           _____  Resolve  Ⓐ Ⓑ Ⓒ Ⓓ    Confidence ___/5

## 10

Recognize _____  Answer Type _____
Restate    _____  Answer Type _____
           _____  Answer Type _____
Recall     _____  Answer Type _____
           _____  Resolve  Ⓐ Ⓑ Ⓒ Ⓓ    Confidence ___/5

## 11

Recognize _____  Answer Type _____
Restate    _____  Answer Type _____
           _____  Answer Type _____
Recall     _____  Answer Type _____
           _____  Resolve  Ⓐ Ⓑ Ⓒ Ⓓ    Confidence ___/5

| Questions | General | Specific | Synthesis | Answers | Reason |
|---|---|---|---|---|---|
| Main Purpose | Purpose | Function | | Wrong | Somewhat right, but too broad |
| Main Idea | Thesis | Topic | | Wrong | Somewhat right, but too narrow |
| Tone | Tone | Attitude | | Wrong | Somewhat right, but too extreme |
| Rhetoric | Structure | Argument | | Wrong | Tempting words, but wrong part |
| Vocabulary | | Vocabulary | | Wrong | Tempting words, but not true |
| Evidence | | Evidence | | Wrong | Tempting words, but irrelevant |
| Detail | | Detail | | Wrong | Flatly false |
| Inference | | Inference | | Right (general) | Give identify evidence |
| Data | | Data Specific | Data Synthesis | Right (specific) | Give line or annotation evidence |
| Paired | | Paired Specific | Paired Synthesis | Right (synthesis) | Give identify evidence |

Lesson 9: Mastering Khan Academy

## Review

1. What was the purpose of the passage?

2. What was the author's central claim? Which questions were related to that claim?

3. What questions did you find hardest? What made them hard (e.g., the question itself, the answers, the passage, something else)?

4. What questions did you find easiest)? What made them easy (e.g., the question itself, the answers, the passage, something else)?

5. Are there patterns to the question types you find harder than others? For example, did you find that general or specific are harder? What about individual question types (e.g., detail, inference, vocabulary)?

6. Look at each of the questions you answered incorrectly. Why was your answer wrong? What makes the correct answer right?

## Passage Type: Social Studies

Passage Name: _____ Skill Level: _____ Date: _____ Correct: _____

### Underline, Annotate, and Identify

Line

10

                          Purpose  _____

20

                          Thesis  _____

30

                          Tone  _____

40

                          Data  _____

50

60

70

80

Lesson 9: Mastering Khan Academy

## Restate, Recall, and Resolve

**1**

Recognize _____  Answer Type _____

Restate _____  Answer Type _____

_____  Answer Type _____

Recall _____  Answer Type _____

_____  Resolve  Ⓐ Ⓑ Ⓒ Ⓓ   Confidence ___/5

**2**

Recognize _____  Answer Type _____

Restate _____  Answer Type _____

_____  Answer Type _____

Recall _____  Answer Type _____

_____  Resolve  Ⓐ Ⓑ Ⓒ Ⓓ   Confidence ___/5

**3**

Recognize _____  Answer Type _____

Restate _____  Answer Type _____

_____  Answer Type _____

Recall _____  Answer Type _____

_____  Resolve  Ⓐ Ⓑ Ⓒ Ⓓ   Confidence ___/5

**4**

Recognize _____  Answer Type _____

Restate _____  Answer Type _____

_____  Answer Type _____

Recall _____  Answer Type _____

_____  Resolve  Ⓐ Ⓑ Ⓒ Ⓓ   Confidence ___/5

## 5

Recognize _____  Answer Type _____

Restate _____  Answer Type _____

_____  Answer Type _____

Recall _____  Answer Type _____

_____  Resolve  Ⓐ Ⓑ Ⓒ Ⓓ    Confidence ___/5

## 6

Recognize _____  Answer Type _____

Restate _____  Answer Type _____

_____  Answer Type _____

Recall _____  Answer Type _____

_____  Resolve  Ⓐ Ⓑ Ⓒ Ⓓ    Confidence ___/5

## 7

Recognize _____  Answer Type _____

Restate _____  Answer Type _____

_____  Answer Type _____

Recall _____  Answer Type _____

_____  Resolve  Ⓐ Ⓑ Ⓒ Ⓓ    Confidence ___/5

## 8

Recognize _____  Answer Type _____

Restate _____  Answer Type _____

_____  Answer Type _____

Recall _____  Answer Type _____

_____  Resolve  Ⓐ Ⓑ Ⓒ Ⓓ    Confidence ___/5

### 9

| | | | |
|---|---|---|---|
| Recognize | _____ | Answer Type | _____ |
| Restate | _____ | Answer Type | _____ |
| | _____ | Answer Type | _____ |
| Recall | _____ | Answer Type | _____ |
| | _____ | Resolve Ⓐ Ⓑ Ⓒ Ⓓ | Confidence ___/5 |

### 10

| | | | |
|---|---|---|---|
| Recognize | _____ | Answer Type | _____ |
| Restate | _____ | Answer Type | _____ |
| | _____ | Answer Type | _____ |
| Recall | _____ | Answer Type | _____ |
| | _____ | Resolve Ⓐ Ⓑ Ⓒ Ⓓ | Confidence ___/5 |

### 11

| | | | |
|---|---|---|---|
| Recognize | _____ | Answer Type | _____ |
| Restate | _____ | Answer Type | _____ |
| | _____ | Answer Type | _____ |
| Recall | _____ | Answer Type | _____ |
| | _____ | Resolve Ⓐ Ⓑ Ⓒ Ⓓ | Confidence ___/5 |

| Questions | General | Specific | Synthesis | Answers | Reason |
|---|---|---|---|---|---|
| Main Purpose | Purpose | Function | | Wrong | Somewhat right, but too broad |
| Main Idea | Thesis | Topic | | Wrong | Somewhat right, but too narrow |
| Tone | Tone | Attitude | | Wrong | Somewhat right, but too extreme |
| Rhetoric | Structure | Argument | | Wrong | Tempting words, but wrong part |
| Vocabulary | | Vocabulary | | Wrong | Tempting words, but not true |
| Evidence | | Evidence | | Wrong | Tempting words, but irrelevant |
| Detail | | Detail | | Wrong | Flatly false |
| Inference | | Inference | | Right (general) | Give identify evidence |
| Data | | Data Specific | Data Synthesis | Right (specific) | Give line or annotation evidence |
| Paired | | Paired Specific | Paired Synthesis | Right (synthesis) | Give identify evidence |

## Review

1. What was the purpose of the passage? What was the author's central claim? Which questions were related to that claim?

2. If there were charts and graphs, how do they support the author's thesis?

3. What questions did you find hardest? What made them hard (e.g., the question itself, the answers, the passage, something else)?

4. What questions did you find easiest)? What made them easy (e.g., the question itself, the answers, the passage, something else)?

5. Are there patterns to the question types you find harder than others? For example, did you find that general or specific are harder? What about individual question types (e.g., detail, inference, vocabulary)?

6. Look at each of the questions you answered incorrectly. Why was your answer wrong? What makes the correct answer right?

## Passage Type: Paired Passage

Passage Name: _____   Skill Level: _____   Date: _____   Correct: _____

## Underline, Annotate, and Identify

Line

10

20

30

40

50

60

70

80

Purpose 1  _____
           _____

Purpose 2  _____
           _____

Agree      _____
           _____

Disagree   _____
           _____

## Restate, Recall, and Resolve

**1**

| | | | |
|---|---|---|---|
| Recognize | _____ | Answer Type | _____ |
| Restate | _____ | Answer Type | _____ |
| | _____ | Answer Type | _____ |
| Recall | _____ | Answer Type | _____ |
| | _____ | Resolve Ⓐ Ⓑ Ⓒ Ⓓ | Confidence ___/5 |

**2**

| | | | |
|---|---|---|---|
| Recognize | _____ | Answer Type | _____ |
| Restate | _____ | Answer Type | _____ |
| | _____ | Answer Type | _____ |
| Recall | _____ | Answer Type | _____ |
| | _____ | Resolve Ⓐ Ⓑ Ⓒ Ⓓ | Confidence ___/5 |

**3**

| | | | |
|---|---|---|---|
| Recognize | _____ | Answer Type | _____ |
| Restate | _____ | Answer Type | _____ |
| | _____ | Answer Type | _____ |
| Recall | _____ | Answer Type | _____ |
| | _____ | Resolve Ⓐ Ⓑ Ⓒ Ⓓ | Confidence ___/5 |

**4**

| | | | |
|---|---|---|---|
| Recognize | _____ | Answer Type | _____ |
| Restate | _____ | Answer Type | _____ |
| | _____ | Answer Type | _____ |
| Recall | _____ | Answer Type | _____ |
| | _____ | Resolve Ⓐ Ⓑ Ⓒ Ⓓ | Confidence ___/5 |

Lesson 9: Mastering Khan Academy

## 5

Recognize _____  Answer Type _____

Restate _____  Answer Type _____

_____  Answer Type _____

Recall _____  Answer Type _____

_____  Resolve  Ⓐ Ⓑ Ⓒ Ⓓ   Confidence ___/5

## 6

Recognize _____  Answer Type _____

Restate _____  Answer Type _____

_____  Answer Type _____

Recall _____  Answer Type _____

_____  Resolve  Ⓐ Ⓑ Ⓒ Ⓓ   Confidence ___/5

## 7

Recognize _____  Answer Type _____

Restate _____  Answer Type _____

_____  Answer Type _____

Recall _____  Answer Type _____

_____  Resolve  Ⓐ Ⓑ Ⓒ Ⓓ   Confidence ___/5

## 8

Recognize _____  Answer Type _____

Restate _____  Answer Type _____

_____  Answer Type _____

Recall _____  Answer Type _____

_____  Resolve  Ⓐ Ⓑ Ⓒ Ⓓ   Confidence ___/5

## 9

Recognize _____  Answer Type _____

Restate _____  Answer Type _____

_____  Answer Type _____

Recall _____  Answer Type _____

_____  Resolve Ⓐ Ⓑ Ⓒ Ⓓ    Confidence ___/5

## 10

Recognize _____  Answer Type _____

Restate _____  Answer Type _____

_____  Answer Type _____

Recall _____  Answer Type _____

_____  Resolve Ⓐ Ⓑ Ⓒ Ⓓ    Confidence ___/5

## 11

Recognize _____  Answer Type _____

Restate _____  Answer Type _____

_____  Answer Type _____

Recall _____  Answer Type _____

_____  Resolve Ⓐ Ⓑ Ⓒ Ⓓ    Confidence ___/5

| Questions | General | Specific | Synthesis | Answers | Reason |
|---|---|---|---|---|---|
| Main Purpose | Purpose | Function | | Wrong | Somewhat right, but too broad |
| Main Idea | Thesis | Topic | | Wrong | Somewhat right, but too narrow |
| Tone | Tone | Attitude | | Wrong | Somewhat right, but too extreme |
| Rhetoric | Structure | Argument | | Wrong | Tempting words, but wrong part |
| Vocabulary | | Vocabulary | | Wrong | Tempting words, but not true |
| Evidence | | Evidence | | Wrong | Tempting words, but irrelevant |
| Detail | | Detail | | Wrong | Flatly false |
| Inference | | Inference | | Right (general) | Give identify evidence |
| Data | | Data Specific | Data Synthesis | Right (specific) | Give line or annotation evidence |
| Paired | | Paired Specific | Paired Synthesis | Right (synthesis) | Give identify evidence |

Lesson 9: Mastering Khan Academy

## Review

1. What was the purpose of Passage 1? What was Passage 1's central claim?

2. What was the purpose of Passage 2? What was Passage 2's central claim?

3. Where do Passage 1 and Passage 2 agree? Where do they disagree?

4. What questions did you find hardest? What made them hard (e.g., the question itself, the answers, the passage, something else)?

5. What questions did you find easiest)? What made them easy (e.g., the question itself, the answers, the passage, something else)?

6. Are there patterns to the question types you find harder than others? For example, did you find that general or specific are harder? What about individual question types (e.g., detail, inference, vocabulary)?

7. Look at each of the questions you answered incorrectly. Why was your answer wrong? What makes the correct answer right?

# PRACTICE TEST REVIEW: TEST 7 AND TEST 8

**Staying motivated isn't always easy, but it's important to keep pushing.** If you haven't done so already, go back and review tests 7 and 8.

- Looking at the passages, did you remember to **underline**? How about **annotating** the passage (two to four words, once or twice per paragraph)? How could you have improved your reading?

- Turning to the questions, what **question types** had you flummoxed? Why were your **incorrect answers wrong** and their **correct answers right**? Do you see any patterns?

If you're this far through the book, you've put in a lot of work. If you don't keep putting in the work, your score can become stagnant. Reviewing old tests is one of the best ways to consolidate your gains and expand your potential. **Don't become complacent. Keep pushing.** You can find review sheets for tests 7 and 8 on page 259 and 265, respectively.

Lesson 9: Mastering Khan Academy

# LESSON 10: UNDERSTANDING THE TEST-MAKERS

Engagement with the material is key to active learning, and while you may have more experience with this in school or at home, it can be applied to the SAT as well. It allows you to retrieve on test day the skills you have been building while preparing for the test.

If you're ever unsure of how to answer a question, ask yourself this deceitfully simple question:

*What are the test-makers testing my ability to do?*

This question may seem straight-forward, and it sits behind the strategies of **recognizing** what they are asking you and **restating** the prompt as a question. Find that the best way to do answer this question is to practice writing your own questions and answers. We worked on this a little in lesson 4 (**Mastering the Questions**, page 47) and lesson 5 (**Mastering the Answers**, page 73). Here, however, you'll have the opportunity to create your own sets of questions and answers. The place you learn to understand the test-makers is in the **Build-a-passage Workshop**.

## LITERATURE BUILD-A-PASSAGE: THE MINISTER'S BLACK VEIL

Let's start by building a literature passage. This passage doesn't include any charts and graphs, so we will have no infographic questions. It isn't paired either, so we'll have no paired questions. The rest of the questions, however, are fair game. Let's give our passage a good distribution of question types.

| Questions | General | Specific | Synthesis |
|---|---|---|---|
| Main Purpose | | 2 Function | |
| Main Idea | | | |
| Tone | 1 Tone | 1 Attitude | |
| Rhetoric | 1 Structure | | |
| Vocabulary | | 2 Vocabulary | |
| Evidence | | 1 Evidence | |
| Detail | | 1 Detail | |
| Inference | | 1 Inference | |
| Data | | | |
| Paired | | | |

To get yourself started, read through the passage the way you always read SAT passages: **Underline**, **Annotate**, and **Identify**.

# Practice Passage: Literature (Antiquated English)

This passage is adapted from Nathaniel Hawthorne, "The Minister's Black Veil," first published in 1832.

The sexton stood in the porch of Milford meetinghouse, pulling busily at the bell rope. The old people of the village came stooping along the street. Children, with bright faces, tripped merrily beside their parents, or mimicked a graver gait, in the conscious dignity of their Sunday clothes. Spruce bachelors looked sidelong at the pretty maidens, and fancied that the Sabbath sunshine made them prettier than on weekdays. When the throng had mostly streamed into the porch, the sexton began to toll the bell, keeping his eye on the Reverend Mr. Hooper's door. The first glimpse of the clergyman's figure was the signal for the bell to cease its summons.

"But what has good Parson Hooper got upon his face?" cried the sexton in astonishment.

All within hearing immediately turned about, and beheld the semblance of Mr. Hooper, pacing slowly his meditative way toward the meetinghouse. With one accord they started, expressing more wonder than if some strange minister were coming to dust the cushions of Mr. Hooper's pulpit.

"Are you sure it is our parson?" inquired Goodman Gray of the sexton.

"Of a certainty it is good Mr. Hooper," replied the sexton. "He was to have exchanged pulpits with Parson Shute, of Westbury; but Parson Shute sent to excuse himself yesterday, being to preach a funeral sermon."

The cause of so much amazement may appear sufficiently slight. Mr. Hooper gentlemanly person, of about thirty, though still a bachelor, was dressed with due clerical neatness, as if a careful wife had starched his band, and brushed the weekly dust from his Sunday's garb. There was but one thing remarkable in his appearance. Swathed about his forehead, and hanging down over his face, so low as to be shaken by his breath Mr. Hooper had on a black veil. On a nearer view it seemed to consist of two folds of crepe, which entirely concealed his features, except the mouth and chin, but probably did not intercept his sight, further than to give a darkened aspect to all living and inanimate things. With this gloomy shade before him, good Mr. Hooper walked onward, at a slow and quiet pace, stooping somewhat, and looking on the ground, as is customary with abstracted men, yet nodding kindly to those of his parishioners who still waited on the meetinghouse steps. But so wonderstruck were they that his greeting hardly met with a return.

"I can't really feel as if good Mr. Hooper's face was behind that piece of crape," said the sexton.

"I don't like it," muttered an old woman, as she hobbled into the meetinghouse. "He has changed himself into something awful, only by hiding his face."

"Our parson has gone mad!" cried Goodman Gray, following him across the threshold.

A rumor of some unaccountable phenomenon had preceded Mr. Hooper into the meetinghouse, and set all the congregation astir. Few could refrain from twisting their heads toward the door; many stood upright, and turned directly about while several little boys clambered upon the seats, and came down again with a terrible racket. There was a general bustle, a rustling of the women's gowns and shuffling of the men's feet, greatly at variance with that hushed repose which should attend the entrance of the minister. But Mr. Hooper appeared not to notice the perturbation of his people. He entered with an almost noiseless step, bent his head mildly to the pews on each side, and bowed as he passed his oldest parishioner, a whitehaired great-grandsire, who occupied an armchair in the center of the aisle. It was strange to observe how slowly this venerable man became conscious of something singular in the appearance of his pastor. He seemed not fully to partake of the prevailing wonder, till Mr. Hooper had ascended the stairs, and showed himself in the pulpit, face to face with his congregation, except for the black veil. That mysterious emblem was never once withdrawn. It shook with his measured breath, as he gave out the psalm; it threw its obscurity between him and the holy page, as he read the Scriptures; and while he prayed, the veil lay heavily on his uplifted countenance. Did he seek to hide it from the dread Being whom he was addressing?

Such was the effect of this simple piece of crepe, that more than one woman of delicate nerves was forced to leave the meetinghouse. Yet perhaps the pale-faced congregation was almost as fearful a sight to the minister, as his black veil to them.

Now, read through the passage again and get the general questions sorted out:

- What's the author's **purpose**? Literature passages describe literary characters. Even though we aren't creating any purpose questions, we'll need this information to write our function questions.

- How does the passage develop? What is the organizational **structure**?

- What is the overall tone of the passage?

You can also start thinking about your specific questions:

- How do the paragraphs **function** to emphasize the author's description?

- What interesting **vocabulary** does the passage use? This isn't just hard words, but words with secondary meanings.

- What **details**, either about the characters, the setting, or the events of the passage, stand out?

- What can we **infer** about the main character and their circumstances?

- Where do you find your **evidence** for the detail and inference questions?

- What's the main character's **attitude** toward their circumstances? Toward another character?

This will take some time, and will likely require you to read the passage two or three times. You may want to read for the general questions first, then go back and sketch out your more specific questions.

## Building Literature Questions

Once you've sketched out your questions, you can start with the questions themselves.

1. Start by figuring out the core questions you are going to ask (**restate**). After you have the core question, write the prompt. Feel free to take a peek at the examples in lesson 3 if you are stuck.

2. Now, you can answer your question (**recall**). Start by giving the best answer to the question you asked. Once you are sure you have the pure answer, you can write the correct test-style question.

3. Finally, come up with three incorrect answers (**resolve**). You should try for a variety of incorrect reasons (they are listed at the beginning and end of the bank). It's easier to avoid the "mostly correct" for now as well. They are almost as hard to write as they are to answer!

Writing questions and answers is a multi-step process, but with time it gets easier. Let's write some questions for our Hawthorne passage.

### 1

Recognize: Structure

Restate:

Prompt:

Recall:

Answer Ⓐ

Answer Ⓑ

Answer Ⓒ

Answer Ⓓ

### 2

Recognize: Function

Restate:

Prompt:

Recall:

Answer Ⓐ

Answer Ⓑ

Answer Ⓒ

Answer Ⓓ

**3**

Recognize  Attitude

Restate

Prompt

Recall

Answer Ⓐ

Answer Ⓑ

Answer Ⓒ

Answer Ⓓ

**4**

Recognize  Vocab

Restate

Prompt

Recall

Answer Ⓐ

Answer Ⓑ

Answer Ⓒ

Answer Ⓓ

**5**

Recognize  Inference/Detail

Restate

Prompt

Recall

Answer Ⓐ

Answer Ⓑ

Answer Ⓒ

Answer Ⓓ

Lesson 10: Understanding the Test-Makers

## 6

Recognize: Evidence for #6

Restate

Prompt

Recall

Answer Ⓐ

Answer Ⓑ

Answer Ⓒ

Answer Ⓓ

## 7

Recognize: Line-number Inference/Detail

Restate

Prompt

Recall

Answer Ⓐ

Answer Ⓑ

Answer Ⓒ

Answer Ⓓ

## 8

Recognize: Vocab

Restate

Prompt

Recall

Answer Ⓐ

Answer Ⓑ

Answer Ⓒ

Answer Ⓓ

## 9

Recognize    Function          Answer Ⓐ _____

Restate      _____

             _____   Answer Ⓑ _____

Prompt       _____

             _____   Answer Ⓒ _____

Recall       _____

             _____   Answer Ⓓ _____

             _____

## 10

Recognize    Tone              Answer Ⓐ _____

Restate      _____

             _____   Answer Ⓑ _____

Prompt       _____

             _____   Answer Ⓒ _____

Recall       _____

             _____   Answer Ⓓ _____

             _____

| Questions | General | Specific | Synthesis | Answers | Reason |
|---|---|---|---|---|---|
| Main Purpose | Purpose | Function | | Wrong | Somewhat right, but too broad |
| Main Idea | Thesis | Topic | | Wrong | Somewhat right, but too narrow |
| Tone | Tone | Attitude | | Wrong | Somewhat right, but too extreme |
| Rhetoric | Structure | Argument | | Wrong | Tempting words, but wrong part |
| Vocabulary | | Vocabulary | | Wrong | Tempting words, but not true |
| Evidence | | Evidence | | Wrong | Tempting words, but irrelevant |
| Detail | | Detail | | Wrong | Flatly false |
| Inference | | Inference | | Right (general) | Give identify evidence |
| Data | | Data Specific | Data Synthesis | Right (specific) | Give line or annotation evidence |
| Paired | | Paired Specific | Paired Synthesis | Right (synthesis) | Give identify evidence |

Lesson 10: Understanding the Test-Makers

## Reviewing Your Creation

Now, consider the process of writing questions and how that has improved your ability to answer the **literature** questions that you'll see on test day.

1. For which question type was it hardest to write the prompt? Did you go back to lesson 3 to look at some example prompts?

2. Which wrong answer type (e.g., somewhat right but too narrow, tempting words, but irrelevant) was hardest to write? Why?

3. Which wrong answer type (e.g., somewhat right but too narrow, tempting words, but irrelevant) was easiest to write? Why?

4. How can you prepare yourself for questions as you read the passage?

5. How can you prepare yourself for the answers as you read the passage?

6. How does writing literature questions change the way you read literature passages?

7. How does writing on antiquated English questions change the way you read the passages with antiquated English?

# SCIENCE BUILD-A-PASSAGE: CIVIL WAR NAVAL DATA

Science! This one has charts and graphs, so we'll need to write some questions that go with the data.

| Questions | General | Specific | Synthesis |
|---|---|---|---|
| Main Purpose | 1 Purpose | | |
| Main Idea | 1 Thesis | | |
| Tone | | | |
| Rhetoric | | 1 Argument | |
| Vocabulary | | 1 Vocabulary | |
| Evidence | | 1 Evidence | |
| Detail | | 1 Detail | |
| Inference | | 1 Inference | |
| Data | | 1 Data (Detail) | 2 Data (Synthesis) |
| Paired | | | |

Read through the passage and get the general question sorted out:

- What's the author's **purpose**? Science passages tend to explain something. What is the author explaining?

- What's the author's **thesis**? What are they arguing?

Start thinking about your specific questions:

- What interesting **vocabulary** does the passage use?

- What **assumptions** supply the background of the scientific discovery?

- What **details** stand out in the passage?

- What are the logical **implications** of the passage?

- Where do you find your **evidence** for the detail and inference questions?

Lesson 10: Understanding the Test-Makers

- What is the attitude of the scientists mentioned in the passage?

Finally, let's create three questions from the data.

- What do the data say? What **details** emerge in the data?

- Where do the data and the passage agree? How can you **synthesize** the data with the text?

- How do the two figures compare with each other?

As with the literature passage, read the passage at least twice: once to understand it and a second time to find your questions.

## Practice Passage: Science (with Data)

This passage is adapted from Hannah Hickey, "Mining Weather Data from Civil War–era Navy Logbooks," 2018, National Oceanic and Atmospheric Administration.

   A new grant will let a University of Washington-based project add a new fleet to its quest to learn more about past climate from the records of long-gone mariners. This will allow the project to digitize the
5  logbooks, muster rolls and related materials from U.S. naval vessels, focusing on the period from 1861 to 1879.
   "Very few of the marine weather observations diligently recorded by Navy officers since the early
10 1800s have been digitized and made accessible for modern climate and weather research," said principal investigator Kevin Wood, a research scientist with the Joint Institute for the Study of the Atmosphere and Ocean, a research center operated by the UW and the
15 National Oceanic and Atmospheric Administration Pacific Marine Environmental Laboratory. "The Civil War- and Reconstruction-era logs we are targeting here are particularly useful to fill in and extend our knowledge of past weather conditions around the
20 world, from the mid-19th century to the beginning of the 20th century."
   Wood is one of the leaders of the Old Weather project, launched in 2010, that has transcribed weather records from the British Royal Navy and later the U.S.
25 Navy, Coast Guard and Coast Survey ships that had sailed Arctic waters. A 2015 addition began to digitize the logbooks of U.S. whaling ships that are now at the New Bedford Whaling Museum.
   After making digital images of the logbooks housed
30 at the National Archives, the project will recover ships' positions, weather records, oceanographic data and other historical information through the Old Weather citizen-science program that trains volunteers to transcribe the logs' handwritten entries. So far
35 volunteers have transcribed more than 3 million new-to-science weather records, and more than 1 million of those have been quality-check and added into global climate databases.
   The new effort fills a gap in the data of past weather
40 conditions. Comparing historic and modern data and rising temperatures allows scientists to understand climate change patterns and improve prediction.

   "A key point about the U.S. Civil War is that it put a stop to [Naval officer] Matthew Maury's pioneering
45 collection of marine weather observations. If you look at the number and coverage of the marine observations we currently have available, you can see a dramatic drop-off in 1861. Coverage didn't get back to pre-war standards until about 1880," said collaborator Philip
50 Brohan, a climate scientist at the U.K.'s national weather office and Old Weather science team leader. "This project will go some way to repairing the damage. And it's a credit to the National Archives that such a repair is still possible, even 150 years later."

The isothermal lines indicate average air temperatures in Kelvin (300 K = 80°F) for July 1871 (above) and 2010 (below). Adapted from the National Oceanic and Atmospheric Administration, https://www.esrl.noaa.gov. Point A indicates the location of Washington, DC. Point B indicates the location of New York City.

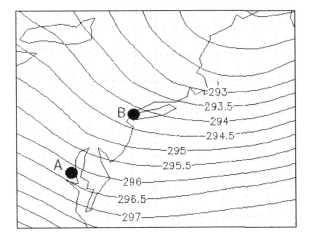

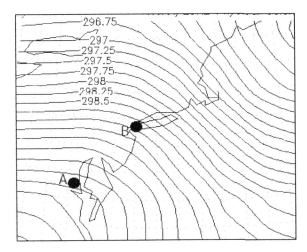

## Building Science Questions

Once again, start on the questions after you've sketched out the passage.

1. What is the core question you are going to ask (**restate**)? What prompt works best with this core question?

2. What is the answer to your core question (**recall**)? After you have the unadorned answer, turn it into an SAT-style question.

3. What are some reasonable incorrect answers (**resolve**)? You can start sprinkling in some "mostly correct" answers, though you can stay in safer waters if you prefer. The answer types are listed at the bottom of the page again.

Ready? On to the questions and answers!

**1**

Recognize: Purpose

Restate:

Prompt:

Recall:

Answer Ⓐ
Answer Ⓑ
Answer Ⓒ
Answer Ⓓ

**2**

Recognize: Thesis

Restate:

Prompt:

Recall:

Answer Ⓐ
Answer Ⓑ
Answer Ⓒ
Answer Ⓓ

### 3

Recognize  Vocabulary          Answer Ⓐ
Restate
                               Answer Ⓑ

Prompt
                               Answer Ⓒ

Recall
                               Answer Ⓓ


### 4

Recognize  Argument            Answer Ⓐ
Restate
                               Answer Ⓑ

Prompt
                               Answer Ⓒ

Recall
                               Answer Ⓓ


### 5

Recognize  Detail              Answer Ⓐ
Restate
                               Answer Ⓑ

Prompt
                               Answer Ⓒ

Recall
                               Answer Ⓓ

Lesson 10: Understanding the Test-Makers

**6**

Recognize   Evidence for #5

Restate

Prompt

Recall

Answer Ⓐ

Answer Ⓑ

Answer Ⓒ

Answer Ⓓ

**7**

Recognize   Line-number Inference

Restate

Prompt

Recall

Answer Ⓐ

Answer Ⓑ

Answer Ⓒ

Answer Ⓓ

**8**

Recognize   Data (Detail)

Restate

Prompt

Recall

Answer Ⓐ

Answer Ⓑ

Answer Ⓒ

Answer Ⓓ

## 9

| | | | |
|---|---|---|---|
| Recognize | Data (Synthesis) | Answer Ⓐ | |
| Restate | | | |
| | | Answer Ⓑ | |
| Prompt | | | |
| | | Answer Ⓒ | |
| Recall | | | |
| | | Answer Ⓓ | |

## 10

| | | | |
|---|---|---|---|
| Recognize | Data (Synthesis) | Answer Ⓐ | |
| Restate | | | |
| | | Answer Ⓑ | |
| Prompt | | | |
| | | Answer Ⓒ | |
| Recall | | | |
| | | Answer Ⓓ | |

| Questions | General | Specific | Synthesis | Answers | Reason |
|---|---|---|---|---|---|
| Main Purpose | Purpose | Function | | Wrong | Somewhat right, but too broad |
| Main Idea | Thesis | Topic | | Wrong | Somewhat right, but too narrow |
| Tone | Tone | Attitude | | Wrong | Somewhat right, but too extreme |
| Rhetoric | Structure | Argument | | Wrong | Tempting words, but wrong part |
| Vocabulary | | Vocabulary | | Wrong | Tempting words, but not true |
| Evidence | | Evidence | | Wrong | Tempting words, but irrelevant |
| Detail | | Detail | | Wrong | Flatly false |
| Inference | | Inference | | Right (general) | Give identify evidence |
| Data | | Data Specific | Data Synthesis | Right (specific) | Give line or annotation evidence |
| Paired | | Paired Specific | Paired Synthesis | Right (synthesis) | Give identify evidence |

Lesson 10: Understanding the Test-Makers

## Reviewing Your Creation

Let's review the question writing process and look for ways you can improve your comprehension of **science** and **data** passages and the questions that accompany them.

1. For which question type was it hardest to write the prompt? Did you go back to lesson 3 to look at some example prompts?

2. Which wrong answer type (e.g., somewhat right but too narrow, tempting words, but irrelevant) was hardest to write? Why?

3. Which wrong answer type (e.g., somewhat right but too narrow, tempting words, but irrelevant) was easiest to write? Why?

4. How can you prepare yourself for questions as you read the passage?

5. How can you prepare yourself for the answers as you read the passage?

6. How does writing science questions change the way you read science passages?

7. How does writing data synthesis questions change the way you read the passages with data?

# SOCIAL STUDIES BUILD-A-PASSAGE: REAL PRICE PARITY

The data questions can be a little tough, so let's try another passage with data. This is a social studies passage.

| Questions | General | Specific | Synthesis |
|---|---|---|---|
| Main Purpose | | 1 Function | |
| Main Idea | 1 Thesis | | |
| Tone | | | |
| Rhetoric | 1 Structure | | |
| Vocabulary | | 1 Vocabulary | |
| Evidence | | 1 Evidence | |
| Detail | | 1 Detail | |
| Inference | | | |
| Data | | 2 Data (Detail) | 2 Data (Synthesis) |
| Paired | | | |

Read through the passage and get the general questions sorted out:

- What's the author's **purpose**? Like the science passages, social studies passages tend to explain something. What is the author explaining?

- What's the author's **thesis**? What are they arguing?

- How would you describe the passage's structure? Do things change at any point?

Start thinking about your specific questions:

- What interesting **vocabulary** does the passage use?

- What **detail** most stands out in the passage? (Pair this detail question with an evidence question.)

- Where do you find your **evidence** for the detail?

- What function do the paragraphs serve?

Lesson 10: Understanding the Test-Makers

Finally, create four questions from the data.

- What do the data say? What **details** emerge in the data?

- Where do the data and the passage agree? How can you **synthesize** the data with the text?

Again, reading the passage twice is a good idea: once to **underline**, **annotate**, and **identify**, and once to find your questions. Don't forget to annotate the data—you're going to need to find 4 questions in the data by the time you're finished.

## Practice Passage: Social Studies (with Data)

This passage is adapted from "We've Got Your Number," 2018, U.S. Chamber of Commerce.

The U.S. Bureau of Economic Analysis (BEA) is a key source of accurate and objective data about the nation's economy. BEA's economists produce some of the world's most closely watched statistics, including
[5] U.S. gross domestic product, better known as GDP. They also produce state and local numbers, too, plus foreign trade and investment stats and industry data.

You might guess that a dollar stretches further in Mississippi than in New York. But do you know how
[10] much further? Or the difference between a dollar in Dallas and a dollar in Dubuque?

The BEA has the numbers for that.

You can compare buying power across the 50 states and the District of Columbia, or across the nation's
[15] metro areas, with BEA's Regional Price Parities, which measure differences in price levels. For example, what you could buy for 86 cents in Mississippi cost $1.15 on average in the state of New York (or $1.19 in Hawaii, the costliest state), price parities for 2015 show. In
[20] other words, prices in New York were 34 percent higher than in Mississippi.

Knowing this can help a worker decide whether to take a job transfer or help a couple choose where to retire. Companies consider differences in price levels
[25] when locating a new office or setting salaries. Local boosters use these numbers to promote their towns.

Regional prices also add perspective to regional pay. In addition to the annual release of Regional Price Parities, BEA produces price-adjusted income data
[30] that show how the per capita incomes of states and metro areas compare when prices are taken into account.

As for those metro areas: 92 cents in Dubuque, Iowa, would buy goods or services that cost $1 in
[35] Dallas. The value of a dollar in Dallas, meanwhile, was right at the national average.

Our trade in goods and services data are best known for capturing the trade gap — the difference between U.S. exports and imports. BEA also estimates
[40] the United States' deficits or surpluses with individual nations and shows what's being traded with whom. Balance of payments numbers (also called the international transactions accounts) give a broader view of the economic activity between the U.S. and
[45] other nations. That includes trade in goods and services, financial investments and associated income, and foreign aid. Among these stats, the current account balance is especially popular as an economic indicator.

[50] International investment position is a statistical balance sheet showing the values of American-owned assets abroad and foreign-owned assets in the United States at a given time.

Direct investment data provide information on the
[55] economic ties between affiliated companies in the U.S. and abroad, including transactions, assets, liabilities, sales, employment and more. Plus, BEA economists publish data on new foreign direct investment that enters the United States each year

[60] International trade numbers help policymakers and the public understand how exports and imports affect the U.S. economy. Negotiators use these stats when making trade agreements. Businesses use them to learn about export markets. Economic boosters use them to
[65] attract foreign investment to their areas. The data provide insight into the effects of foreign ownership inside the United States and the operations of U.S. companies abroad.

Governments of all levels, businesses big and small,
[70] and Americans everywhere rely on our numbers. BEA's work underpins decisions about interest rates and trade policy, taxes and spending, hiring and investing, and more. All from a source that's nonpartisan, nonpolitical and neutral on policy.

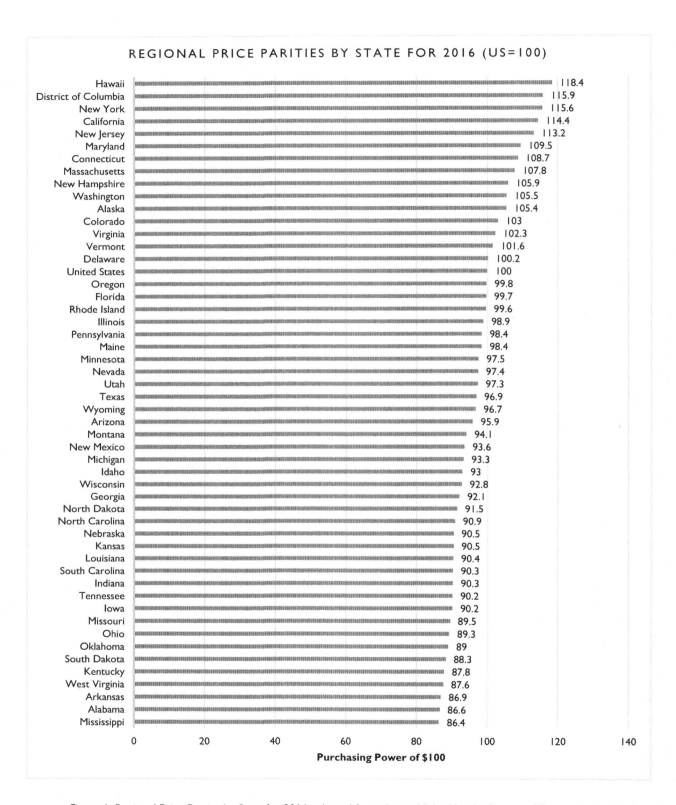

Figure 1: Regional Price Parties by State for 2016, adapted from data published by the Bureau of Economic Analysis.

## Building Social Studies Questions

Once again, start on the questions after you've sketched out the passage.

1. What is the core question you are going to ask (**restate**)? Do any of the stock prompts stand out as best for this question type?

2. What is the answer to your core question (**recall**)? After you have the cleanest answer, turn it into an SAT-style question.

3. What are some reasonable incorrect answers (**resolve**)? You should be getting more comfortable here, so feel free to stretch yourself. The answer types are listed at the bottom of the page again.

### 1

Recognize    Thesis                                Answer Ⓐ  _____

Restate      _____                              _____

             _____        Answer Ⓑ  _____

Prompt       _____                              _____

             _____        Answer Ⓒ  _____

Recall       _____                              _____

             _____        Answer Ⓓ  _____

                                                              _____

### 2

Recognize    Structure                             Answer Ⓐ  _____

Restate      _____                              _____

             _____        Answer Ⓑ  _____

Prompt       _____                              _____

             _____        Answer Ⓒ  _____

Recall       _____                              _____

             _____        Answer Ⓓ  _____

                                                              _____

Lesson 10: Understanding the Test-Makers

## 3

Recognize — Vocabulary

Restate

Prompt

Recall

Answer Ⓐ

Answer Ⓑ

Answer Ⓒ

Answer Ⓓ

## 4

Recognize — Detail

Restate

Prompt

Recall

Answer Ⓐ

Answer Ⓑ

Answer Ⓒ

Answer Ⓓ

## 5

Recognize — Evidence for #4

Restate

Prompt

Recall

Answer Ⓐ

Answer Ⓑ

Answer Ⓒ

Answer Ⓓ

## 6

Recognize: Function

Restate:

Prompt:

Recall:

Answer Ⓐ
Answer Ⓑ
Answer Ⓒ
Answer Ⓓ

## 7

Recognize: Data (Synthesis)

Restate:

Prompt:

Recall:

Answer Ⓐ
Answer Ⓑ
Answer Ⓒ
Answer Ⓓ

## 8

Recognize: Data (Detail)

Restate:

Prompt:

Recall:

Answer Ⓐ
Answer Ⓑ
Answer Ⓒ
Answer Ⓓ

Lesson 10: Understanding the Test-Makers

## 9

Recognize: Data (Detail)

Restate:

Prompt:

Recall:

Answer Ⓐ

Answer Ⓑ

Answer Ⓒ

Answer Ⓓ

## 10

Recognize: Data (Synthesis)

Restate:

Prompt:

Recall:

Answer Ⓐ

Answer Ⓑ

Answer Ⓒ

Answer Ⓓ

| Questions | General | Specific | Synthesis | Answers | Reason |
|---|---|---|---|---|---|
| Main Purpose | Purpose | Function | | Wrong | Somewhat right, but too broad |
| Main Idea | Thesis | Topic | | Wrong | Somewhat right, but too narrow |
| Tone | Tone | Attitude | | Wrong | Somewhat right, but too extreme |
| Rhetoric | Structure | Argument | | Wrong | Tempting words, but wrong part |
| Vocabulary | | Vocabulary | | Wrong | Tempting words, but not true |
| Evidence | | Evidence | | Wrong | Tempting words, but irrelevant |
| Detail | | Detail | | Wrong | Flatly false |
| Inference | | Inference | | Right (general) | Give identify evidence |
| Data | | Data Specific | Data Synthesis | Right (specific) | Give line or annotation evidence |
| Paired | | Paired Specific | Paired Synthesis | Right (synthesis) | Give identify evidence |

## Reviewing Your Creation

Let's review the question writing process and look for ways you can improve your comprehension of **social studies** and **data** passages and the questions that accompany them.

1. For which question type was it hardest to write the prompt? Did you go back to lesson 3 to look at some example prompts?

2. Which wrong answer type (e.g., somewhat right but too narrow, tempting words, but irrelevant) was hardest to write? Why?

3. Which wrong answer type (e.g., somewhat right but too narrow, tempting words, but irrelevant) was easiest to write? Why?

4. How can you prepare yourself for questions as you read the passage?

5. How can you prepare yourself for the answers as you read the passage?

6. How does writing social studies questions change the way you read social studies passages?

7. How does writing data synthesis questions change the way you read the passages with data?

# PAIRED HISTORY BUILD-A-PASSAGE: WOMEN'S SUFFRAGE

Ready for a paired passage? Here's a set of passages on women's rights. We'll need three paired questions.

| Questions | General | Specific | Synthesis |
|---|---|---|---|
| Main Purpose | | | |
| Main Idea | | | |
| Tone | 1 Tone | | |
| Rhetoric | | 1 Argument | |
| Vocabulary | | 1 Vocabulary | |
| Evidence | | 2 Evidence | |
| Detail | | 1 Detail | |
| Inference | | 1 Inference | |
| Data | | | |
| Paired | | 1 Paired Inference | 2 Paired Synthesis |

Once again, read through the passages and get a sense for the author's arguments:

- What's the **purpose** of each passage? History passages are often arguing for something.

- What's the **tone** of each passage? Are the authors arguing with heat or are they level-headed? Maybe they have different tactics based on the circumstances of their writing.

- What's the **thesis** of each passage?

Now, look for agreement and disagreement so you can write your paired synthesis questions.

- What do they agree on? One of the questions can ask about their **shared purpose** (to argue about women's suffrage), but you'll need another question.

- What do they disagree on?

Lastly, let's look at regular questions that accompany passages, paired or not.

- How do the paragraphs **function** in the author's argument?

- What interesting **vocabulary** does the passage use? Look for secondary meanings.

- How do the authors support their argument? What **assumptions** do they make?

- What **details** stand out in the passage?

- What can we **infer** about the authors or their arguments from the passage?

- Where do you find your **evidence** for the detail and inference questions?

Like with the literature passage, this takes some time. Make sure you have the authors' positions down before you move on to the question construction.

# Practice Passage: History (Paired and Antiquated)

Passage 1 is adapted from Susan B. Anthony, "On Women's Right to Vote." Anthony gave this speech in 1873 after being arrested for voting in the 1872. Passage 2 is a petition written by Ellen Ewing Sherman and Madeleine Victor Dahlgreen in 1872.

**Passage 1**

Fellow people in this here world:

I stand before you tonight under indictment for the alleged crime of having voted at the last presidential election, without having a lawful right to vote. It shall be my work this evening to prove to you that me thus voting, I not only committed no crime, but, instead, simply exercised my citizen's rights, guaranteed to me and all United States citizens by the National Constitution, beyond the power of any state to deny.

The preamble of the Federal Constitution says: "We, the people of the United States, in order to form a more perfect union, establish justice, insure domestic tranquillity, provide for the common defense, promote the general welfare, and secure the blessings of liberty to ourselves and our posterity, do ordain and establish this Constitution for the United States of America."

It was we, the people; not we, the white male citizens; nor yet we, the male citizens; but we, the whole people, who formed the Union. And we formed it, not to give the blessings of liberty, but to secure them; not to the half of ourselves and the half of our posterity, but to the whole people - women as well as men. And it is a downright mockery to talk to women of their enjoyment of the blessings of liberty while they are denied the use of the only means of securing them provided by this democratic-republican government - the ballot.

For any state to make sex a qualification that must ever result in the disfranchisement of one entire half of the people, is to pass a bill of attainder, or, an ex post facto law, and is therefore a violation of the supreme law of the land. By it the blessings of liberty are forever withheld from women and their female posterity.

To them this government has no just powers derived from the consent of the governed. To them this government is not a democracy. It is not a republic. It is an odious aristocracy; a hateful oligarchy of sex; the most hateful aristocracy ever established on the face of the globe; an oligarchy of wealth, where the rich govern the poor. An oligarchy of learning, where the educated govern the ignorant, or even an oligarchy of race, where the Saxon rules the African, might be endured; but this oligarchy of sex, which makes father, brothers, husband, sons, the oligarchs over the mother and sisters, the wife and daughters, of every household—which ordains all men sovereigns, all women subjects, carries dissension, discord, and rebellion into every home of the nation.

Webster, Worcester, and Bouvier all define a citizen to be a person in the United States, entitled to vote and hold office. The only question left to be settled now is: Are women persons? And I hardly believe any of our opponents will have the hardihood to say they are not. Being persons, then, women are citizens; and no state has a right to make any law, or to enforce any old law, that shall abridge their privileges or immunities. Hence, every discrimination against women in the constitutions and laws of the several states is today null and void, precisely as is every one against Negroes."

**Passage 2**

To the Congress of the United States, protesting against an Extension of Suffrage to Women:

We, the undersigned, do hereby appeal to your honorable body, and desire respectfully to enter our protest against an extension of Suffrage to Women; and in the firm belief that our petition represents the sober convictions of the majority of the women of the country.

Although we shrink from the notoriety of the public eye, yet we are too deeply and painfully impressed by the grave perils which threaten our peace and happiness in these proposed changes in our civil and political rights, longer to remain silent.

Because Holy Scripture inculcates a different, and for us, higher sphere, apart from public life.

Because as women we find a full measure of duties, cares and responsibilities developing upon us, and we are therefore unwilling to bear other and heavier burdens, and those unsuited to our physical organization.

Because we hold that an extension of suffrage would be averse to the interest of the working women of the country, with whom we heartily sympathize.

Because these changes must introduce a fruitful element of discord in the existing marriage relation, which would tend to the infinite detriment of children, and increase the already alarming prevalence of divorce throughout the land.

Because no general law, affecting the condition of all women, should be framed to meet exceptional discontent.

For these, and many more reasons, do we beg of your wisdom that no law extending suffrage to women may be passed, as the passage of such a law would be fraught with danger so grave to the general order of the country.

## Building History Questions

Again, follow the three-step process for question writing:

1. What's the core question (**restate**)? Adapt this into an SAT prompt.

2. What the simple answer (**recall**)? Turn this into an SAT answer.

3. What are your incorrect answers (**resolve**)? Use the incorrect answer types to give your choices more realism.

Let's get to the questions on the question of suffrage. Good luck!

### 1

Recognize: Argument

Restate:

Prompt:

Recall:

Answer Ⓐ
Answer Ⓑ
Answer Ⓒ
Answer Ⓓ

### 2

Recognize: Tone

Restate:

Prompt:

Recall:

Answer Ⓐ
Answer Ⓑ
Answer Ⓒ
Answer Ⓓ

Lesson 10: Understanding the Test-Makers

## 3

Recognize: Inference

Restate:

Prompt:

Recall:

Answer Ⓐ
Answer Ⓑ
Answer Ⓒ
Answer Ⓓ

## 4

Recognize: Evidence for #3

Restate:

Prompt:

Recall:

Answer Ⓐ
Answer Ⓑ
Answer Ⓒ
Answer Ⓓ

## 5

Recognize: Detail

Restate:

Prompt:

Recall:

Answer Ⓐ
Answer Ⓑ
Answer Ⓒ
Answer Ⓓ

**6**

Recognize   Evidence for #5          Answer Ⓐ

Restate
                                     Answer Ⓑ

Prompt
                                     Answer Ⓒ

Recall
                                     Answer Ⓓ


**7**

Recognize   Vocab                    Answer Ⓐ

Restate
                                     Answer Ⓑ

Prompt
                                     Answer Ⓒ

Recall
                                     Answer Ⓓ


**8**

Recognize   Paired (Inference)       Answer Ⓐ

Restate
                                     Answer Ⓑ

Prompt
                                     Answer Ⓒ

Recall
                                     Answer Ⓓ

Lesson 10: Understanding the Test-Makers

## 9

**Recognize** Paired (Synthesis)

**Restate**

**Prompt**

**Recall**

Answer Ⓐ

Answer Ⓑ

Answer Ⓒ

Answer Ⓓ

## 10

**Recognize** Paired (Synthesis)

**Restate**

**Prompt**

**Recall**

Answer Ⓐ

Answer Ⓑ

Answer Ⓒ

Answer Ⓓ

| Questions | General | Specific | Synthesis | Answers | Reason |
|---|---|---|---|---|---|
| Main Purpose | Purpose | Function | | Wrong | Somewhat right, but too broad |
| Main Idea | Thesis | Topic | | Wrong | Somewhat right, but too narrow |
| Tone | Tone | Attitude | | Wrong | Somewhat right, but too extreme |
| Rhetoric | Structure | Argument | | Wrong | Tempting words, but wrong part |
| Vocabulary | | Vocabulary | | Wrong | Tempting words, but not true |
| Evidence | | Evidence | | Wrong | Tempting words, but irrelevant |
| Detail | | Detail | | Wrong | Flatly false |
| Inference | | Inference | | Right (general) | Give identify evidence |
| Data | | Data Specific | Data Synthesis | Right (specific) | Give line or annotation evidence |
| Paired | | Paired Specific | Paired Synthesis | Right (synthesis) | Give identify evidence |

## Reviewing Your Creation

Now, consider the process of writing questions and how that has improved your ability to answer the **history, paired passage,** and **antiquated English** questions that you'll see on test day.

1. For which question type was it hardest to write the prompt? Did you go back to lesson 3 to look at some example prompts?

2. Which wrong answer type (e.g., somewhat right but too narrow, tempting words, but irrelevant) was hardest to write? Why?

3. Which wrong answer type (e.g., somewhat right but too narrow, tempting words, but irrelevant) was easiest to write? Why?

4. How can you prepare yourself for questions as you read the passage?

5. How can you prepare yourself for the answers as you read the passage?

6. How does writing history questions change the way you read history passages?

7. How does writing paired questions change the way you read paired passages?

8. How does writing antiquated English questions change the way you read paired passages?

Lesson 10: Understanding the Test-Makers

## BUILDING PASSAGES AND INCREASING YOU READING SKILLS

Writing SAT questions is more art than science, but familiarity with how the test makers create their questions will help you analyze what they are asking you. You can even practice rewriting questions for the official practice tests, creating a new set of 10 problems to challenge yourself.

To have a true mastery of the test, make sure you know how the test-*makers* think.

# LESSON 11: MASTERING THE TEST

If you want to master the test, you have to **review your old tests**. Back in Lesson 5, we talked about how looking over your mistakes is a necessary step in improving your test-taking skills. I can certainly understand the desire to put a test away and never think about it again, especially if that test didn't quite go according to plan. On the other hand, if you've spent the hour plus taking the test, you owe it to yourself to maximize its utility.

Deciding to review your old tests can sometimes feel tedious. Students have told me that they'd rather just take more tests and practice than look back at what they did wrong. This is a human impulse. But if you aren't fixing the mistakes you made on test 6, you will make similar mistakes on test 7; if you make those mistakes on the practice tests, you will make similar mistakes on the real test. Nobody likes tedious tasks. But reviewing practices before test day can prevent you from needing to take the test all over again in a few months. A few hours now can save you weeks later.

This isn't limited to standardized tests, of course. All sorts of situations, from the trivial to the life-and-death, merit review. Here's how LeBron James talked about looking over game tape after the Cavaliers won game one of a seven-game playoff series.

> We executed our defensive plan and made some big shots. Offensively, we got a little stagnant and started playing isolation, which we were very good at, but no matter what happened, we came out with the win. In a series, I think you get better with time. You see what teams are capable of, what they want to do, what we want to do, how we can be successful at both ends, and so I'm looking forward to actually watching the film tomorrow to see how we can be better going into game two. (April 15, 2017)

Dan Keenan, a project manager who ran NASA's "Human Error–Based Process Failure Modes and Effects Analysis" team described reviewing NASA's mistakes:

> Anyone who has ever had the courage to go out into the world and do something knows there are only two kinds of mistakes: ones we *can* recover from and ones we *cannot* recover from. Mistakes are where many of our new journeys begin, and what we learn can help us return safely. (Dan Keenan, "Where Journeys Begin")

Taking the SAT isn't sending a human into space and hoping they return alive, and your performance on a random Saturday morning doesn't have the hopes and dreams of the city of Cleveland riding on it. But doing your best can help you achieve *your* hopes and dreams.

# HOW TO REVIEW

## Self-Evaluation, Passage Review, and Question Review

We start with our old friend, the self-evaluation. You may have been filling these out as you go, but they're duplicated here just in case.

### SELF-EVALUATION TEST 1

| | | | | | | |
|---|---|---|---|---|---|---|
| **Passage 1** | I felt confident during the first passage. | Strongly Agree | Somewhat Agree | No Opinion | Somewhat Disagree | Strongly Disagree |
| | Describe in two to three sentences how you felt on the first passage | | | | | |
| **Passage 2** | I felt confident during the second passage. | Strongly Agree | Somewhat Agree | No Opinion | Somewhat Disagree | Strongly Disagree |
| | Describe in two to three sentences how you felt on the second passage | | | | | |
| **Passage 3** | I felt confident during the third passage. | Strongly Agree | Somewhat Agree | No Opinion | Somewhat Disagree | Strongly Disagree |
| | Describe in two to three sentences how you felt on the third passage | | | | | |
| **Passage 4** | I felt confident during the fourth passage. | Strongly Agree | Somewhat Agree | No Opinion | Somewhat Disagree | Strongly Disagree |
| | Describe in two to three sentences how you felt on the fourth passage | | | | | |
| **Passage 5** | I felt confident during the fifth passage. | Strongly Agree | Somewhat Agree | No Opinion | Somewhat Disagree | Strongly Disagree |
| | Describe in two to three sentences how you felt on the fifth passage | | | | | |
| **Overall** | I felt confident during the reading section. | Strongly Agree | Somewhat Agree | No Opinion | Somewhat Disagree | Strongly Disagree |
| | I had enough time for the reading section. | Strongly Agree | Somewhat Agree | No Opinion | Somewhat Disagree | Strongly Disagree |
| | I cared about the passages I read. | Strongly Agree | Somewhat Agree | No Opinion | Somewhat Disagree | Strongly Disagree |
| | In three to four sentences, describe how you feel about the reading section | | | | | |

After reviewing the test in general, turn to reviewing the passages and questions specifically.

## Passage Review

Start by skimming the passage. You don't necessarily need to reread it for all of its nitty-gritty details, but you should have a sense for what the passage is about. As you go, ask yourself the following questions related to **Underline**, **Annotate**, and **Identify**:

- What type of passage is it (literature, sciences, history, or social studies)?
- What is the purpose of the passage?
- What is its thesis or main idea?
- What was the author's tone?
- If it's a **paired passage**, where do the authors agree and disagree?
- If it's a **data passage**, what information does the chart provide?

On the following pages, you'll find my annotations and identification for each of the passages on all ten practice tests. While I don't print out the passages and my underlining, you will find my answers to each of the questions above plus a running account of my annotations. These are, of course, my answers and annotations. If you have a different response, that doesn't mean that your wrong. If, however, I say the passage is about ethics and economics, but you say it's about the economics of fair trade coffee, you may want to double check your reading to see if you're too broad, too narrow, or too extreme.

## Question Review

After you have reviewed the passage, you can start looking over the questions. While you can certainly review all of the questions, it is typically best to focused on the questions that you answered incorrectly and the questions where confidence was less than 4 out of 5. For each of these questions, ask yourself the following:

- What type of question is it? What are they asking you?
- Why is my answer wrong?
    - If you answered correctly but weren't confident, why is your second choice wrong?
- Why is their answer right? What evidence supports this answer?

In effect, this is a quick check of your **Restate**, **Recall**, and **Resolve** skills.

The amount of time you spend on each passage will vary, but something like ten to fifteen minutes is fairly typical. If you are done after two minutes, you are going to want to spend more time reviewing the passage before moving on to the questions. If it takes you more than twenty minutes, you're probably worrying about too many details.

On the pages that follow, I give my **recognition** of each question type for every question in the test.

### Online Bonus Content

If you're looking for a deep dive into a passage, you can use adapted worksheets from Lesson 9 (Mastering Khan Academy) to breakdown the passage (**Underline**, **Annotate**, and **Identify**) and the questions (**Recognize**, **Restate**, **Recall**, and **Resolve**). When you are done with the passage, answer the review questions at the end.

A book of these worksheets would be 250 pages long (!), so I've posted them in the bonus content at www.professorscompanion.com/reading.

# OFFICIAL TEST REVIEW: TESTS 1-10

## Test 1 Review

### SELF-EVALUATION TEST 1

| | | | | | | |
|---|---|---|---|---|---|---|
| **Passage 1** | I felt confident during the first passage. | Strongly Agree | Somewhat Agree | No Opinion | Somewhat Disagree | Strongly Disagree |
| | Describe in two to three sentences how you felt on the first passage | | | | | |
| **Passage 2** | I felt confident during the second passage. | Strongly Agree | Somewhat Agree | No Opinion | Somewhat Disagree | Strongly Disagree |
| | Describe in two to three sentences how you felt on the second passage | | | | | |
| **Passage 3** | I felt confident during the third passage. | Strongly Agree | Somewhat Agree | No Opinion | Somewhat Disagree | Strongly Disagree |
| | Describe in two to three sentences how you felt on the third passage | | | | | |
| **Passage 4** | I felt confident during the fourth passage. | Strongly Agree | Somewhat Agree | No Opinion | Somewhat Disagree | Strongly Disagree |
| | Describe in two to three sentences how you felt on the fourth passage | | | | | |
| **Passage 5** | I felt confident during the fifth passage. | Strongly Agree | Somewhat Agree | No Opinion | Somewhat Disagree | Strongly Disagree |
| | Describe in two to three sentences how you felt on the fifth passage | | | | | |
| **Overall** | I felt confident during the reading section. | Strongly Agree | Somewhat Agree | No Opinion | Somewhat Disagree | Strongly Disagree |
| | I had enough time for the reading section. | Strongly Agree | Somewhat Agree | No Opinion | Somewhat Disagree | Strongly Disagree |
| | I cared about the passages I read. | Strongly Agree | Somewhat Agree | No Opinion | Somewhat Disagree | Strongly Disagree |
| | In three to four sentences, describe how you feel about the reading section | | | | | |

Lesson 11: Mastering Your Review

## Passage Review (Annotations and Identification)

| Questions 1-10 | The Strangeness of Beauty |
|---|---|
| Type | Literature |
| Purpose | To describe a man asking a woman for her daughter's hand in marriage |
| Thesis/Topic | Akira asks Chie for Naomi's hand in marriage, which she rejects. Naomi spurns her mother. |
| Tone/Attitude | Chilly relationship between Akira and Chie, Naomi is defiant |
| Annotations | Entrance formal - frosty - description - urgent? - child - marriage - disapproval - it's going to happen |

| Questions 11-21 | Gift Giving |
|---|---|
| Type | Social Studies (with Data) |
| Purpose | To explain how gift givers and gift recipients value gifts |
| Thesis/Topic | Gift givers think gift recipients like valuable gifts, but they overstate this |
| Tone/Attitude | Conversational, asks questions |
| Annotations | $ - gift buying, bonds and fears - deadweight - why? - overspend - appreciate gifts - ritual - $$ = signal? - perspective |
| Data | Givers appreciate more expensive gift, recipients slightly opposite |

| Questions 22-31 | DNA |
|---|---|
| Type | Science (with Data) |
| Purpose | To explain the biological properties of DNA |
| Thesis/Topic | DNA is formed by chemical chains of paired bases in an irregular sequence |
| Tone/Attitude | Scientific, confident |
| Annotations | DNA Base - sequences - 2 chains - structure - pairs - sequences |
| Data | Different species have different % of bases; pairs add to 50% |

| Questions 32-41 | Three Guineas |
|---|---|
| Type | History |
| Purpose | To argue that women should have a greater role in society |
| Thesis/Topic | Men have been in control, but women are becoming more important to public life |
| Tone/Attitude | Discontented, questioning |
| Annotations | Women & society - industry - men - 20 yrs - women can do this too - ?'s - procession of men - women have thought - expansion of thinking |

| Questions 42-52 | Space Mining |
|---|---|
| Type | Science (Paired, without Data) |
| Purpose | To explain the economic realities and implication of space mining |
| Thesis/Topic | Slezak: Space mining will provide new economic opportunities for business <br> Editors: Space mining brings new ethical questions about wealth, stewardship, and exploitation |
| Tone/Attitude | Slezak: optimistic, opportunistic <br> Editors: cautiously optimistic, measured |
| Annotations | Slezak: space mining - forum - non-Earth economy - water? - what people want <br> Editors: we could all be enriched - consequences - environment - hard to get - consensus |
| Agree/Disagree | Agree: Space mining has the opportunity to create a new economy <br> Disagree: Slezak is much more optimistic, editors are much more cautious about if this is good |

Lesson 11: Mastering Your Review

## Question Review (Question and Answer Types)

| Questions | General | Specific | Synthesis | Answers | Reason |
|---|---|---|---|---|---|
| Main Purpose | Purpose | Function | | Wrong | Somewhat right, but too broad |
| Main Idea | Thesis | Topic | | Wrong | Somewhat right, but too narrow |
| Tone | Tone | Attitude | | Wrong | Somewhat right, but too extreme |
| Rhetoric | Structure | Argument | | Wrong | Tempting words, but wrong part |
| Vocabulary | | Vocabulary | | Wrong | Tempting words, but not true |
| Evidence | | Evidence | | Wrong | Tempting words, but irrelevant |
| Detail | | Detail | | Wrong | Flatly false |
| Inference | | Inference | | Right (general) | Give identify evidence |
| Data | | Data Specific | Data Synthesis | Right (specific) | Give line or annotation evidence |
| Paired | | Paired Specific | Paired Synthesis | Right (synthesis) | Give identify evidence |

| | Recognize | Why My Answer Is Wrong | Why the Correct Answer Is Right |
|---|---|---|---|
| 1 | | | |
| 2 | | | |
| 4 | | | |
| 5 | | | |
| 6 | | | |
| 7 | | | |
| 8 | | | |
| 9 | | | |
| 10 | | | |
| 11 | | | |
| 12 | | | |
| 13 | | | |
| 14 | | | |
| 15 | | | |
| 16 | | | |
| 17 | | | |
| 18 | | | |
| 19 | | | |
| 20 | | | |
| 21 | | | |

| Recognize | Why My Answer Is Wrong | Why the Correct Answer Is Right |
|---|---|---|
| 22 | | |
| 23 | | |
| 24 | | |
| 25 | | |
| 26 | | |
| 27 | | |
| 28 | | |
| 29 | | |
| 30 | | |
| 31 | | |
| 32 | | |
| 33 | | |
| 34 | | |
| 35 | | |
| 36 | | |
| 37 | | |
| 38 | | |
| 39 | | |
| 40 | | |
| 41 | | |
| 42 | | |
| 43 | | |
| 44 | | |
| 45 | | |
| 46 | | |
| 47 | | |
| 48 | | |
| 49 | | |
| 50 | | |
| 51 | | |
| 52 | | |

|  | The Strangeness of Beauty | Gift Giving | DNA | Three Guineas | Space Mining |
|---|---|---|---|---|---|
| Purpose |  |  |  | 1.1.32 |  |
| Function | 1.1.7 | 1.1.11<br>1.1.19 | 1.1.22<br>1.1.25<br>1.1.27 | 1.1.34<br>1.1.41 | 1.1.46 |
| Thesis |  |  |  | 1.1.33 | 1.1.47 |
| Topic |  |  |  |  | 1.1.42 |
| Tone |  |  |  | 1.1.38 |  |
| Attitude | 1.1.6 |  |  |  |  |
| Structure | 1.1.1<br>1.1.2 |  |  |  |  |
| Argument |  |  | 1.1.23 |  |  |
| Vocab | 1.1.3<br>1.1.8 | 1.1.12<br>1.1.18 |  | 1.1.40 | 1.1.45<br>1.1.48 |
| Evidence | 1.1.5<br>1.1.10 | 1.1.14<br>1.1.17 | 1.1.24 | 1.1.37<br>1.1.39 | 1.1.44<br>1.1.51 |
| Detail | 1.1.4<br>1.1.9 | 1.1.13<br>1.1.16 |  | 1.1.35<br>1.1.36 | 1.1.43 |
| Inference |  | 1.1.15 | 1.1.26 |  |  |
| Data (Detail) |  | 1.1.20 | 1.1.28<br>1.1.30 |  |  |
| Data (Synthesis) |  | 1.1.21 | 1.1.29<br>1.1.31 |  |  |
| Paired (Inference) |  |  |  |  | 1.1.50 |
| Paired (Synthesis) |  |  |  |  | 1.1.49<br>1.1.52 |

## Test 2 Review

## SELF-EVALUATION TEST 2

| | | | | | | |
|---|---|---|---|---|---|---|
| **Passage 1** | I felt confident during the first passage. | Strongly Agree | Somewhat Agree | No Opinion | Somewhat Disagree | Strongly Disagree |
| | Describe in two to three sentences how you felt on the first passage | | | | | |
| **Passage 2** | I felt confident during the second passage. | Strongly Agree | Somewhat Agree | No Opinion | Somewhat Disagree | Strongly Disagree |
| | Describe in two to three sentences how you felt on the second passage | | | | | |
| **Passage 3** | I felt confident during the third passage. | Strongly Agree | Somewhat Agree | No Opinion | Somewhat Disagree | Strongly Disagree |
| | Describe in two to three sentences how you felt on the third passage | | | | | |
| **Passage 4** | I felt confident during the fourth passage. | Strongly Agree | Somewhat Agree | No Opinion | Somewhat Disagree | Strongly Disagree |
| | Describe in two to three sentences how you felt on the fourth passage | | | | | |
| **Passage 5** | I felt confident during the fifth passage. | Strongly Agree | Somewhat Agree | No Opinion | Somewhat Disagree | Strongly Disagree |
| | Describe in two to three sentences how you felt on the fifth passage | | | | | |
| **Overall** | I felt confident during the reading section. | Strongly Agree | Somewhat Agree | No Opinion | Somewhat Disagree | Strongly Disagree |
| | I had enough time for the reading section. | Strongly Agree | Somewhat Agree | No Opinion | Somewhat Disagree | Strongly Disagree |
| | I cared about the passages I read. | Strongly Agree | Somewhat Agree | No Opinion | Somewhat Disagree | Strongly Disagree |
| | In three to four sentences, describe how you feel about the reading section | | | | | |

Lesson 11: Mastering Your Review

## Passage Review (Annotations and Identification)

| Questions 1-10 | The Professor |
|---|---|
| Type | Literature |
| Purpose | To describe a man and his hatred of his job and his co-worker |
| Thesis/Topic | A man has made a mistake with his job, which requires him to work with a man he once admired but not loathes. |
| Tone/Attitude | Superiority; thinks he's better than other people |
| Annotations | Mistake - I should be better - antipathy - EC doesn't like me - William - how to change |

| Questions 11-21 | Ethics in Business |
|---|---|
| Type | Social Studies (with Data) |
| Purpose | To explain different ethical approaches to business |
| Thesis/Topic | Moral dilemmas arise when figuring out how to behave both ethically an economically |
| Tone/Attitude | Inquisitive, probing |
| Annotations | Ethics in business - empathy - empathy in business - virtues - judgment - actions - dilemmas not inevitable - herd mentality - psychology |
| Data | Fair trade prices consistent, always higher than regular coffee; regular coffee dipped in mid-2000s |

| Questions 22-31 | Rewired Brains |
|---|---|
| Type | Science (Paired, without Data)) |
| Purpose | To explain how the web can/can't rewire our brains |
| Thesis/Topic | Carr: Using the web trains our brains to be faster but also less patient <br> Pinker: The effects of web and new media use are greatly exaggerated |
| Tone/Attitude | Carr: informative, surprised by findings? <br> Pinker: skeptical, responding |
| Annotations | Carr: Good things with internet - brain training - trade off - adaptive brains <br> Pinker: brain less plastic - brain training doesn't work - immersion |
| Agree/Disagree | Agree: The brain can adapt <br> Disagree: Pinker disagrees with the Carr's conclusions on the extent to which the brain adapts |

| Questions 32-41 | Women's Suffrage |
|---|---|
| Type | History (Antiquated English) |
| Purpose | To argue that women's suffrage is a good thing |
| Thesis/Topic | Women's suffrage |
| Tone/Attitude | Strong, impassioned |
| Annotations | Problem with men - women's power - negative manhood - too many masculine women - women forced to be like men - suffrage and peace - not all men |

| Questions 42-52 | Undersea Waves |
|---|---|
| Type | Science (with Data) |
| Purpose | To explain how undersea waves form |
| Thesis/Topic | Undersea waves and their formation at Luzon Strait |
| Tone/Attitude | Appreciation |
| Annotations | Underwater waves - huge - models - study - giant facility - model cause - expansion |
| Data | Bands of temperature, drops at 13, little 9 degree |

## Question Review (Question and Answer Types)

| Questions | General | Specific | Synthesis | Answers | Reason |
|---|---|---|---|---|---|
| Main Purpose | Purpose | Function | | Wrong | Somewhat right, but too broad |
| Main Idea | Thesis | Topic | | Wrong | Somewhat right, but too narrow |
| Tone | Tone | Attitude | | Wrong | Somewhat right, but too extreme |
| Rhetoric | Structure | Argument | | Wrong | Tempting words, but wrong part |
| Vocabulary | | Vocabulary | | Wrong | Tempting words, but not true |
| Evidence | | Evidence | | Wrong | Tempting words, but irrelevant |
| Detail | | Detail | | Wrong | Flatly false |
| Inference | | Inference | | Right (general) | Give identify evidence |
| Data | | Data Specific | Data Synthesis | Right (specific) | Give line or annotation evidence |
| Paired | | Paired Specific | Paired Synthesis | Right (synthesis) | Give identify evidence |

| | Recognize | Why My Answer Is Wrong | Why the Correct Answer Is Right |
|---|---|---|---|
| 1 | | | |
| 2 | | | |
| 4 | | | |
| 5 | | | |
| 6 | | | |
| 7 | | | |
| 8 | | | |
| 9 | | | |
| 10 | | | |
| 11 | | | |
| 12 | | | |
| 13 | | | |
| 14 | | | |
| 15 | | | |
| 16 | | | |
| 17 | | | |
| 18 | | | |
| 19 | | | |
| 20 | | | |
| 21 | | | |

| Recognize | Why My Answer Is Wrong | Why the Correct Answer Is Right |
|---|---|---|
| 22 | | |
| 23 | | |
| 24 | | |
| 25 | | |
| 26 | | |
| 27 | | |
| 28 | | |
| 29 | | |
| 30 | | |
| 31 | | |
| 32 | | |
| 33 | | |
| 34 | | |
| 35 | | |
| 36 | | |
| 37 | | |
| 38 | | |
| 39 | | |
| 40 | | |
| 41 | | |
| 42 | | |
| 43 | | |
| 44 | | |
| 45 | | |
| 46 | | |
| 47 | | |
| 48 | | |
| 49 | | |
| 50 | | |
| 51 | | |
| 52 | | |

|  | The Professor | Ethics in Business | Rewired Brains | Women's Suffrage | Undersea Waves |
|---|---|---|---|---|---|
| Purpose |  | 2.1.11 |  |  |  |
| Function | 2.1.2<br>2.1.4<br>2.1.8 | 2.1.15 | 2.1.26 | 2.1.34 | 2.1.43 |
| Thesis |  |  |  | 2.1.33 |  |
| Topic |  | 2.1.18 |  | 2.1.42 |  |
| Tone |  |  |  |  |  |
| Attitude |  |  |  |  |  |
| Structure | 2.1.1<br>2.1.3 |  |  |  |  |
| Argument |  | 2.1.12<br>2.1.17 | 2.1.28 |  |  |
| Vocab |  | 2.1.14<br>2.1.16 | 2.1.25 | 2.1.37<br>2.1.39 | 2.1.44<br>2.1.47 |
| Evidence | 2.1.7<br>2.1.10 | 2.1.13 | 2.1.23 | 2.1.36<br>2.1.41 | 2.1.46<br>2.1.49 |
| Detail | 2.1.5<br>2.1.6<br>2.1.9 |  | 2.1.22<br>2.1.24<br>2.1.27 | 2.1.35<br>2.1.40 | 2.1.45 |
| Inference |  |  |  | 2.1.38 | 2.1.48 |
| Data (Detail) |  | 2.1.19<br>2.1.20 |  |  | 2.1.50 |
| Data (Synthesis) |  | 2.1.21 |  |  | 2.1.51<br>2.1.52 |
| Paired (Inference) |  |  | 2.1.31<br>2.1.32 |  |  |
| Paired (Synthesis) |  |  | 2.1.29<br>2.1.30 |  |  |

## Test 3 Review

## SELF-EVALUATION TEST 3

| | | | | | | |
|---|---|---|---|---|---|---|
| **Passage 1** | I felt confident during the first passage. | Strongly Agree | Somewhat Agree | No Opinion | Somewhat Disagree | Strongly Disagree |
| | Describe in two to three sentences how you felt on the first passage | | | | | |
| **Passage 2** | I felt confident during the second passage. | Strongly Agree | Somewhat Agree | No Opinion | Somewhat Disagree | Strongly Disagree |
| | Describe in two to three sentences how you felt on the second passage | | | | | |
| **Passage 3** | I felt confident during the third passage. | Strongly Agree | Somewhat Agree | No Opinion | Somewhat Disagree | Strongly Disagree |
| | Describe in two to three sentences how you felt on the third passage | | | | | |
| **Passage 4** | I felt confident during the fourth passage. | Strongly Agree | Somewhat Agree | No Opinion | Somewhat Disagree | Strongly Disagree |
| | Describe in two to three sentences how you felt on the fourth passage | | | | | |
| **Passage 5** | I felt confident during the fifth passage. | Strongly Agree | Somewhat Agree | No Opinion | Somewhat Disagree | Strongly Disagree |
| | Describe in two to three sentences how you felt on the fifth passage | | | | | |
| **Overall** | I felt confident during the reading section. | Strongly Agree | Somewhat Agree | No Opinion | Somewhat Disagree | Strongly Disagree |
| | I had enough time for the reading section. | Strongly Agree | Somewhat Agree | No Opinion | Somewhat Disagree | Strongly Disagree |
| | I cared about the passages I read. | Strongly Agree | Somewhat Agree | No Opinion | Somewhat Disagree | Strongly Disagree |
| | In three to four sentences, describe how you feel about the reading section | | | | | |

## Passage Review (Annotations and Identification)

| Questions 1-10 | Lady Carlotta and Mrs. Quabarl |
|---|---|
| Type | Literature (Antiquated English) |
| Purpose | To describe Lady Carlotta and her stolen job of governess |
| Thesis/Topic | Lady Carlotta abandons her train to go off with Mrs. Quabarl pretending to be the nanny |
| Tone/Attitude | Sardonic; Lady Carlotta is perfectly willing to mislead people |
| Annotations | Passing time - meddlesome - doesn't help - train leaves - Miss Hope? - governess? - the children - not that interesting - French - Russian - Mrs. Quabarl cut down |

| Questions 11-21 | Public Transportation |
|---|---|
| Type | Social Studies (with Data) |
| Purpose | To explain and evaluate global trends in public transportation |
| Thesis/Topic | Public transportation is more effective and efficient than private transportation outside the US |
| Tone/Attitude | Colloquial, conversational, optimistic |
| Annotations | Public transport - $430B/yr. - problems with PT - benefits - bicycles - millennials - seniors |
| Data | Figure 1: the primary occupation of public transportation passengers in the US is outside the home; Figure 2: most people taking public transportation in the US do so for work |

| Questions 22-31 | Bird Man |
|---|---|
| Type | Science (without Data) |
| Purpose | To explain a scientific breakthrough on bird flight |
| Thesis/Topic | How one scientist (and his son) made a breakthrough on the evolution of bird flight |
| Tone/Attitude | Narrative, uses colorful asides |
| Annotations | Field sites - ground-up and tree-down - cowboy - ground? perches! - observations - data - ramps and fins - WAIR - tree-down and ground-up |

| Questions 32-41 | Women's Education |
| --- | --- |
| Type | History (Paired, antiquated English) |
| Purpose | To argue over the rights of women to receive an equal education |
| Thesis/Topic | Tallyrand: society is best served by maintaining the status quo, not pitting men against women<br>Wollstonecraft: women, and society, are best served by giving women equal education rights |
| Tone/Attitude | Tallyrand: informative, surprised by findings?<br>Wollstonecraft: skeptical, responding |
| Annotations | Tallyrand: Half the population - why? - greater good - best for women - good of the all<br>Wollstonecraft: women must be virtuous - why not? - women's autonomy - tyrants |
| Agree/Disagree | Agree: the greater good is important<br>Disagree: Tallyrand thinks the greater good is served by excluding women from public service (and thus education). Wollstonecraft believes women are entitled to the same rights. |

| Questions 42-52 | Honey Bees |
| --- | --- |
| Type | Science (with Data) |
| Purpose | To explain how bad bee nutrition results in infestations of mites and harms bee colony health |
| Thesis/Topic | Bees with poor diets and commercial insecticides are more likely to be infested and have lower overall health |
| Tone/Attitude | Scientific, speculative |
| Annotations | Bees - mite infestations - plants - creams - diet - secondary infections - bee controls - trial w/ and w/o P - wild honey |
| Data | Colonies with collapse more susceptible; colonies without collapse are safer |

## Question Review (Question and Answer Types)

| Questions | General | Specific | Synthesis | Answers | Reason |
|---|---|---|---|---|---|
| Main Purpose | Purpose | Function | | Wrong | Somewhat right, but too broad |
| Main Idea | Thesis | Topic | | Wrong | Somewhat right, but too narrow |
| Tone | Tone | Attitude | | Wrong | Somewhat right, but too extreme |
| Rhetoric | Structure | Argument | | Wrong | Tempting words, but wrong part |
| Vocabulary | | Vocabulary | | Wrong | Tempting words, but not true |
| Evidence | | Evidence | | Wrong | Tempting words, but irrelevant |
| Detail | | Detail | | Wrong | Flatly false |
| Inference | | Inference | | Right (general) | Give identify evidence |
| Data | | Data Specific | Data Synthesis | Right (specific) | Give line or annotation evidence |
| Paired | | Paired Specific | Paired Synthesis | Right (synthesis) | Give identify evidence |

| | Recognize | Why My Answer Is Wrong | Why the Correct Answer Is Right |
|---|---|---|---|
| 1 | | | |
| 2 | | | |
| 4 | | | |
| 5 | | | |
| 6 | | | |
| 7 | | | |
| 8 | | | |
| 9 | | | |
| 10 | | | |
| 11 | | | |
| 12 | | | |
| 13 | | | |
| 14 | | | |
| 15 | | | |
| 16 | | | |
| 17 | | | |
| 18 | | | |
| 19 | | | |
| 20 | | | |
| 21 | | | |

| Recognize | Why My Answer Is Wrong | Why the Correct Answer Is Right |
|---|---|---|
| 22 | | |
| 23 | | |
| 24 | | |
| 25 | | |
| 26 | | |
| 27 | | |
| 28 | | |
| 29 | | |
| 30 | | |
| 31 | | |
| 32 | | |
| 33 | | |
| 34 | | |
| 35 | | |
| 36 | | |
| 37 | | |
| 38 | | |
| 39 | | |
| 40 | | |
| 41 | | |
| 42 | | |
| 43 | | |
| 44 | | |
| 45 | | |
| 46 | | |
| 47 | | |
| 48 | | |
| 49 | | |
| 50 | | |
| 51 | | |
| 52 | | |

Lesson 11: Mastering Your Review

|  | Lady Carlotta & Mrs. Quabarl | Public Transportation | Bird Man | Women's Education | Honey Bees |
|---|---|---|---|---|---|
| Purpose | | | | | |
| Function | 3.1.5 | 3.1.11 | 3.1.25 | | 3.1.48 |
| Thesis | | | | | |
| Topic | | 3.1.14 | | | |
| Tone | | | | | 3.1.42 |
| Attitude | | | | | |
| Structure | 3.1.1 | | 3.1.21 | | |
| Argument | | 3.1.18 | | | 3.1.49 |
| Vocab | 3.1.2 | 3.1.16 | 3.1.22 | 3.1.31 | 3.1.47 |
|  | 3.1.6 | 3.1.17 | 3.1.28 | 3.1.35 | |
| Evidence | 3.1.4 | 3.1.13 | 3.1.24 | 3.1.33 | 3.4.44 |
|  | 3.1.10 | | 3.1.30 | 3.1.37 | 3.1.46 |
| Detail | 3.1.7 | 3.1.12 | 3.1.26 | 3.1.34 | |
|  | 3.1.9 | 3.1.15 | 3.1.27 | 3.1.36 | |
| Inference | 3.1.3 | | 3.1.23 | 3.1.32 | 3.1.43 |
|  | 3.1.8 | | 3.1.29 | | 3.1.45 |
| Data (Detail) | | 3.1.19 | | | 3.1.50 |
|  | | | | | 3.1.51 |
| Data (Synthesis) | | 3.1.29 | | | 3.1.52 |
| Paired (Inference) | | | | 3.1.38 | |
|  | | | | 3.1.40 | |
| Paired (Synthesis) | | | | 3.1.39 | |

## Test 4 Review

## SELF-EVALUATION TEST 4

| | | | | | | |
|---|---|---|---|---|---|---|
| **Passage 1** | I felt confident during the first passage. | Strongly Agree | Somewhat Agree | No Opinion | Somewhat Disagree | Strongly Disagree |
| | Describe in two to three sentences how you felt on the first passage | | | | | |
| **Passage 2** | I felt confident during the second passage. | Strongly Agree | Somewhat Agree | No Opinion | Somewhat Disagree | Strongly Disagree |
| | Describe in two to three sentences how you felt on the second passage | | | | | |
| **Passage 3** | I felt confident during the third passage. | Strongly Agree | Somewhat Agree | No Opinion | Somewhat Disagree | Strongly Disagree |
| | Describe in two to three sentences how you felt on the third passage | | | | | |
| **Passage 4** | I felt confident during the fourth passage. | Strongly Agree | Somewhat Agree | No Opinion | Somewhat Disagree | Strongly Disagree |
| | Describe in two to three sentences how you felt on the fourth passage | | | | | |
| **Passage 5** | I felt confident during the fifth passage. | Strongly Agree | Somewhat Agree | No Opinion | Somewhat Disagree | Strongly Disagree |
| | Describe in two to three sentences how you felt on the fifth passage | | | | | |
| **Overall** | I felt confident during the reading section. | Strongly Agree | Somewhat Agree | No Opinion | Somewhat Disagree | Strongly Disagree |
| | I had enough time for the reading section. | Strongly Agree | Somewhat Agree | No Opinion | Somewhat Disagree | Strongly Disagree |
| | I cared about the passages I read. | Strongly Agree | Somewhat Agree | No Opinion | Somewhat Disagree | Strongly Disagree |
| | In three to four sentences, describe how you feel about the reading section | | | | | |

Lesson 11: Mastering Your Review

## Passage Review (Annotations and Identification)

| Questions 1-10 | The Mad Balloonist |
|---|---|
| Type | Literature |
| Purpose | To describe an explorer and his mad quest for the North Pole |
| Thesis/Topic | Destiny has brought the scientist to seek the North Pole despite its dangers. |
| Tone/Attitude | Shifts from confusion to certainty |
| Annotations | Not clear - fate - why go - what's there? - others who have gone before |

| Questions 11-21 | The Great Inversion |
|---|---|
| Type | Social Studies (with Data) |
| Purpose | To explain the shifts in metropolitan demographics |
| Thesis/Topic | Shifts metropolitan demographics will be bad for taxes, wealth, and health in urban centers |
| Tone/Attitude | Forceful, bordering on urgent |
| Annotations | Migration - raw - AA immigration - demographic inversion - pensions - adjust perception - ring - 1925 - 1974 - migration - no factory - start in suburbs |
| Data | Chart 1: 2010 more large metro, roughly equal small and non-metro <br> Chart 2: Growth rates higher across the board in 1990-2000; large metro growth greatest |

| Questions 22-31 | Goat Milk |
|---|---|
| Type | Science (without Data) |
| Purpose | To explain the development of ATryn, the liquid gold goat milk |
| Thesis/Topic | How scientists developed medicine for humans that can be grown in livestock (transgenic medicine) |
| Tone/Attitude | Excited by the new possibilities |
| Annotations | Animals and pharma factories - medication - healing milk? - thrombin - clots - liquid gold |

| Questions 32-41 | Democracy and Revolution |
|---|---|
| Type | History (Paired, antiquated English) |
| Purpose | To argue about the responsibilities of the present to the past and the future |
| Thesis/Topic | Burke: in times of instability, we have an obligation to slow down change<br>Paine: every generation should act in its own interest regardless of the past |
| Tone/Attitude | Burke: argumentative in favor of slow change<br>Paine: argumentative in favor of revolution |
| Annotations | Burke: sacred state – don't do it! – more than a trade good – partnership – cannot be separated<br>Paine: the past (1688) – the living not the dead – past/future should not control |
| Agree/Disagree | Burke: society binds the living, dead, and not yet born; be careful with society<br>Paine: the present owes nothing to the past or future; all generations are free |

| Questions 42-52 | Medieval Volcano |
|---|---|
| Type | Science (with Data) |
| Purpose | To explain how a volcano brought about the Little Ice Age |
| Thesis/Topic | An eruption in Indonesia caused the earth to cool over almost 200 years |
| Tone/Attitude | Excited, somewhat casual |
| Annotations | Medieval Volcano – proof – carbon dating – other volcanoes too – history – massive – late 13th c. equator? – Ecuador? |
| Data | Big dips from 1200 to 1700, spike at 1680 |

Lesson 11: Mastering Your Review

## Question Review (Question and Answer Types)

| Questions | General | Specific | Synthesis | Answers | Reason |
|---|---|---|---|---|---|
| Main Purpose | Purpose | Function | | Wrong | Somewhat right, but too broad |
| Main Idea | Thesis | Topic | | Wrong | Somewhat right, but too narrow |
| Tone | Tone | Attitude | | Wrong | Somewhat right, but too extreme |
| Rhetoric | Structure | Argument | | Wrong | Tempting words, but wrong part |
| Vocabulary | | Vocabulary | | Wrong | Tempting words, but not true |
| Evidence | | Evidence | | Wrong | Tempting words, but irrelevant |
| Detail | | Detail | | Wrong | Flatly false |
| Inference | | Inference | | Right (general) | Give identify evidence |
| Data | | Data Specific | Data Synthesis | Right (specific) | Give line or annotation evidence |
| Paired | | Paired Specific | Paired Synthesis | Right (synthesis) | Give identify evidence |

| | Recognize | Why My Answer Is Wrong | Why the Correct Answer Is Right |
|---|---|---|---|
| 1 | | | |
| 2 | | | |
| 4 | | | |
| 5 | | | |
| 6 | | | |
| 7 | | | |
| 8 | | | |
| 9 | | | |
| 10 | | | |
| 11 | | | |
| 12 | | | |
| 13 | | | |
| 14 | | | |
| 15 | | | |
| 16 | | | |
| 17 | | | |
| 18 | | | |
| 19 | | | |
| 20 | | | |
| 21 | | | |

| Questions 32-41 | Democracy and Revolution |
| --- | --- |
| Type | History (Paired, antiquated English) |
| Purpose | To argue about the responsibilities of the present to the past and the future |
| Thesis/Topic | Burke: in times of instability, we have an obligation to slow down change <br> Paine: every generation should act in its own interest regardless of the past |
| Tone/Attitude | Burke: argumentative in favor of slow change <br> Paine: argumentative in favor of revolution |
| Annotations | Burke: sacred state - don't do it! - more than a trade good - partnership - cannot be separated <br> Paine: the past (1688) - the living not the dead - past/future should not control |
| Agree/Disagree | Burke: society binds the living, dead, and not yet born; be careful with society <br> Paine: the present owes nothing to the past or future; all generations are free |

| Questions 42-52 | Medieval Volcano |
| --- | --- |
| Type | Science (with Data) |
| Purpose | To explain how a volcano brought about the Little Ice Age |
| Thesis/Topic | An eruption in Indonesia caused the earth to cool over almost 200 years |
| Tone/Attitude | Excited, somewhat casual |
| Annotations | Medieval Volcano - proof - carbon dating - other volcanoes too - history - massive - late 13th c. equator? - Ecuador? |
| Data | Big dips from 1200 to 1700, spike at 1680 |

Lesson 11: Mastering Your Review

## Question Review (Question and Answer Types)

| Questions | General | Specific | Synthesis | Answers | Reason |
|---|---|---|---|---|---|
| Main Purpose | Purpose | Function | | Wrong | Somewhat right, but too broad |
| Main Idea | Thesis | Topic | | Wrong | Somewhat right, but too narrow |
| Tone | Tone | Attitude | | Wrong | Somewhat right, but too extreme |
| Rhetoric | Structure | Argument | | Wrong | Tempting words, but wrong part |
| Vocabulary | | Vocabulary | | Wrong | Tempting words, but not true |
| Evidence | | Evidence | | Wrong | Tempting words, but irrelevant |
| Detail | | Detail | | Wrong | Flatly false |
| Inference | | Inference | | Right (general) | Give identify evidence |
| Data | | Data Specific | Data Synthesis | Right (specific) | Give line or annotation evidence |
| Paired | | Paired Specific | Paired Synthesis | Right (synthesis) | Give identify evidence |

| | Recognize | Why My Answer Is Wrong | Why the Correct Answer Is Right |
|---|---|---|---|
| 1 | | | |
| 2 | | | |
| 4 | | | |
| 5 | | | |
| 6 | | | |
| 7 | | | |
| 8 | | | |
| 9 | | | |
| 10 | | | |
| 11 | | | |
| 12 | | | |
| 13 | | | |
| 14 | | | |
| 15 | | | |
| 16 | | | |
| 17 | | | |
| 18 | | | |
| 19 | | | |
| 20 | | | |
| 21 | | | |

| Recognize | Why My Answer Is Wrong | Why the Correct Answer Is Right |
|---|---|---|
| 22 | | |
| 23 | | |
| 24 | | |
| 25 | | |
| 26 | | |
| 27 | | |
| 28 | | |
| 29 | | |
| 30 | | |
| 31 | | |
| 32 | | |
| 33 | | |
| 34 | | |
| 35 | | |
| 36 | | |
| 37 | | |
| 38 | | |
| 39 | | |
| 40 | | |
| 41 | | |
| 42 | | |
| 43 | | |
| 44 | | |
| 45 | | |
| 46 | | |
| 47 | | |
| 48 | | |
| 49 | | |
| 50 | | |
| 51 | | |
| 52 | | |

Lesson 11: Mastering Your Review

|  | The Mad Balloonist | The Great Inversion | Goat Milk | Democracy and Revolution | Medieval Volcano |
|---|---|---|---|---|---|
| Purpose |  |  | 4.1.22 |  | 4.1.42 |
| Function | 4.1.4 |  | 4.1.30 |  | 4.1.45 |
| Thesis |  |  |  |  |  |
| Topic |  | 4.1.11 |  |  |  |
| Tone |  |  | 4.1.23 |  |  |
| Attitude | 4.1.1<br>4.1.7 |  |  |  |  |
| Structure |  |  |  |  | 4.1.43 |
| Argument |  |  |  |  | 4.1.49 |
| Vocab | 4.1.3<br>4.1.9<br>4.1.10 | 4.1.13<br>4.1.18 | 4.1.24 | 4.1.33<br>4.1.34 |  |
| Evidence | 4.1.2<br>4.1.6 | 4.1.15<br>4.1.17 | 4.1.26<br>4.1.28 | 4.1.37<br>4.1.39 | 4.1.44<br>4.1.47 |
| Detail | 4.1.5 | 4.1.12<br>4.1.14 | 4.1.27 | 4.1.32 | 4.1.46 |
| Inference | 4.1.8 | 4.1.16 | 4.1.25<br>4.1.29<br>4.1.31 | 4.1.35 | 4.1.48 |
| Data (Detail) |  | 4.1.20<br>4.1.21 |  |  | 4.1.50 |
| Data (Synthesis) |  | 4.1.19 |  |  | 4.1.51<br>4.1.52 |
| Paired (Inference) |  |  |  | 4.1.36<br>4.1.38 |  |
| Paired (Synthesis) |  |  |  | 4.1.40<br>4.1.40 |  |

## Test 5 Review

## SELF-EVALUATION TEST 5

| | | | | | | |
|---|---|---|---|---|---|---|
| Passage 1 | I felt confident during the first passage. | Strongly Agree | Somewhat Agree | No Opinion | Somewhat Disagree | Strongly Disagree |
| | Describe in two to three sentences how you felt on the first passage | | | | | |
| Passage 2 | I felt confident during the second passage. | Strongly Agree | Somewhat Agree | No Opinion | Somewhat Disagree | Strongly Disagree |
| | Describe in two to three sentences how you felt on the second passage | | | | | |
| Passage 3 | I felt confident during the third passage. | Strongly Agree | Somewhat Agree | No Opinion | Somewhat Disagree | Strongly Disagree |
| | Describe in two to three sentences how you felt on the third passage | | | | | |
| Passage 4 | I felt confident during the fourth passage. | Strongly Agree | Somewhat Agree | No Opinion | Somewhat Disagree | Strongly Disagree |
| | Describe in two to three sentences how you felt on the fourth passage | | | | | |
| Passage 5 | I felt confident during the fifth passage. | Strongly Agree | Somewhat Agree | No Opinion | Somewhat Disagree | Strongly Disagree |
| | Describe in two to three sentences how you felt on the fifth passage | | | | | |
| Overall | I felt confident during the reading section. | Strongly Agree | Somewhat Agree | No Opinion | Somewhat Disagree | Strongly Disagree |
| | I had enough time for the reading section. | Strongly Agree | Somewhat Agree | No Opinion | Somewhat Disagree | Strongly Disagree |
| | I cared about the passages I read. | Strongly Agree | Somewhat Agree | No Opinion | Somewhat Disagree | Strongly Disagree |
| | In three to four sentences, describe how you feel about the reading section | | | | | |

Lesson 11: Mastering Your Review

## Passage Review (Annotations and Identification)

| Questions 1-10 | Lunch with Dad |
|---|---|
| Type | Literature |
| Purpose | To describe Lymie's wait and then lunch with his Dad |
| Thesis/Topic | A man is reading a history book while waiting for his father |
| Tone/Attitude | Lymie is irritated with the other guests; his father has aged and somewhat vain |
| Annotations | Restaurant – book – Paris – Vienna – newcomers – skims – old/disheveled – thinks good of himself |

| Questions 11-21 | Women and Abolitionism |
|---|---|
| Type | History (Paired, antiquated English) |
| Purpose | To argue whether or not women should play a public role in the abolition movement |
| Thesis/Topic | Beecher: Women should play a public role in the abolitionist debate; women and men have different functions<br>Grimke: Women should play an active role in the abolitionist debate; they have the same rights as men |
| Tone/Attitude | Grimke is more combative than Beecher; both are persuasive |
| Annotations | Beecher: Gender – public ways for men – kind ways for women – non-combative<br>Grimke: human rights – gender doesn't matter – animal nature – her doctrine |
| Agree/Disagree | Agree: Abolition is an important question that women can address<br>Disagree: Where should women play a role? Beecher says in domestic and social circles. Grimke says publicly. |

| Questions 22-31 | Organic Food |
|---|---|
| Type | Science (with Data) |
| Purpose | To explain the trade-offs for conventional and organic farming |
| Thesis/Topic | Conventional food is more efficient than organic food, but not across all food types |
| Tone/Attitude | Author: Challenging, but conversational<br>Foley: measured response, wants to see innovation |
| Annotations | Efficiency in energy – but not food – big agra – environmentalists – conventional vs. organic – legumes and cereals – fertilizer, nitrogen – but – blend |
| Data | Various yields of crop types<br>Various yields for species; range 60%-100% |

| Questions 32-41 | Internet Comments |
|---|---|
| Type | Social Studies (with Data) |
| Purpose | To explain why internet comments are inaccurate |
| Thesis/Topic | Internet comments are affected by a herd mentality, can be manipulated |
| Tone/Attitude | Scientific, Inquisitive (use of rhetorical questions)<br>Researcher 2 (Watts) was surprised by results |
| Annotations | Herd behavior – crowd wisdom – steering crowd – news aggregate – random up/down votes data – willingness to go up – real world applications – artificially increased |
| Data | Different categories of news had different responses to artificial up votes |

| Questions 42-52 | MRI's and Memory |
|---|---|
| Type | Science (without Data) |
| Purpose | To explain how the brain responds (or not) to training |
| Thesis/Topic | Training and practice affect our brain activity, against prevailing thesis |
| Tone/Attitude | Author: Memory; Second study: Mental athletes was surprising |
| Annotations | Physical changes – static brain – memory – no difference – different circuits – similar to cabbies – training and practice |

## Question Review (Question and Answer Types)

| Questions | General | Specific | Synthesis | Answers | Reason |
|---|---|---|---|---|---|
| Main Purpose | Purpose | Function | | Wrong | Somewhat right, but too broad |
| Main Idea | Thesis | Topic | | Wrong | Somewhat right, but too narrow |
| Tone | Tone | Attitude | | Wrong | Somewhat right, but too extreme |
| Rhetoric | Structure | Argument | | Wrong | Tempting words, but wrong part |
| Vocabulary | | Vocabulary | | Wrong | Tempting words, but not true |
| Evidence | | Evidence | | Wrong | Tempting words, but irrelevant |
| Detail | | Detail | | Wrong | Flatly false |
| Inference | | Inference | | Right (general) | Give identify evidence |
| Data | | Data Specific | Data Synthesis | Right (specific) | Give line or annotation evidence |
| Paired | | Paired Specific | Paired Synthesis | Right (synthesis) | Give identify evidence |

| | Recognize | Why My Answer Is Wrong | Why the Correct Answer Is Right |
|---|---|---|---|
| 1 | | | |
| 2 | | | |
| 4 | | | |
| 5 | | | |
| 6 | | | |
| 7 | | | |
| 8 | | | |
| 9 | | | |
| 10 | | | |
| 11 | | | |
| 12 | | | |
| 13 | | | |
| 14 | | | |
| 15 | | | |
| 16 | | | |
| 17 | | | |
| 18 | | | |
| 19 | | | |
| 20 | | | |
| 21 | | | |

| Recognize | Why My Answer Is Wrong | Why the Correct Answer Is Right |
|---|---|---|
| 22 | | |
| 23 | | |
| 24 | | |
| 25 | | |
| 26 | | |
| 27 | | |
| 28 | | |
| 29 | | |
| 30 | | |
| 31 | | |
| 32 | | |
| 33 | | |
| 34 | | |
| 35 | | |
| 36 | | |
| 37 | | |
| 38 | | |
| 39 | | |
| 40 | | |
| 41 | | |
| 42 | | |
| 43 | | |
| 44 | | |
| 45 | | |
| 46 | | |
| 47 | | |
| 48 | | |
| 49 | | |
| 50 | | |
| 51 | | |
| 52 | | |

|  | Lunch with Dad | Women and Abolitionism | Organic Food | Internet Comments | MRIs and Memory |
|---|---|---|---|---|---|
| **Purpose** | | | | | |
| Function | 5.1.2 | | | | 5.1.48 |
| | | | | | 5.1.52 |
| **Thesis** | | 5.1.16 | | | |
| Topic | 5.1.8 | | | | |
| **Tone** | | | | | |
| Attitude | 5.1.4 | | 5.1.24 | | |
| Structure | 5.1.1 | | | 5.1.32 | |
| Argument | 5.1.9 | | | | |
| Vocab | 5.1.10 | 5.1.14 | 5.1.22 | 5.1.37 | 5.1.44 |
| | | 5.1.15 | 5.1.29 | 5.1.38 | 5.1.47 |
| Evidence | 5.1.5 | 5.1.12 | 5.1.25 | 5.1.34 | 5.1.43 |
| | | 5.1.18 | 5.1.27 | | 5.1.46 |
| | | | | | 5.1.47 |
| Detail | 5.1.6 | 5.1.11 | 5.1.26 | 5.1.35 | 5.1.42 |
| | 5.1.7 | 5.1.17 | 5.1.28 | | 5.1.45 |
| | | | | | 5.1.49 |
| Inference | 5.1.3 | 5.1.13 | | 5.1.33 | 5.1.50 |
| | | | | 5.1.36 | |
| Data (Detail) | | | 5.1.30 | 5.1.39 | |
| | | | 5.1.31 | 5.1.40 | |
| Data (Synthesis) | | | | 5.1.41 | |
| Paired (Inference) | | 5.1.21 | | | |
| Paired (Synthesis) | | 5.1.19 | | | |
| | | 5.1.20 | | | |

## Test 6 Review

## SELF-EVALUATION TEST 6

| | | | | | | |
|---|---|---|---|---|---|---|
| **Passage 1** | I felt confident during the first passage. | Strongly Agree | Somewhat Agree | No Opinion | Somewhat Disagree | Strongly Disagree |
| | Describe in two to three sentences how you felt on the first passage | | | | | |
| **Passage 2** | I felt confident during the second passage. | Strongly Agree | Somewhat Agree | No Opinion | Somewhat Disagree | Strongly Disagree |
| | Describe in two to three sentences how you felt on the second passage | | | | | |
| **Passage 3** | I felt confident during the third passage. | Strongly Agree | Somewhat Agree | No Opinion | Somewhat Disagree | Strongly Disagree |
| | Describe in two to three sentences how you felt on the third passage | | | | | |
| **Passage 4** | I felt confident during the fourth passage. | Strongly Agree | Somewhat Agree | No Opinion | Somewhat Disagree | Strongly Disagree |
| | Describe in two to three sentences how you felt on the fourth passage | | | | | |
| **Passage 5** | I felt confident during the fifth passage. | Strongly Agree | Somewhat Agree | No Opinion | Somewhat Disagree | Strongly Disagree |
| | Describe in two to three sentences how you felt on the fifth passage | | | | | |
| **Overall** | I felt confident during the reading section. | Strongly Agree | Somewhat Agree | No Opinion | Somewhat Disagree | Strongly Disagree |
| | I had enough time for the reading section. | Strongly Agree | Somewhat Agree | No Opinion | Somewhat Disagree | Strongly Disagree |
| | I cared about the passages I read. | Strongly Agree | Somewhat Agree | No Opinion | Somewhat Disagree | Strongly Disagree |
| | In three to four sentences, describe how you feel about the reading section | | | | | |

Lesson 11: Mastering Your Review

## Passage Review (Annotations and Identification)

| Questions 1-10 | Nawabdin Electrician |
|---|---|
| Type | Literature |
| Purpose | To describe an old fix-it man and his rich employer |
| Thesis/Topic | A man asks his boss for a motorcycle and the boss agrees to keep himself happy |
| Tone/Attitude | Nawabdin is deferential; Harouni just wants to be comfortable |
| Annotations | Fix-it guy — salary not enough — side work — watches — Harouni — household — everywhere — wants out? — too old — motorcycle — what this does — wife |

| Questions 11-21 | Fake News |
|---|---|
| Type | Social Studies (with Data) |
| Purpose | To explain two how the news and news experts are perceived by the public |
| Thesis/Topic | The public distrusts the media and expects more transparency |
| Tone/Attitude | Informative, but also critical |
| Annotations | public vs private — public important — complete process — authority — quote — experts — opinions |
| Data | Independent variables: accuracy/independence/bias<br>Dependent variable: time<br>Decreasing trust in accuracy distrust, decreasing trust in independence, decreasing trust in favoritism |

| Questions 22-31 | Beetles, Bees, and Dung |
|---|---|
| Type | Science (without Data) |
| Purpose | To explain an experiment on how pollen affects bees, beetles, and plant growth |
| Thesis/Topic | Plants that had a greater fragrance attracted more beetles, and thus fewer bees. |
| Tone/Attitude | Descriptive opening, then scientific |
| Annotations | pollen — beetles — fragrance — experiment — remove beetles — benchmark — results — beetles deter bees — odd result |

| | | |
|---|---|---|
| Questions 32-41 | Civil Disobedience | |
| Type | History (Paired, antiquated English) | |
| Purpose | To argue (debate) when bad laws should be observed and when they should be broken | |
| Thesis/Topic | Lincoln: Unjust laws should be followed until the laws are changed | |
| | Thoreau: Unjust laws should be broken if they will not change on their own | |
| Tone/Attitude | Lincoln: solemn, pointed | |
| | Thoreau: rhetorical questions, impatient | |
| Annotations | Lincoln: patriots – laws – political religion – there are bad laws – mob rule is bad – abolition | |
| | Thoreau: they say (Lincoln) – but … – when to break the law – justice delayed – abolition | |
| Agree/Disagree | Agree: slavery is one pressing example of a law that is bad | |
| | Disagree: abolitionists are right/wrong to disobey unjust laws. Lincoln says wait; Thoreau says withdraw from bad government | |

| | | |
|---|---|---|
| Questions 42-52 | Solar Power | |
| Type | Science (with Data) | |
| Purpose | To explain cost and efficiency advancements in solar tech | |
| Thesis/Topic | The cost of solar cells is decreasing as their efficiency is increasing | |
| Tone/Attitude | Author: Argues against pessimism | |
| | Green: Optimistic future, beyond expectations | |
| Annotations | Too much supply – prospects – cheap – target – cut costs – thin lines – willow glass – flexible – reflective? – extra watts – Green bets – efficiency | |
| Data | Figure 1: | |
| | Independent variable: type | |
| | Dependent variable: cost | |
| | Solar is most expensive; natural gas and wind are least expensive | |
| | Figure 2: | |
| | Independent variable: time | |
| | Dependent variable: cost | |
| | Solar costs are rapidly decreasing | |

Lesson 11: Mastering Your Review

## Question Review (Question and Answer Types)

| Questions | General | Specific | Synthesis | Answers | Reason |
|---|---|---|---|---|---|
| Main Purpose | Purpose | Function | | Wrong | Somewhat right, but too broad |
| Main Idea | Thesis | Topic | | Wrong | Somewhat right, but too narrow |
| Tone | Tone | Attitude | | Wrong | Somewhat right, but too extreme |
| Rhetoric | Structure | Argument | | Wrong | Tempting words, but wrong part |
| Vocabulary | | Vocabulary | | Wrong | Tempting words, but not true |
| Evidence | | Evidence | | Wrong | Tempting words, but irrelevant |
| Detail | | Detail | | Wrong | Flatly false |
| Inference | | Inference | | Right (general) | Give identify evidence |
| Data | | Data Specific | Data Synthesis | Right (specific) | Give line or annotation evidence |
| Paired | | Paired Specific | Paired Synthesis | Right (synthesis) | Give identify evidence |

| | Recognize | Why My Answer Is Wrong | Why the Correct Answer Is Right |
|---|---|---|---|
| 1 | | | |
| 2 | | | |
| 4 | | | |
| 5 | | | |
| 6 | | | |
| 7 | | | |
| 8 | | | |
| 9 | | | |
| 10 | | | |
| 11 | | | |
| 12 | | | |
| 13 | | | |
| 14 | | | |
| 15 | | | |
| 16 | | | |
| 17 | | | |
| 18 | | | |
| 19 | | | |
| 20 | | | |
| 21 | | | |

| | Recognize | Why My Answer Is Wrong | Why the Correct Answer Is Right |
|---|---|---|---|
| 22 | | | |
| 23 | | | |
| 24 | | | |
| 25 | | | |
| 26 | | | |
| 27 | | | |
| 28 | | | |
| 29 | | | |
| 30 | | | |
| 31 | | | |
| 32 | | | |
| 33 | | | |
| 34 | | | |
| 35 | | | |
| 36 | | | |
| 37 | | | |
| 38 | | | |
| 39 | | | |
| 40 | | | |
| 41 | | | |
| 42 | | | |
| 43 | | | |
| 44 | | | |
| 45 | | | |
| 46 | | | |
| 47 | | | |
| 48 | | | |
| 49 | | | |
| 50 | | | |
| 51 | | | |
| 52 | | | |

Lesson 11: Mastering Your Review

| | Nawabdin Electrician | Fake News | Beetles, Bees, and Dung | Civil Disobedience | Solar Power |
|---|---|---|---|---|---|
| Purpose | | 6.1.11 | 6.1.22 | | |
| Function | 6.1.1<br>6.1.3<br>6.1.5<br>6.1.6 | | 6.1.29 | 6.1.36 | 6.1.50 |
| Thesis | | | | | |
| Topic | | | | | |
| Tone | 6.1.9 | | | | |
| Attitude | | | | | |
| Structure | | | | | |
| Argument | 6.1.4 | 6.1.15 | 6.1.31 | | 6.1.43 |
| Vocab | 6.1.2 | 6.1.14<br>6.1.18 | 6.1.26<br>6.1.30 | 6.1.35<br>6.1.37 | 6.1.44<br>6.1.49 |
| Evidence | 6.1.8 | 6.1.13<br>6.1.17 | 6.1.28<br>6.1.32 | 6.1.34<br>6.1.39 | 6.1.46<br>6.1.48 |
| Detail | 6.1.10 | 6.1.12<br>6.1.16 | 6.1.23<br>6.1.25<br>6.1.27 | 6.1.33<br>6.1.38 | 6.1.47 |
| Inference | 6.1.7 | | 6.1.24 | | 6.1.45 |
| Data (Detail) | | 6.1.19<br>6.1.20 | | | 6.1.52 |
| Data (Synthesis) | | 6.1.21 | | | 6.1.51 |
| Paired (Inference) | | | | 6.1.41 | |
| Paired (Synthesis) | | | | 6.1.40<br>6.1.42 | |

## Test 7 Review

## SELF-EVALUATION TEST 7

| | | | | | | |
|---|---|---|---|---|---|---|
| Passage 1 | I felt confident during the first passage. | Strongly Agree | Somewhat Agree | No Opinion | Somewhat Disagree | Strongly Disagree |
| | Describe in two to three sentences how you felt on the first passage | | | | | |
| Passage 2 | I felt confident during the second passage. | Strongly Agree | Somewhat Agree | No Opinion | Somewhat Disagree | Strongly Disagree |
| | Describe in two to three sentences how you felt on the second passage | | | | | |
| Passage 3 | I felt confident during the third passage. | Strongly Agree | Somewhat Agree | No Opinion | Somewhat Disagree | Strongly Disagree |
| | Describe in two to three sentences how you felt on the third passage | | | | | |
| Passage 4 | I felt confident during the fourth passage. | Strongly Agree | Somewhat Agree | No Opinion | Somewhat Disagree | Strongly Disagree |
| | Describe in two to three sentences how you felt on the fourth passage | | | | | |
| Passage 5 | I felt confident during the fifth passage. | Strongly Agree | Somewhat Agree | No Opinion | Somewhat Disagree | Strongly Disagree |
| | Describe in two to three sentences how you felt on the fifth passage | | | | | |
| Overall | I felt confident during the reading section. | Strongly Agree | Somewhat Agree | No Opinion | Somewhat Disagree | Strongly Disagree |
| | I had enough time for the reading section. | Strongly Agree | Somewhat Agree | No Opinion | Somewhat Disagree | Strongly Disagree |
| | I cared about the passages I read. | Strongly Agree | Somewhat Agree | No Opinion | Somewhat Disagree | Strongly Disagree |
| | In three to four sentences, describe how you feel about the reading section | | | | | |

Lesson 11: Mastering Your Review

## Passage Review (Annotations and Identification)

| Questions 1-10 | Silas Marner |
|---|---|
| Type | Literature |
| Purpose | To describe how Eppie changes Silas Marner |
| Thesis/Topic | Eppie's love has turned Silas from a miser into a warm person |
| Tone/Attitude | Eppie is warm and bubbly; Silas is becoming that way |
| Annotations | Gold – Eppie – Sunshine – Gold vs. Eppie – Field Trip – Flowers – Bird Watching – He grows as well – growth and love |

| Questions 11-21 | Jobs and Tech |
|---|---|
| Type | Social Studies (with Data) |
| Purpose | To explain advancements in tech and employment |
| Thesis/Topic | Unlike what was expected, advancements in tech have not produced more jobs and may be decreasing employment |
| Tone/Attitude | Author: Surprised? <br> Katz: uncertain |
| Annotations | Tech – professions – wage stagnation – job growth – "great decoupling" – $ but ☹ – or not? – stability – questioning the future |
| Data | Figure 1: <br> Independent variable: productivity and employment <br> Dependent variable: time <br> Productivity rises faster than employment <br> Figure 2: <br> Independent variable: output per worker <br> Dependent variable: time <br> US/Germany/Japan have all grown, but US output more in last decade |

| Questions 22-31 | Flying V |
|---|---|
| Type | Science (without Data) |
| Purpose | To explain why birds fly in V |
| Thesis/Topic | Birds find an aerodynamic sweet spot that decreases drag and conserve energy |
| Tone/Attitude | Scientists: Breakthrough! |
| Annotations | Why V? – Drafting? – GPS Data – other birds – aerodynamics – common birds |

| Questions 32-41 | Gender and American Democracy |
|---|---|
| Type | History (Paired, antiquated English) |
| Purpose | To argue (debate) whether there should be a division of labor between men and women |
| Thesis/Topic | Tocqueville: Disregarding nature's differences hurts both men and women<br>Mill: All people, regardless of gender, should be able to do whatever than can attain |
| Tone/Attitude | Tocqueville: rhetorical questions, strongly opposed to the fanciful and degrading equality<br>Mill: dismissive of tradition, forceful proponent of equality |
| Annotations | Tocqueville: men + women – but bad! – consequences – division of labor<br>Mill: superiority – whatever you can attain – injustice – bad for society |
| Agree/Disagree | Agree: gender equality is a growing issue in the United States<br>Disagree: is gender equality a good thing or bad thing? Tocqueville: Hurts everyone. Mill: Good for everyone |

| Questions 42-52 | Higgs-Boson Particle |
|---|---|
| Type | Science (with Data) |
| Purpose | To explain the history of the Higgs-Boson |
| Thesis/Topic | The Higgs-Boson particle was accepted long (1964) before it was successfully observed (2013) |
| Tone/Attitude | Author: excited, once surprised it wasn't known |
| Annotations | Where does mass come from? – puzzle – metaphor – rejected – mass from environment – studied – true before data |
| Data | Independent variable: Particle type<br>Dependent variable: Time between [ and confirmation<br>Higgs-Boson was supposed but not proven much longer than any other particle |

## Question Review (Question and Answer Types)

| Questions | General | Specific | Synthesis | Answers | Reason |
|---|---|---|---|---|---|
| Main Purpose | Purpose | Function | | Wrong | Somewhat right, but <u>too broad</u> |
| Main Idea | Thesis | Topic | | Wrong | Somewhat right, but <u>too narrow</u> |
| Tone | Tone | Attitude | | Wrong | Somewhat right, but <u>too extreme</u> |
| Rhetoric | Structure | Argument | | Wrong | Tempting words, but <u>wrong part</u> |
| Vocabulary | | Vocabulary | | Wrong | Tempting words, but <u>not true</u> |
| Evidence | | Evidence | | Wrong | Tempting words, but <u>irrelevant</u> |
| Detail | | Detail | | Wrong | Flatly false |
| Inference | | Inference | | Right (general) | Give identify evidence |
| Data | | Data Specific | Data Synthesis | Right (specific) | Give line or annotation evidence |
| Paired | | Paired Specific | Paired Synthesis | Right (synthesis) | Give identify evidence |

| | Recognize | Why My Answer Is Wrong | Why the Correct Answer Is Right |
|---|---|---|---|
| 1 | | | |
| 2 | | | |
| 4 | | | |
| 5 | | | |
| 6 | | | |
| 7 | | | |
| 8 | | | |
| 9 | | | |
| 10 | | | |
| 11 | | | |
| 12 | | | |
| 13 | | | |
| 14 | | | |
| 15 | | | |
| 16 | | | |
| 17 | | | |
| 18 | | | |
| 19 | | | |
| 20 | | | |
| 21 | | | |

| Recognize | Why My Answer Is Wrong | Why the Correct Answer Is Right |
|---|---|---|
| 22 | | |
| 23 | | |
| 24 | | |
| 25 | | |
| 26 | | |
| 27 | | |
| 28 | | |
| 29 | | |
| 30 | | |
| 31 | | |
| 32 | | |
| 33 | | |
| 34 | | |
| 35 | | |
| 36 | | |
| 37 | | |
| 38 | | |
| 39 | | |
| 40 | | |
| 41 | | |
| 42 | | |
| 43 | | |
| 44 | | |
| 45 | | |
| 46 | | |
| 47 | | |
| 48 | | |
| 49 | | |
| 50 | | |
| 51 | | |
| 52 | | |

Lesson 11: Mastering Your Review

|                   | Silas Marner | Jobs and Tech | Flying V | Gender and Democracy | Higgs-Boson Particle |
|-------------------|--------------|---------------|----------|----------------------|----------------------|
| Purpose           |              | 7.1.11        | 7.1.22   |                      |                      |
| Function          | 7.1.4        | 7.1.14        | 7.1.23   |                      | 7.1.43               |
|                   | 7.1.7        |               | 7.1.26   |                      |                      |
|                   |              |               | 7.1.29   |                      |                      |
| Thesis            | 7.1.1        |               |          |                      |                      |
| Topic             |              |               | 7.1.29   |                      |                      |
| Tone              |              |               |          |                      |                      |
| Attitude          | 7.1.5        | 7.1.16        |          |                      |                      |
| Structure         |              |               |          |                      | 7.1.42               |
| Argument          | 7.1.3        |               |          |                      | 7.1.48               |
| Vocab             | 7.1.10       | 7.1.15        | 7.1.31   | 7.1.32               | 7.1.49               |
|                   |              | 7.1.18        |          | 7.1.35               |                      |
| Evidence          | 7.1.6        | 7.1.13        | 7.1.25   | 7.1.34               | 7.1.45               |
|                   | 7.1.9        | 7.1.17        | 7.1.28   | 7.1.37               | 7.1.47               |
| Detail            | 7.1.2        | 7.1.12        |          |                      | 7.1.46               |
|                   | 7.1.8        |               |          |                      |                      |
| Inference         |              |               | 7.1.24   | 7.1.33               | 7.1.44               |
|                   |              |               | 7.1.27   | 7.1.36               |                      |
| Data (Detail)     |              | 7.1.19        |          |                      | 7.1.51               |
|                   |              | 7.1.20        |          |                      |                      |
| Data (Synthesis)  |              | 7.1.21        |          |                      | 7.1.50               |
|                   |              |               |          |                      | 7.1.52               |
| Paired (Inference)|              |               |          | 7.1.39               |                      |
|                   |              |               |          | 7.1.41               |                      |
| Paired (Synthesis)|              |               |          | 7.1.38               |                      |
|                   |              |               |          | 7.1.40               |                      |

## Test 8 Review

## SELF-EVALUATION TEST 8

| | | | | | | |
|---|---|---|---|---|---|---|
| **Passage 1** | I felt confident during the first passage. | Strongly Agree | Somewhat Agree | No Opinion | Somewhat Disagree | Strongly Disagree |
| | Describe in two to three sentences how you felt on the first passage | | | | | |
| **Passage 2** | I felt confident during the second passage. | Strongly Agree | Somewhat Agree | No Opinion | Somewhat Disagree | Strongly Disagree |
| | Describe in two to three sentences how you felt on the second passage | | | | | |
| **Passage 3** | I felt confident during the third passage. | Strongly Agree | Somewhat Agree | No Opinion | Somewhat Disagree | Strongly Disagree |
| | Describe in two to three sentences how you felt on the third passage | | | | | |
| **Passage 4** | I felt confident during the fourth passage. | Strongly Agree | Somewhat Agree | No Opinion | Somewhat Disagree | Strongly Disagree |
| | Describe in two to three sentences how you felt on the fourth passage | | | | | |
| **Passage 5** | I felt confident during the fifth passage. | Strongly Agree | Somewhat Agree | No Opinion | Somewhat Disagree | Strongly Disagree |
| | Describe in two to three sentences how you felt on the fifth passage | | | | | |
| **Overall** | I felt confident during the reading section. | Strongly Agree | Somewhat Agree | No Opinion | Somewhat Disagree | Strongly Disagree |
| | I had enough time for the reading section. | Strongly Agree | Somewhat Agree | No Opinion | Somewhat Disagree | Strongly Disagree |
| | I cared about the passages I read. | Strongly Agree | Somewhat Agree | No Opinion | Somewhat Disagree | Strongly Disagree |
| | In three to four sentences, describe how you feel about the reading section | | | | | |

## Passage Review (Annotations and Identification)

| Questions 1-10 | My Best Friend |
|---|---|
| Type | Literature |
| Purpose | To describe the author's love of books, his father's hatred of them, and his receiving great expectations |
| Thesis/Topic | The author's best friends are books and a bookstore owner, when he got great expectations it changed his life. |
| Tone/Attitude | Author loves books. Father hates books. Sempere loves books and wants to pass that love on to the author |
| Annotations | Reading + friends – reading + father – sheets – bookstore – Dickens – rereading |

| Questions 11-21 | Null Results |
|---|---|
| Type | Social studies (with Data) |
| Purpose | Explain why null results matter |
| Thesis/Topic | Publishing null results saves money and leads to better scientific data in the long run |
| Tone/Attitude | Author: Null results aren't exciting, but are important<br>Researchers: Social Scientists don't like null results, hard to interpret |
| Annotations | What null data is – what does it mean – TESS – null don't interest – expectations – praise – publish less strong data – pre-analysis |
| Data | Independent variable: Results<br>Dependent variable: Publication status<br>The more conclusive the data, the more likely the study is to be published with prestige, published, or written |

| Questions 22-31 | Nano Salt Wires |
|---|---|
| Type | Science (with Data) |
| Purpose | To explain how salt nano wires and how they behave at the nano level |
| Thesis/Topic | Nano wires, which are observed in the nano world, have similar behavior in the macroworld and worth studying |
| Tone/Attitude | Author: challenging, but conversational <br> Foley: measured response, wants to see innovation |
| Annotations | Salt wires – common – no gravity – observations – rearrange atoms – prospects |
| Data | Independent variable: Distance to surface <br> Dependent variable: Force on tip <br> Forces are prolonged if tip moving away. Breaks away farther away than it attaches |

| Questions 32-41 | Lincoln-Douglas |
|---|---|
| Type | History (Paired, Antiquated) |
| Purpose | To argue whether or not the US can exist as with both free and slave States |
| Thesis/Topic | Douglas: as long as States are governing themselves, the republic will thrive <br> Lincoln: slavery has always divided us. |
| Tone/Attitude | Douglass: Sarcastic, maybe a little taunting <br> Lincoln: heavy use of rhetorical questions |
| Annotations | Douglass: evidence – constitution a volition? – states' rights <br> Lincoln: response – different from sugar and wheat – slavery different – spread slavery |
| Agree/Disagree | Agree: free and slave states have different legal structures <br> Disagree: this legal division can continue to exist. |

| Questions 42-52 | Venus Flytrap |
|---|---|
| Type | Science (without Data) |
| Purpose | Explain how the Venus flytrap knows when to close |
| Thesis/Topic | Electric charges on a leaf induce calcium ions to concentrate until a threshold is reached |
| Attitude: | Explanatory; especially appreciative of first study |
| Annotations | Energy + time – springs into action – forgotten – chemistry – calcium – calcium threshold – verification – remains open |

Lesson 11: Mastering Your Review

## Question Review (Question and Answer Types)

| Questions | General | Specific | Synthesis | Answers | Reason |
|---|---|---|---|---|---|
| Main Purpose | Purpose | Function | | Wrong | Somewhat right, but too broad |
| Main Idea | Thesis | Topic | | Wrong | Somewhat right, but too narrow |
| Tone | Tone | Attitude | | Wrong | Somewhat right, but too extreme |
| Rhetoric | Structure | Argument | | Wrong | Tempting words, but wrong part |
| Vocabulary | | Vocabulary | | Wrong | Tempting words, but not true |
| Evidence | | Evidence | | Wrong | Tempting words, but irrelevant |
| Detail | | Detail | | Wrong | Flatly false |
| Inference | | Inference | | Right (general) | Give identify evidence |
| Data | | Data Specific | Data Synthesis | Right (specific) | Give line or annotation evidence |
| Paired | | Paired Specific | Paired Synthesis | Right (synthesis) | Give identify evidence |

| | Recognize | Why My Answer Is Wrong | Why the Correct Answer Is Right |
|---|---|---|---|
| 1 | | | |
| 2 | | | |
| 4 | | | |
| 5 | | | |
| 6 | | | |
| 7 | | | |
| 8 | | | |
| 9 | | | |
| 10 | | | |
| 11 | | | |
| 12 | | | |
| 13 | | | |
| 14 | | | |
| 15 | | | |
| 16 | | | |
| 17 | | | |
| 18 | | | |
| 19 | | | |
| 20 | | | |
| 21 | | | |
| 22 | | | |
| 23 | | | |

| | Recognize | Why My Answer Is Wrong | Why the Correct Answer Is Right |
|---|---|---|---|
| 24 | | | |
| 25 | | | |
| 26 | | | |
| 27 | | | |
| 28 | | | |
| 29 | | | |
| 30 | | | |
| 31 | | | |
| 32 | | | |
| 33 | | | |
| 34 | | | |
| 35 | | | |
| 36 | | | |
| 37 | | | |
| 38 | | | |
| 39 | | | |
| 40 | | | |
| 41 | | | |
| 42 | | | |
| 43 | | | |
| 44 | | | |
| 45 | | | |
| 46 | | | |
| 47 | | | |
| 48 | | | |
| 49 | | | |
| 50 | | | |
| 51 | | | |
| 52 | | | |

|  | My Best Friend | Null Results | Nano Salt Wires | Lincoln-Douglas Debates | Venus Flytrap |
|---|---|---|---|---|---|
| Purpose |  | 8.1.11 |  |  | 8.1.42 |
| Function | 8.1.2<br>8.1.9 | 8.1.18 |  | 8.1.32 | 8.1.46 |
| Thesis |  |  | 8.1.22 |  |  |
| Topic |  |  |  |  |  |
| Tone |  |  |  |  | 8.1.45 |
| Attitude |  |  |  |  |  |
| Structure | 8.1.1 |  | 8.1.23 |  |  |
| Argument |  |  | 8.1.24 |  | 8.1.50 |
| Vocab | 8.1.8 | 8.1.12<br>8.1.13 | 8.1.25<br>8.1.42 | 8.1.35<br>8.1.38 | 8.1.49 |
| Evidence | 8.1.4<br>8.1.6 | 8.1.15<br>8.1.17 | 8.1.29 | 8.1.34<br>8.1.37 | 8.1.44<br>8.1.50 |
| Detail | 8.1.7<br>8.1.10 | 8.1.14 | 8.1.26<br>8.1.28 |  | 8.1.43<br>8.1.47<br>8.1.52 |
| Inference | 8.1.3<br>8.1.5 | 8.1.16 |  | 8.1.33<br>8.1.36 | 8.1.48 |
| Data (Detail) |  | 8.1.19<br>8.1.19 | 8.1.30<br>8.1.31 |  |  |
| Data (Synthesis) |  | 8.1.21 |  |  |  |
| Paired (Inference) |  |  |  |  |  |
| Paired (Synthesis) |  |  |  | 8.1.39<br>8.1.40<br>8.1.41 |  |

## Test 9 Review

## SELF-EVALUATION TEST 9

| | | | | | | |
|---|---|---|---|---|---|---|
| **Passage 1** | I felt confident during the first passage. | Strongly Agree | Somewhat Agree | No Opinion | Somewhat Disagree | Strongly Disagree |
| | Describe in two to three sentences how you felt on the first passage | | | | | |
| **Passage 2** | I felt confident during the second passage. | Strongly Agree | Somewhat Agree | No Opinion | Somewhat Disagree | Strongly Disagree |
| | Describe in two to three sentences how you felt on the second passage | | | | | |
| **Passage 3** | I felt confident during the third passage. | Strongly Agree | Somewhat Agree | No Opinion | Somewhat Disagree | Strongly Disagree |
| | Describe in two to three sentences how you felt on the third passage | | | | | |
| **Passage 4** | I felt confident during the fourth passage. | Strongly Agree | Somewhat Agree | No Opinion | Somewhat Disagree | Strongly Disagree |
| | Describe in two to three sentences how you felt on the fourth passage | | | | | |
| **Passage 5** | I felt confident during the fifth passage. | Strongly Agree | Somewhat Agree | No Opinion | Somewhat Disagree | Strongly Disagree |
| | Describe in two to three sentences how you felt on the fifth passage | | | | | |
| **Overall** | I felt confident during the reading section. | Strongly Agree | Somewhat Agree | No Opinion | Somewhat Disagree | Strongly Disagree |
| | I had enough time for the reading section. | Strongly Agree | Somewhat Agree | No Opinion | Somewhat Disagree | Strongly Disagree |
| | I cared about the passages I read. | Strongly Agree | Somewhat Agree | No Opinion | Somewhat Disagree | Strongly Disagree |
| | In three to four sentences, describe how you feel about the reading section | | | | | |

Lesson 11: Mastering Your Review

## Passage Review (Annotations and Identification)

| Questions 1-10 | Ink Family |
|---|---|
| Type | Literature |
| Purpose | To describe the author's family and the family ink business |
| Thesis/Topic | A girl ventures with an older widow to father's business |
| Tone/Attitude | Girl is mesmerized by the shop; family follow custom |
| Annotations | Father - Big Uncle - Little Uncle - envy? - decoration - boxes - customer - ink metaphor? - ink shop - ink x2 - $$ - pride |

| Questions 11-20 | Memory and Google |
|---|---|
| Type | Social studies (with Data) |
| Purpose | Explain how internet searches affect memory |
| Thesis/Topic | The internet has decreased our ability to remember facts, but increased our ability to find these facts |
| Tone/Attitude | Formal but approachable |
| Annotations | Memory - memory - less memory - transactive memory - habits - research partners - studies - not saved - effects - access |
| Data | Most people remember nothing, about half remember locations, about a third remember statements |

| Questions 21-31 | Guppy Evolution |
| --- | --- |
| Type | Science (with Data) |
| Purpose | To explain how predators can affect the genes and evolution of guppies |
| Thesis/Topic | The presence of predators affects the size of guppy litters and the mass of guppy offspring |
| Tone/Attitude | Scientific, probing |
| Annotations | Sex diet evolve - guppies - luck - predators - pred & reproduction evolution - larger litter smaller fish - genes not context - manipulation - some small predators - faster evolutions - 4 gens |
| Data | Figure 1: high predators = high offspring |
| | Independent variable: location and predators; Dependent variable: number of offspring |
| | Figure 2 high predators = smaller embryo mass |
| | Independent variable: location and predators; Dependent variable: mass of embryos |

| Questions 32-42 | Woman and Slavery |
| --- | --- |
| Type | History (Antiquated English) |
| Purpose | To argue that women can and should be opposed to slavery |
| Thesis/Topic | Woman can oppose slavery while maintaining their femininity |
| Tone/Attitude | Argumentative, rhetorical questions |
| Annotations | Slavery and women - they tell us - but no - liberty and slavery - can we not contribute - North vs. tyrants - ruin domestic happiness - women & national affairs - rushing to destruction - USA dear to women - onward! |

| Questions 43-52 | Antibiotics and Bacteria |
| --- | --- |
| Type | Science (Paired without Data) |
| Purpose | Handwerk 1: to explain an innovated antibiotic and its implications |
| | Livermore: to argue that the method of the study is promising even if the drug may not be |
| Thesis/Topic | Handwerk: Lewis's research has produced a drug diseases are not resistant to |
| | Livermore: Lewis's research has methodological elegance, but Teix may be too costly |
| Attitude: | Handwerk: laudatory |
| | Livermore: Cautious and qualified optimism |
| Annotations | Drug resistance & antibiotics - new drug - no resistance - fungi - environment - experiment - uncultured soil - lipid v. proteins - antibiotics - elegance - less exciting - pros & cons - big, difficult to grow - trials - costly |
| Agree/Disagree | Agree: We need antibiotics that bacteria are not resistant to |
| | Disagree: Teixobactin is a breakthrough drug |

Lesson 11: Mastering Your Review

## Question Review (Question and Answer Types)

| Questions | General | Specific | Synthesis | Answers | Reason |
|---|---|---|---|---|---|
| Main Purpose | Purpose | Function | | Wrong | Somewhat right, but too broad |
| Main Idea | Thesis | Topic | | Wrong | Somewhat right, but too narrow |
| Tone | Tone | Attitude | | Wrong | Somewhat right, but too extreme |
| Rhetoric | Structure | Argument | | Wrong | Tempting words, but wrong part |
| Vocabulary | | Vocabulary | | Wrong | Tempting words, but not true |
| Evidence | | Evidence | | Wrong | Tempting words, but irrelevant |
| Detail | | Detail | | Wrong | Flatly false |
| Inference | | Inference | | Right (general) | Give identify evidence |
| Data | | Data Specific | Data Synthesis | Right (specific) | Give line or annotation evidence |
| Paired | | Paired Specific | Paired Synthesis | Right (synthesis) | Give identify evidence |

| | Recognize | Why My Answer Is Wrong | Why the Correct Answer Is Right |
|---|---|---|---|
| 1 | | | |
| 2 | | | |
| 4 | | | |
| 5 | | | |
| 6 | | | |
| 7 | | | |
| 8 | | | |
| 9 | | | |
| 10 | | | |
| 11 | | | |
| 12 | | | |
| 13 | | | |
| 14 | | | |
| 15 | | | |
| 16 | | | |
| 17 | | | |
| 18 | | | |
| 19 | | | |
| 20 | | | |
| 21 | | | |

| Recognize | Why My Answer Is Wrong | Why the Correct Answer Is Right |
|---|---|---|
| 22 | | |
| 23 | | |
| 24 | | |
| 25 | | |
| 26 | | |
| 27 | | |
| 28 | | |
| 29 | | |
| 30 | | |
| 31 | | |
| 32 | | |
| 33 | | |
| 34 | | |
| 35 | | |
| 36 | | |
| 37 | | |
| 38 | | |
| 39 | | |
| 40 | | |
| 41 | | |
| 42 | | |
| 43 | | |
| 44 | | |
| 45 | | |
| 46 | | |
| 47 | | |
| 48 | | |
| 49 | | |
| 50 | | |
| 51 | | |
| 52 | | |

|  | Family Ink | Null Results | Guppy Evolution | Woman and Slavery | Antibiotics and Bacteria |
|---|---|---|---|---|---|
| Purpose |  | 9.1.11 |  | 9.1.32 |  |
| Function |  | 9.1.13 | 9.1.21 |  | 9.1.43 |
|  |  |  | 9.1.24 |  | 9.1.48 |
| Thesis | 9.1.2 |  |  |  |  |
| Topic |  |  |  | 9.1.35 |  |
| Tone |  |  |  |  |  |
| Attitude | 9.1.3 |  |  |  |  |
| Structure | 9.1.1 |  |  |  |  |
| Argument |  | 9.1.12 | 9.1.23 | 9.1.33 |  |
|  |  |  | 9.1.26 | 9.1.34 |  |
| Vocab | 9.1.9 | 9.1.15 | 9.1.25 | 9.1.39 | 9.1.47 |
|  | 9.1.10 | 9.1.18 |  | 9.1.40 |  |
| Evidence | 9.1.5 | 9.1.17 | 9.1.28 | 9.1.37 | 9.1.45 |
|  | 9.1.8 |  |  | 9.1.42 | 9.1.52 |
| Detail | 9.1.6 |  | 9.1.22 | 9.1.36 | 9.1.44 |
|  |  |  |  | 9.1.38 |  |
| Inference | 9.1.4 | 9.1.14 | 9.1.27 | 9.1.41 | 9.1.46 |
|  | 9.1.7 | 9.1.16 |  |  |  |
| Data (Detail) |  | 9.1.19 | 9.1.29 |  |  |
|  |  |  | 9.1.30 |  |  |
| Data (Synthesis) |  | 9.1.20 | 9.1.31 |  |  |
| Paired (Inference) |  |  |  |  | 9.1.51 |
| Paired (Synthesis) |  |  |  |  | 9.1.49 |
|  |  |  |  |  | 9.1.50 |

## Test 10 Review

## SELF-EVALUATION TEST 10

| | | | | | | |
|---|---|---|---|---|---|---|
| **Passage 1** | I felt confident during the first passage. | Strongly Agree | Somewhat Agree | No Opinion | Somewhat Disagree | Strongly Disagree |
| | Describe in two to three sentences how you felt on the first passage | | | | | |
| **Passage 2** | I felt confident during the second passage. | Strongly Agree | Somewhat Agree | No Opinion | Somewhat Disagree | Strongly Disagree |
| | Describe in two to three sentences how you felt on the second passage | | | | | |
| **Passage 3** | I felt confident during the third passage. | Strongly Agree | Somewhat Agree | No Opinion | Somewhat Disagree | Strongly Disagree |
| | Describe in two to three sentences how you felt on the third passage | | | | | |
| **Passage 4** | I felt confident during the fourth passage. | Strongly Agree | Somewhat Agree | No Opinion | Somewhat Disagree | Strongly Disagree |
| | Describe in two to three sentences how you felt on the fourth passage | | | | | |
| **Passage 5** | I felt confident during the fifth passage. | Strongly Agree | Somewhat Agree | No Opinion | Somewhat Disagree | Strongly Disagree |
| | Describe in two to three sentences how you felt on the fifth passage | | | | | |
| **Overall** | I felt confident during the reading section. | Strongly Agree | Somewhat Agree | No Opinion | Somewhat Disagree | Strongly Disagree |
| | I had enough time for the reading section. | Strongly Agree | Somewhat Agree | No Opinion | Somewhat Disagree | Strongly Disagree |
| | I cared about the passages I read. | Strongly Agree | Somewhat Agree | No Opinion | Somewhat Disagree | Strongly Disagree |
| | In three to four sentences, describe how you feel about the reading section | | | | | |

Lesson 11: Mastering Your Review

## Passage Review (Annotations and Identification)

| Questions 1-10 | Baghdad, Georgia |
|---|---|
| Type | Literature |
| Purpose | To describe the arrival of the worldly new school-teacher |
| Thesis/Topic | A well-traveled outsider comes to a small town to teach |
| Tone/Attitude | Miss Spivey is confident/brash/arrogant; the townspeople are simpler |
| Annotations | Miss Spivey - confident - school-teacher - worldly - education - pompous - famous - transition to Threestep - old map - sailing - North Africa - camels - ?? - mistake |

| Questions 11-21 | Traffic and the Environment |
|---|---|
| Type | Science (with Data) |
| Purpose | To explain a surprising relationship between mass transportation and the environment |
| Thesis/Topic | To decrease transportation pollution, transportation needs to be less convenient |
| Tone/Attitude | Surprising, startling |
| Annotations | Get worse - backfire - replace - commuters - steps - worse - expansion - incentives - spaces led to use - inconvenience is the goal |
| Data | Figure 1: Independent variable: alteration of traffic |
| | Dependent variable: overall change in traffic |
| | Decreasing access leads to an overall reduction in vehicle use |
| | Figure 2: How might changing traffic affect driving behavior? |

| Questions 22-32 | Nerve Fibers |
|---|---|
| Type | Science (without Data) |
| Purpose | To explain how fast and slow nerve fibers respond to stimuli |
| Thesis/Topic | Slow nerve fibers respond to touch and carry emotional information |
| Tone/Attitude | Technical, probing |
| Annotations | Fast + slow nerves - 1993 study - delayed signals - 2nd study - why? - hair - more ?'s - patient GL - results - emotion |

| Questions 33-42 | American Imperialism |
|---|---|
| Type | History (Paired, Antiquated) |
| Purpose | To argue whether or not an American Empire would be a good (and liberating) thing |
| Thesis/Topic | Beveridge: God has given America the gifts and rights to govern a global empire |
| | Bryan: America has always stood for liberty and freedom from empires |
| Tone/Attitude | Beveridge: Glorious account of America's history |
| | Bryan: Condemnation of imperial attitudes |
| Annotations | Beveridge: Noble USA - imperialism - blood - working folk - God - history of expansion - American invasions of liberty - Cuba |
| | Bryan: Republican - history - is this liberty? - America opposed to colonialism - not liberty affects |
| Agree/Disagree | Agree: America's history supports the ideals of liberty |
| | Disagree: American imperialism is not liberty if the natives don't want it |

| Questions 43-52 | Weed Control |
|---|---|
| Type | Science (with Data) |
| Purpose | Explain how plowing fields at different times affects weed growth |
| Thesis/Topic | Plowing fields at night dramatically reduces the number of weeds that grow in a field |
| Attitude: | Straightforward, but shocking results |
| Annotations | weeds + plowing - weed seeds - question - test - results - plow in day - plow @ night - effective? - YES! - dramatic results - more studies |
| Data | Independent variable - time of plowing |
| | Dependent variable - weed growth |
| | Almost all darkness had fewer seeds than light (only G) |

Lesson 11: Mastering Your Review

## Question Review (Question and Answer Types)

| Questions | General | Specific | Synthesis | Answers | Reason |
|---|---|---|---|---|---|
| Main Purpose | Purpose | Function | | Wrong | Somewhat right, but too broad |
| Main Idea | Thesis | Topic | | Wrong | Somewhat right, but too narrow |
| Tone | Tone | Attitude | | Wrong | Somewhat right, but too extreme |
| Rhetoric | Structure | Argument | | Wrong | Tempting words, but wrong part |
| Vocabulary | | Vocabulary | | Wrong | Tempting words, but not true |
| Evidence | | Evidence | | Wrong | Tempting words, but irrelevant |
| Detail | | Detail | | Wrong | Flatly false |
| Inference | | Inference | | Right (general) | Give identify evidence |
| Data | | Data Specific | Data Synthesis | Right (specific) | Give line or annotation evidence |
| Paired | | Paired Specific | Paired Synthesis | Right (synthesis) | Give identify evidence |

| | Recognize | Why My Answer Is Wrong | Why the Correct Answer Is Right |
|---|---|---|---|
| 1 | | | |
| 2 | | | |
| 4 | | | |
| 5 | | | |
| 6 | | | |
| 7 | | | |
| 8 | | | |
| 9 | | | |
| 10 | | | |
| 11 | | | |
| 12 | | | |
| 13 | | | |
| 14 | | | |
| 15 | | | |
| 16 | | | |
| 17 | | | |
| 18 | | | |
| 19 | | | |
| 20 | | | |
| 21 | | | |

| | Recognize | Why My Answer Is Wrong | Why the Correct Answer Is Right |
|---|---|---|---|
| 22 | | | |
| 23 | | | |
| 24 | | | |
| 25 | | | |
| 26 | | | |
| 27 | | | |
| 28 | | | |
| 29 | | | |
| 30 | | | |
| 31 | | | |
| 32 | | | |
| 33 | | | |
| 34 | | | |
| 35 | | | |
| 36 | | | |
| 37 | | | |
| 38 | | | |
| 39 | | | |
| 40 | | | |
| 41 | | | |
| 42 | | | |
| 43 | | | |
| 44 | | | |
| 45 | | | |
| 46 | | | |
| 47 | | | |
| 48 | | | |
| 49 | | | |
| 50 | | | |
| 51 | | | |
| 52 | | | |

|  | Baghdad, Georgia | Traffic and the Environment | Nerve Fibers | American Imperialism | Weed Control |
| --- | --- | --- | --- | --- | --- |
| Purpose |  | 10.1.11 |  |  |  |
| Function | 10.1.5<br>10.1.6 |  | 10.1.28<br>10.1.30 | 10.1.34 | 10.1.44 |
| Thesis |  |  |  | 10.1.33 |  |
| Topic |  |  |  |  |  |
| Tone |  |  |  |  |  |
| Attitude | 10.1.2 |  |  |  |  |
| Structure | 10.1.1 |  |  |  |  |
| Argument |  | 10.1.12<br>10.0.14 |  |  | 10.1.46 |
| Vocab |  | 10.1.13<br>10.1.18 | 10.1.24<br>10.1.25 | 10.1.35<br>10.1.38 | 10.1.45<br>10.1.49 |
| Evidence | 10.1.4<br>10.1.10 | 10.1.16 | 10.1.23<br>10.1.27 | 10.1.37<br>10.1.42 | 10.1.48 |
| Detail | 10.1.8<br>10.1.9 | 10.1.17 | 10.1.26<br>10.1.30<br>10.1.32 |  | 10.1.43 |
| Inference | 10.1.3<br>10.1.7 | 10.1.15 | 10.1.22<br>10.1.29 | 10.1.36 | 10.1.47 |
| Data (Detail) |  | 10.1.19<br>10.1.20 |  |  | 10.1.50<br>10.1.51 |
| Data (Synthesis) |  | 10.1.20 |  |  | 10.1.52 |
| Paired (Inference) |  |  |  | 10.1.41 |  |
| Paired (Synthesis) |  |  |  | 10.1.39<br>10.1.40 |  |

# LESSON 12: UNDERSTANDING WHAT'S NEXT

You've done the hardest part: **You studied hard and fought the beast**. Now comes the second hardest part: waiting for your scores to come back.

First, the you should **give yourself a few days to recover** from the test. The SAT is a big deal! Give yourself a break if you need it.

Second, **don't be afraid to take the SAT a second or third time**. This is common. in fact, more than half the people who take the test will take it multiple times. It doesn't show weakness; if anything, it shows perseverance and determination. I've tutored some students whose schools *required* them to take the test three times.

When you're figuring out what comes next, there are some things to do before you get your scores and some things to do after your get your sores.

## BEFORE YOU GET YOUR SCORES

Typically, scores are returned two to three weeks after the test date. Historically, the June scores have come back a little later (the College Board puts a priority on scoring AP tests), but most of the time you can expect to get your scores a few weeks before the next test. However, this short timeline doesn't always give you time to prepare. It's good to have a plan ready before you get your scores.

From an admissions perspective, there is little reason not to take the test again. Schools don't look down on your persistence. There are, however, some questions to ask yourself as you wait:

- **What score would you be happy with?** You can reasonably expect a score on the SAT that is within 30 to 50 points of your practice test scores. Some students find the adrenaline of test day sharpens their focus and their scores go up a touch, while others find they score better at home that on test day. You may also find some 50/50 guesses go your way and some don't. If you wouldn't be happy with a 50-point jump, you should prepare to take the test again.

- **Are you going to do anything differently this time?** Taking the test again without changing anything is likely to give you the same results. Do you have the time between tests to review practice tests, refine your test-taking strategies, or try out some of the online bonus content available at www.professorscompanion.com? If you're not going to change anything, you shouldn't expect a score boost. You may gain a couple of points by calming nerves, but without studying, things don't usually improve much.

- **What is the opportunity cost of taking the test again?** In economics, "opportunity cost" is the value of your next best alternative. For example, let's say you have the choice to go to the beach with your friends or pick up a few hours at your summer job. If you go to the beach, you'll pay for parking and a hamburger and soda ($15). If you work a few hours, you'll make $40. The opportunity cost of the beach is that $40 (meaning you bank account has $55 less in it), while the opportunity cost of working is the time at the beach. You have to choose what you'd rather do. It's the same with the SAT. If you have to choose between studying for your AP U.S. History test or taking the SAT, you may want to focus on the AP. If you have to choose between taking the test and going to the beach, you may want to buckle down for one more run at the SAT.

## AFTER YOU GET YOUR SCORES

Good news! Whatever your score was on test day, this is the lowest possible score admissions offices will ever see. If you take the test again and score lower, they'll take this test score when they consider your application. If your score goes up, those are bonus points!

In addition to the questions above, you should ask yourself these questions as you consider whether or not to take the test again.

- **Was your score from this test in keeping with your practice test scores?** Practice test scores are the best indication of how you will score on test day. If your practice test scores are consistently higher than your score on the official test, it isn't unreasonable to project a better score if you take the test again. If, on the other hand, your test score is in line with practice tests, you can't just assume that the scores will get better the next time around without putting in effort.

- **Did something out of the ordinary happen on test day to affect your scores?** Sometimes life conspires against you. Students get the flu or go through break-ups. One of my students slipped on the ice on her way to the test and gave herself a concussion. These sort of things are unfortunate, but there really isn't anything you can do to prevent them from happening. Taking the test again because of things outside of your control is frustrating, but it's also often the right choice.

- **Do you have anything left to prove to yourself?** This can be the hardest question of all to answer, but it's also the one that is most important. When I was in high school, my parents were happy with my score, but I wasn't. I knew I could do better. I let them talk me out of taking the test again. I'm happy with the college I attended, but I'll never know what my best score could have been.

In the end, the question of whether or not you should take the test again comes down boils down to two questions.

1. Are you happy with your score?

2. Are you willing and able to do the work to improve?

If the answer to the first question is "yes" and the answer to the second question is "no"—**congratulations**! Keep your grades up, get that application essay in order, and work on the skills you'll need for college.

If you're looking for more, however, you'll need to take the test again.

## TAKING THE TEST AGAIN: STUDYING AND REVIEWING

**The best thing you can do to study is to read**. It is a reading test, after all. Whether your reading for school or pleasure, reading every day, even if only for 5 to 10 minutes, will help.

Reading on your own will hone your ability to concentrate on test day. In lesson 8, we worked on focusing as you read. I also recommended some books for you to check out (page 148). You should also check out the bonus passages at www.professorscompanion.com/reading.

You may also want to pick up a copy of The Professor's Companion's *SAT & ACT Reading Workbook: 50 Passages for You to Read, Enjoy, and Prep for the Test*. You can find this on amazon.com or directly at www.professorscompanion.com/reading-workbook. You'll get 50 passages keyed to things you already like America history, superhero movies, or dystopian literature. You'll also get 300+ questions designed to help you work on your questions-answering skills.

### If You Did the Crash Course

It's a classic "good news, bad news" situation. The good news is that you've plenty of material to study. You've only done about 30% of the book, which means you've got 70% of the book left to do.

Whether or you think this is good news or bad news is up to you, I suppose. Nobody gets better without working at it. Take a look back at page 6 and plot out lessons until the next test. If you have the time, work through the whole of the book. If you are waiting for test scores to be released, focus on **lesson 4** on **mastering question types**, lesson 7 on **mastering passage types** and **lesson 8** on **mastering the clock**.

### If You Did the Complete Course

If you're going to take the test again, make sure you are pushing yourself to do your best. This means **reviewing everything:** old tests, Khan Academy practice passages, the practice passages in this book, and the bonus passages at www.professorscompanion.com/reading.

As you review, look for patterns in the passages:

- If you want to review passages, head t **lesson 2** and your **underline**, **annotate**, and **identify** skills.

- If you are finding one type of passage, review **lesson 7** to hone your **passage strategies.**

You should also review your work with the questions:

Epilogue: Taking the Test Again

- If you are feeling like the passages are going well, but that the questions are tripping you up, review **lesson 3** on **restate** and **recall** and **lesson 4** on **recognizing** questions

- If the answers are tripping you up, review **lesson 5** on **correct and incorrect answers** and **resolving questions**.

- If you want to hone the questions and answers further, spend more time with **lesson 9** and the **Khan Academy** worksheets.

For a more comprehensive overview, look at the whole test:

- If your timing needs work, review **lesson 6** on **pacing each passage**.

- If you want to keep yourself engaged, you can also review **lesson 8** on **focusing for 13 minutes**.

Finally, you can look at the passage, questions, and answers as a composite.

- If you want to stretch yourself, work on **lesson 10** and the **Build-a-Passage Workshop**.

- If you need to review it all, go through everything in **lesson 11**. Review **your old tests**; check your **annotations and identifications** against my samples. Look at all the questions and figure out why their **correct answers are right** and your **incorrect answers are wrong**.

## TAKING THE TEST AGAIN: DOING YOUR BEST

Taking the test again can be frustrating, but it's also your chance to cash in on all the work you've done. **Keep pushing yourself.** You won't improve if you don't work at it. **Do what you can to do your best.** Study hard, and good luck!


-Tom

# SOLUTIONS

## HOW TO USE THE SOLUTION MANUAL

In the solutions that follow, you'll get a lot of information, but it's information that matches the way you've been prepped for the test. This means that you'll see how I would read the passage and answer the questions using the lessons from this book. If this is a little confusing at first, that's okay. As you work your way through the book (especially lessons 2-5) the solutions should make more sense.

### Underline, Annotate, and Identify (Lesson 2)

On the first page, you'll get my solutions for **underline**, **annotate**, and **identify** (Lesson 2). These passages are the actual annotations that I use when I teach students. I try to practice what I preach. This means a few things.

- You'll see that I sometimes underline things that don't factor into the questions. *That's okay!* In fact, if all of your underlining matches the questions, it's not very realistic.

- My annotates are brief: again, 2-4 words is 1-2 times per paragraph. Yours may be different. *That's okay!* These were the things that stuck out to me when I was reading. Other things may have stuck out to you.

- I identify the purpose (explain/argue/describe characters). I also identify the author's main topic or thesis and the tone. *Minor differences are fine* (I said to explain brine, you said to explain liquid), but *major differences* (to explain life) may have led to errors.

### Quick Answer Key

On the next pages, you'll look over the questions. You can start with looking at the questions, checking to see why your incorrect answers are wrong and the correct answers are right.

|    |   | Question Type | Why My Incorrect Answer Is Wrong | Why the Correct Answer is Right |
|----|---|---------------|----------------------------------|--------------------------------|
| 1  | C |               |                                  |                                |
| 2  | D |               |                                  |                                |
| 4  | A |               |                                  |                                |
| 5  | A |               |                                  |                                |
| 6  | C |               |                                  |                                |
| 7  | B |               |                                  |                                |
| 8  | A |               |                                  |                                |
| 9  | B |               |                                  |                                |
| 10 | C |               |                                  |                                |

# Recognize, Recognize, Restate, Recall, and Resolve (Lessons 3, 4, and 5)

Next, you'll get a deeper look at the questions, starting with **Recognize, Restate, Recall, and Resolve** to answer each question. On the following pages, you'll find filled out solutions using this template.

**2**

| Recognize | _____ | Answer Type | _____ |
| Restate   | _____ | Answer Type | _____ |
|           |                | Answer Type | _____ |
| Recall    | _____ | Answer Type | _____ |
|           | _____ | Resolve  Ⓐ Ⓑ Ⓒ ● | Confidence ___/5 |

Let's use question 2 on *A Jury of Her Peers* as an example.

**2**

The second paragraph (lines 11-17) indicates that

Typically, I **recognize** the question type (Lesson 4) for every question.

If you haven't read Lesson 4 yet, especially if you're doing the crash course, that's okay. You may have some differences between your question identification and mine. I may call something a detail question that you call a topic question. Consider, for example, question 2 from *A Jury of Her Peers*.

Question 2 could reasonably be called a topic or a detail question, but it's not an attitude or structure question.

| Questions | General | Specific | Synthesis |
|---|---|---|---|
| Main Purpose | Purpose | Function | |
| Main Idea | Thesis | Topic | |
| Tone | Tone | Attitude | |
| Rhetoric | Structure | Argument | |
| Vocabulary | | Vocabulary | |
| Evidence | | Evidence | |
| Detail | | Detail | |
| Inference | | Inference | |
| Data | | Data Specific | Data Synthesis |
| Paired | | Paired Specific | Paired Synthesis |

After I have my shorthand question type identification, I move on to **restate**, **recall** (Lesson 3) and **resolve** (Lesson 5). When I'm taking a test, I usually do this in my head, but I will write out my paraphrasing and answering when I'm less confident.

**Restate:** I write out my paraphrased question from the prompt. I try to keep these short; I'm trying to jolt my brain to answering their prompt, not writing the perfect question. (Lesson 3)

**Recall:** I answer my paraphrased question. I try to keep these brief as well. These are my guide to the correct multiple choice answer, not a complete answer that I might would want to turn in on a reading quiz. (Lesson 3)

## 2

| | | | |
|---|---|---|---|
| Recognize | Detail | Answer Type | |
| Restate | What does ¶2 say? | Answer Type | |
| | | Answer Type | |
| Recall | She went with the group | Answer Type | |
| | | Resolve  Ⓐ Ⓑ Ⓒ ● | Confidence ___/5 |

**Resolve** I go through each of the four answer choices, deciding which ones are right (and what my evidence for this is) and which ones are wrong (and why).

The primary goal here is that you see why the correct answer is right and the incorrect answers are wrong. (Lesson 5). As with the question types, we may disagree on some of the reasons for answers being incorrect or evidence. Again, *this is okay*. I might think that lines 16-17 give the best evidence, but you think its lines 11-14. Perhaps the best answer would have been 11-17 (though this would be longer than they give for evidence questions). I might see an answer choice as "tempting words, but <u>not true</u>" that you see as "<u>not true</u>." Our thresholds for "right words" may be different. Some variation is to be expected.

| Answers | Reason |
|---|---|
| Wrong | Somewhat right, but <u>too broad</u> |
| Wrong | Somewhat right, but <u>too narrow</u> |
| Wrong | Somewhat right, but <u>too extreme</u> |
| Wrong | Tempting words, but <u>wrong part</u> |
| Wrong | Tempting words, but <u>not true</u> |
| Wrong | Tempting words, but <u>irrelevant</u> |
| Wrong | Flatly false |
| Right (general): | Give identify evidence |
| Right (specific): | Give line or annotation evidence |
| Right (synthesis): | Give identify evidence |

On the other hand, if you're saying that everything is "<u>not true</u>," you may want to see why a reasonable person could have arrived at this wrong answer.

## 2

| | | | |
|---|---|---|---|
| Recognize | Detail | Answer Type | Flatly false |
| Restate | What does ¶2 say? | Answer Type | Flatly false |
| | | Answer Type | Tempting words, but not true |
| Recall | She went with the group | Answer Type | Right (lines 16-17) |
| | | Resolve  Ⓐ Ⓑ Ⓒ ● | Confidence ___/5 |

I hope these solutions are helpful to you as you are working through the book. If you have questions about them, feel free to email me at tom@professorscompanion.com or check for updates at www.professorscompanion.com/reading. I'm always happy to help students score their best.

# ***LET US CALCULATE! (SOLUTION)***
## Underline, Annotate, and Identify

This passage is adapted from Jonathan Gray, "'Let Us Calculate!' Leibniz, Llull, and the Computational Imagination." 2016, Public Domain Review. Gottfried Wilhelm Leibniz (1646-1716) was a German mathematician and philosopher.

The seventeenth-century German polymath Gottfried Wilhelm Leibniz is best known for developing differential calculus, a mathematical innovation independent from that of the more famous
5 English mathematician and scientist Isaac Newton. Lesser known, however, are Leibniz's invention of the "stepped reckoner," an early precursor of the modern computer, and the crucial role Leibniz played in the history of computation and computational thinking.
10 In 1879, workmen fixing a leaking roof discovered a mysterious machine discarded in the corner of an attic at the University of Göttingen, Germany. With its cylinders of polished brass and oaken handles, the artifact was identified as one of a number of early
15 mechanical calculating devices that an aged Leibniz invented.

Supported by a network of professors, preachers, and friends—and developed with the technical assistance of a series of itinerant and precariously
20 employed clockmakers, mechanics, artisans, and even a butler—Leibniz's instrument aspired to provide less function than even the most basic of today's calculators. Through an intricate system of different sized wheels, the hand-crank operated device modestly
25 expanded the repertoire of possible operations to include multiplication and division as well as addition and subtraction.

The machine faltered through live demonstrations in London and Paris. Costing a small fortune to
30 construct, it suffered from a series of financial setbacks and technical issues. The Royal Society invited Leibniz to come back once it was fully operational. There is even speculation that—despite Leibniz's rhetoric spanning an impressive volume of letters and
35 publications—the machine never actually worked as intended.

Nevertheless, the instrument exercised a powerful grip on the imagination of later technicians. Leibniz's machine became part of textbook and industry
40 narratives about the development of computation. It was retrospectively integrated into the way that practitioners envisaged the history of their work. IBM acquired a functioning replica for their "antiques attic" collection. Scientist and inventor Stephen Wolfram
45 credits Leibniz with anticipating contemporary projects by "imagining a whole architecture for how knowledge would … be made computational." Recent writers have called Leibniz the "patron saint" of cybernetics and the "godfather of the modern
50 algorithm."

While Leibniz made groundbreaking contributions towards the modern binary number system as well as integral and differential calculus, his role in the history of computing amounts to more than the sum of his
55 scientific and technological accomplishments. He also advanced what we might consider a kind of "computational imaginary"—reflecting on the analytical and generative possibilities of rendering the world computable.

60 Leibniz believed that, just as all words in a language could be represented by the comparatively small number of letters in an alphabet, so the whole world of nature and thought could be considered in terms of a number of fundamental elements—an "alphabet of
65 human thought." By reformulating arguments and ideas in terms of a *characteristica universalis*, or universal language, all could be rendered computable. The combinatorial art would not only facilitate such analysis, but would also provide means to compose
70 new ideas, entities, inventions, and worlds.

Ultimately Leibniz hoped that a thought language of "pure" concepts, combined with formalized processes and methods akin to those used in mathematics, would lead to the mechanization and
75 automation of reason itself. By means of new artificial languages and methods, our ordinary and imperfect ways of reasoning with words and ideas would give way to a formal, symbolic, rule-governed science— conceived of as a computational process. Disputes,
80 conflict, and grievances arising from ill-formed opinions, emotional hunches, biases, prejudices, and misunderstandings would give way to consensus, peace, and progress.

## Quick Answer Key

| | Question Type | Why My Incorrect Answer Is Wrong | Why the Correct Answer is Right |
|---|---|---|---|
| 1 | C | | |
| 2 | A | | |
| 3 | B | | |
| 4 | A | | |
| 5 | D | | |
| 6 | C | | |
| 7 | B | | |
| 8 | D | | |
| 9 | C | | |
| 10 | C | | |

## Recognize, Restate, Recall, and Resolve

| Questions | General | Specific | Synthesis | Answers | Reason |
|---|---|---|---|---|---|
| Main Purpose | Purpose | Function | | Wrong | Somewhat right, but too broad |
| Main Idea | Thesis | Topic | | Wrong | Somewhat right, but too narrow |
| Tone | Tone | Attitude | | Wrong | Somewhat right, but too extreme |
| Rhetoric | Structure | Argument | | Wrong | Tempting words, but wrong part |
| Vocabulary | | Vocabulary | | Wrong | Tempting words, but not true |
| Evidence | | Evidence | | Wrong | Tempting words, but irrelevant |
| Detail | | Detail | | Wrong | Flatly false |
| Inference | | Inference | | Right (general): | Give identify evidence |
| Data | | Data Specific | Data Synthesis | Right (specific): | Give line or annotation evidence |
| Paired | | Paired Specific | Paired Synthesis | Right (synthesis): | Give identify evidence |

### 1

| | | | | |
|---|---|---|---|---|
| Recognize | Purpose | | Answer Type | Tempting words, but wrong part |
| Restate | What is the author's purpose? | | Answer Type | Somewhat right, but too broad |
| | | | Answer Type | Right (annotations) |
| Recall | To explain Leibniz's machine and its legacy | | Answer Type | Somewhat right, but too extreme |
| | | | Resolve | Ⓐ Ⓑ ● Ⓓ         Confidence ___/5 |

Solutions

## 2

| | | | |
|---|---|---|---|
| Recognize | Inference | Answer Type | Right (Lines 38-42) |
| Restate | What does the passage imply about Leibniz? | Answer Type | Tempting words, but <u>not</u> true |
| | | Answer Type | Tempting words, but <u>not</u> true |
| Recall | He had importance beyond the machine | Answer Type | Tempting words, but <u>not</u> true |
| | | Resolve | ● Ⓑ Ⓒ Ⓓ    Confidence ___/5 |

## 3

| | | | |
|---|---|---|---|
| Recognize | Evidence | Answer Type | Tempting words, but <u>not</u> true (C) |
| Restate | What is your evidence? | Answer Type | Right (lines) |
| | | Answer Type | Tempting words, but <u>not</u> true (B) |
| Recall | Lines 38-42 | Answer Type | Tempting words, but <u>not</u> true (D) |
| | | Resolve | Ⓐ ● Ⓒ Ⓓ    Confidence ___/5 |

## 4

| | | | |
|---|---|---|---|
| Recognize | Function | Answer Type | Right (annotations) |
| Restate | What's the function of ¶3 | Answer Type | Somewhat right, but <u>too extreme</u> |
| | | Answer Type | Flatly <u>false</u> |
| Recall | To describe Leibniz's machine | Answer Type | Flatly <u>false</u> |
| | | Resolve | ● Ⓑ Ⓒ Ⓓ    Confidence ___/5 |

## 5

| | | | |
|---|---|---|---|
| Recognize | Vocab | Answer Type | Tempting words, but <u>not</u> true |
| Restate | What does "exercised" mean? | Answer Type | Tempting words, but <u>not</u> true |
| | | Answer Type | Tempting words, but <u>not</u> true |
| Recall | had | Answer Type | Right (annotations) |
| | | Resolve | Ⓐ Ⓑ Ⓒ ●    Confidence ___/5 |

## 6

| | | | |
|---|---|---|---|
| Recognize | Inference | Answer Type | Tempting words, but <u>not</u> true |
| Restate | What does the final paragraph say? | Answer Type | Flatly <u>false</u> |
| | | Answer Type | Right (annotations) |
| Recall | Reason will make things better | Answer Type | Flatly <u>false</u> |
| | | Resolve | Ⓐ Ⓑ ● Ⓓ    Confidence ___/5 |

## 7

| | | | |
|---|---|---|---|
| Recognize | Attitude | Answer Type | Flatly false |
| Restate | What do they think about Leibniz | Answer Type | Right (annotations) |
| | | Answer Type | Somewhat right, but too extreme |
| Recall | They really like him | Answer Type | Flatly false |
| | | Resolve | Ⓐ ● Ⓒ Ⓓ    Confidence ___/5 |

## 8

| | | | |
|---|---|---|---|
| Recognize | Topic | Answer Type | Tempting words, but irrelevant |
| Restate | What is ¶5 about? | Answer Type | Somewhat right, but too broad |
| | | Answer Type | Flatly false |
| Recall | The machine's legacy | Answer Type | Right (annotations) |
| | | Resolve | Ⓐ Ⓑ Ⓒ ●    Confidence ___/5 |

## 9

| | | | |
|---|---|---|---|
| Recognize | Detail | Answer Type | Flatly false |
| Restate | How did Leibniz build his machine? | Answer Type | Tempting words, but not true |
| | | Answer Type | Right (¶3) |
| Recall | He had help | Answer Type | Tempting words, but irrelevant |
| | | Resolve | Ⓐ Ⓑ ● Ⓓ    Confidence ___/5 |

## 10

| | | | |
|---|---|---|---|
| Recognize | Evidence | Answer Type | Flatly false |
| Restate | What is your evidence? | Answer Type | Tempting words, but wrong part (D) |
| | | Answer Type | Right (annotations) |
| Recall | ¶3 | Answer Type | Tempting words, but not true (B) |
| | | Resolve | Ⓐ Ⓑ ● Ⓓ    Confidence ___/5 |

---

### Online Bonus Content

Want to see what other students how other students classified the correct and incorrect answers to "Let Us Calculate"? Submit your questions to tom@professorscompanion.com to add your work and to see other students' creations.

Solutions

***A JURY OF HER PEERS (SOLUTION)***

Underline, Annotate, and Identify

This passage is adapted from Susan Glaspell, "A Jury of Her Peers," written in 1917. The story takes place in early twentieth-century Iowa.

When Martha Hale opened the storm-door and got a cut of the north wind, she ran back for her big woolen scarf. As she hurriedly wound that round her head her eye made a scandalized sweep of her kitchen. It was no ordinary thing that called her away--it was probably further from ordinary than anything that had ever happened in Dickson County. But what her eye took in was that her kitchen was in no shape for leaving: her bread all ready for mixing, half the flour sifted and half unsifted.

She hated to see things half done; but she had been at that when the team from town stopped to get Mr. Hale, and then the sheriff came running in to say his wife wished Mrs. Hale would come too—adding, with a grin, that he guessed she was getting scared and wanted another woman along. So she had dropped everything right where it was.

"Martha!" now came her husband's impatient voice. "Don't keep folks waiting out here in the cold."

She again opened the storm-door, and this time joined the three men and the one woman waiting for her in the big two-seated buggy.

After she had the robes tucked around her, she took another look at the woman who sat beside her on the back seat. She had met Mrs. Peters the year before at the county fair, and the thing she remembered about her was that she didn't seem like a sheriff's wife. She was small and thin and didn't have a strong voice. Mrs. Gorman, sheriff's wife before Gorman went out and Peters came in, had a voice that somehow seemed to be backing up the law with every word. But if Mrs. Peters didn't look like a sheriff's wife, Peters made it up in looking like a sheriff. He was to a dot the kind of man who could get himself elected sheriff—a heavy man with a big voice, who was particularly genial with the law-abiding, as if to make it plain that he knew the difference between criminals and non-criminals. And right there it came into Mrs. Hale's mind, with a stab, that this man who was so pleasant and lively with all of them was going to the Wrights' now as a sheriff.

"The country's not very pleasant this time of year," Mrs. Peters at last ventured, as if she felt they ought to be talking as well as the men.

Mrs. Hale scarcely finished her reply, for they had gone up a little hill and could see the Wright place now, and seeing it did not make her feel like talking. It looked very lonesome this cold March morning. It had always been a lonesome-looking place. It was down in a hollow, and the poplar trees around it were lonesome-looking trees. The men were looking at it and talking about what had happened. The county attorney was bending to one side of the buggy, and kept looking steadily at the place as they drew up to it.

"I'm glad you came with me," Mrs. Peters said nervously, as the two women were about to follow the men in through the kitchen door.

Even after she had her foot on the door-step, her hand on the knob, Martha Hale had a moment of feeling she could not cross that threshold. And the reason it seemed she couldn't cross it now was simply because she hadn't crossed it before. Time and time again it had been in her mind, "I ought to go over and see Minnie Foster"—she still thought of her as Minnie Foster, though for twenty years she had been Mrs. Wright. And then there was always something to do and Minnie Foster would go from her mind. But now she could come.

The men went over to the stove. The women stood close together by the door. Young Henderson, the county attorney, turned around and said, "Come up to the fire, ladies."

Mrs. Peters took a step forward, then stopped. "I'm not—cold," she said.

And so the two women stood by the door, at first not even so much as looking around the kitchen.

The men talked for a minute about what a good thing it was the sheriff had sent his deputy out that morning to make a fire for them, and then Sheriff Peters stepped back from the stove, unbuttoned his outer coat, and leaned his hands on the kitchen table in a way that seemed to mark the beginning of official business. "Now, Mr. Hale," he said in a sort of semi-official voice, "before we move things about, you tell Mr. Henderson just what it was you saw when you came here yesterday morning."

## Quick Answer Key

| | Question Type | Why My Incorrect Answer Is Wrong | Why the Correct Answer is Right |
|---|---|---|---|
| 1 | B | | |
| 2 | D | | |
| 3 | C | | |
| 4 | A | | |
| 5 | D | | |
| 6 | A | | |
| 7 | B | | |
| 8 | D | | |
| 9 | A | | |
| 10 | C | | |

## Recognize, Restate, Recall, and Resolve

| Questions | General | Specific | Synthesis | Answers | Reason |
|---|---|---|---|---|---|
| Main Purpose | Purpose | Function | | Wrong | Somewhat right, but too broad |
| Main Idea | Thesis | Topic | | Wrong | Somewhat right, but too narrow |
| Tone | Tone | Attitude | | Wrong | Somewhat right, but too extreme |
| Rhetoric | Structure | Argument | | Wrong | Tempting words, but wrong part |
| Vocabulary | | Vocabulary | | Wrong | Tempting words, but not true |
| Evidence | | Evidence | | Wrong | Tempting words, but irrelevant |
| Detail | | Detail | | Wrong | Flatly false |
| Inference | | Inference | | Right (general): | Give identify evidence |
| Data | | Data Specific | Data Synthesis | Right (specific): | Give line or annotation evidence |
| Paired | | Paired Specific | Paired Synthesis | Right (synthesis): | Give identify evidence |

### 1

| | | | | |
|---|---|---|---|---|
| Recognize | Structure | Answer Type | Tempting words, but not true |
| Restate | How would you describe the passage? | Answer Type | Right (identify) |
| | | Answer Type | Tempting words, but not true |
| Recall | A woman journeys to her friend's house | Answer Type | Tempting words, but not true |
| | | Resolve | Ⓐ ● Ⓒ Ⓓ     Confidence ___/5 |

Solutions

## 2

| | | | |
|---|---|---|---|
| Recognize | Detail | Answer Type | Flatly false |
| Restate | What does ¶2 say? | Answer Type | Flatly false |
| | | Answer Type | Tempting words, but <u>not true</u> |
| Recall | She went with the group | Answer Type | Right (lines 16-17) |
| | | Resolve | ⒶⒷⓒ●     Confidence ___/5 |

## 3

| | | | |
|---|---|---|---|
| Recognize | Vocabulary | Answer Type | Tempting words, but <u>not true</u> |
| Restate | What does "dropped" mean? | Answer Type | Tempting words, but <u>not true</u> |
| | | Answer Type | Right (annotations) |
| Recall | Left | Answer Type | Flatly false |
| | | Resolve | ⒶⒷ●Ⓓ     Confidence ___/5 |

## 4

| | | | |
|---|---|---|---|
| Recognize | Vocabulary | Answer Type | Right (annotations) |
| Restate | What does "plain" mean? | Answer Type | Tempting words, but <u>not true</u> |
| | | Answer Type | Tempting words, but <u>not true</u> |
| Recall | Clear | Answer Type | Tempting words, but <u>not true</u> |
| | | Resolve | ●ⒷⒸⒹ     Confidence ___/5 |

## 5

| | | | |
|---|---|---|---|
| Recognize | Function | Answer Type | Somewhat right, but <u>too extreme</u> |
| Restate | What does the description of the voices do? | Answer Type | Flatly false |
| | | Answer Type | Tempting words, but <u>irrelevant</u> |
| Recall | Describe Mrs. Peters & Mrs. Gorman | Answer Type | Right (annotations) |
| | | Resolve | ⒶⒷⓒ●     Confidence ___/5 |

## 6

| | | | |
|---|---|---|---|
| Recognize | Inference | Answer Type | Right (annotations) |
| Restate | What does lines 41-43 suggest? | Answer Type | Flatly false |
| | | Answer Type | Flatly false |
| Recall | The men had been talking, but the women hadn't been | Answer Type | Somewhat right, but <u>too broad</u> |
| | | Resolve | ●ⒷⒸⒹ     Confidence ___/5 |

## 7

| | | | |
|---|---|---|---|
| Recognize | Attitude | Answer Type | Somewhat right, but too extreme |
| Restate | What is Mrs. Hale's attitude toward the house? | Answer Type | Right (lines 61-66) |
| | | Answer Type | Flatly false |
| Recall | She can't enter | Answer Type | Somewhat right, but too extreme |
| | | Resolve | Ⓐ ● Ⓒ Ⓓ       Confidence ___/5 |

## 8

| | | | |
|---|---|---|---|
| Recognize | Inference | Answer Type | Flatly false |
| Restate | What does ¶9 say about Mrs. Hale & Mrs. Wright | Answer Type | Tempting words, but not true |
| | | Answer Type | Flatly false |
| Recall | Mrs. Hale knew her when she was Minnie Foster | Answer Type | Right (lines 63-65) |
| | | Resolve | Ⓐ Ⓑ Ⓒ ●       Confidence ___/5 |

## 9

| | | | |
|---|---|---|---|
| Recognize | Inference | Answer Type | Right (lines 76-78) |
| Restate | What does the passage imply about the Wrights' house? | Answer Type | Tempting words, but not true |
| | | Answer Type | Tempting words, but not true |
| Recall | The deputy's fire warmed the kitchen | Answer Type | Flatly false |
| | | Resolve | ● Ⓑ Ⓒ Ⓓ       Confidence ___/5 |

## 10

| | | | |
|---|---|---|---|
| Recognize | Evidence | Answer Type | Tempting words, but wrong part (C) |
| Restate | What is your evidence? | Answer Type | Tempting words, but wrong part (B) |
| | | Answer Type | Right (annotations) |
| Recall | Lines 76-85 | Answer Type | Flatly false |
| | | Resolve | Ⓐ Ⓑ ● Ⓓ       Confidence ___/5 |

---

### Online Bonus Content

Want to see what other students how other students classified the correct and incorrect answers to "A Jury of Her Peers"? Submit your questions to tom@professorscompanion.com to add your work and to see other students' creations.

Solutions

# ***CIVIL RIGHTS ADDRESS (SOLUTION)***
## Underline, Annotate, and Identify

The following passage is adapted from President John F. Kennedy, "Civil Rights Address," originally delivered 11 June 1963. Kennedy addressed the nation after he federalized the Alabama National Guard to enforce the desegregation of the University of Alabama against the wishes of Alabama governor George Wallace.

This Nation was founded by men of many nations and backgrounds. It was founded on the principle that all men are created equal, and that the rights of every man are diminished when the rights of one man are threatened.

Today we are committed to a worldwide struggle to promote and protect the rights of all who wish to be free. And when Americans are sent to Vietnam or West Berlin, we do not ask for whites only. It ought to be possible, therefore, for American students of any color to attend any public institution they select without having to be backed up by troops.

It ought to be possible for American consumers of any color to receive equal service in places of public accommodation, such as hotels and restaurants and theaters and retail stores, without being forced to resort to demonstrations in the street, and it ought to be possible for American citizens of any color to register and to vote in a free election without interference or fear of reprisal.

It ought to be possible, in short, for every American to enjoy the privileges of being American without regard to his race or his color. In short, every American ought to have the right to be treated as he would wish to be treated, as one would wish his children to be treated. But this is not the case.

The Negro baby born in America today, regardless of the section of the Nation in which he is born, has about one-half as much chance of completing a high school as a white baby born in the same place on the same day, one-third as much chance of completing college, one-third as much chance of becoming a professional man, twice as much chance of becoming unemployed, about one-seventh as much chance of earning $10,000 a year, a life expectancy which is 7 years shorter, and the prospects of earning only half as much.

This is not a sectional issue. Difficulties over segregation and discrimination exist in every city, in every State of the Union, producing in many cities a rising tide of discontent that threatens the public safety. Nor is this a partisan issue. In a time of domestic crisis men of good will and generosity should be able to unite regardless of party or politics. This is not even a legal or legislative issue alone. It is better to settle these matters in the courts than on the streets, and new laws are needed at every level, but law alone cannot make men see right.

We are confronted primarily with a moral issue. It is as old as the scriptures and is as clear as the American Constitution.

The heart of the question is whether all Americans are to be afforded equal rights and equal opportunities, whether we are going to treat our fellow Americans as we want to be treated. If an American, because his skin is dark, cannot eat lunch in a restaurant open to the public, if he cannot send his children to the best public school available, if he cannot vote for the public officials who represent him, if, in short, he cannot enjoy the full and free life which all of us want, then who among us would be content to have the color of his skin changed and stand in his place? Who among us would then be content with the counsels of patience and delay?

One hundred years of delay have passed since President Lincoln freed the slaves, yet their heirs, their grandsons, are not fully free. They are not yet freed from the bonds of injustice. They are not yet freed from social and economic oppression. And this Nation, for all its hopes and all its boasts, will not be fully free until all its citizens are free.

We preach freedom around the world, and we mean it, and we cherish our freedom here at home, but are we to say to the world, and much more importantly, to each other that this is a land of the free except for the Negroes; that we have no second-class citizens except Negroes; that we have no class or caste system, no ghettoes, no master race except with respect to Negroes?

Now the time has come for this Nation to fulfill its promise. The events in Birmingham and elsewhere have so increased the cries for equality that no city or State or legislative body can prudently choose to ignore them

## Quick Answer Key

| | Question Type | Why My Incorrect Answer Is Wrong | Why the Correct Answer is Right |
|---|---|---|---|
| 1 | A | | |
| 2 | C | | |
| 3 | A | | |
| 4 | A | | |
| 5 | D | | |
| 6 | C | | |
| 7 | C | | |
| 8 | B | | |
| 9 | B | | |
| 10 | A | | |

## Recognize, Restate, Recall, and Resolve

| Questions | General | Specific | Synthesis | Answers | Reason |
|---|---|---|---|---|---|
| Main Purpose | Purpose | Function | | Wrong | Somewhat right, but too broad |
| Main Idea | Thesis | Topic | | Wrong | Somewhat right, but too narrow |
| Tone | Tone | Attitude | | Wrong | Somewhat right, but too extreme |
| Rhetoric | Structure | Argument | | Wrong | Tempting words, but wrong part |
| Vocabulary | | Vocabulary | | Wrong | Tempting words, but not true |
| Evidence | | Evidence | | Wrong | Tempting words, but irrelevant |
| Detail | | Detail | | Wrong | Flatly false |
| Inference | | Inference | | Right (general): | Give identify evidence |
| Data | | Data Specific | Data Synthesis | Right (specific): | Give line or annotation evidence |
| Paired | | Paired Specific | Paired Synthesis | Right (synthesis): | Give identify evidence |

### 1

| | | | |
|---|---|---|---|
| Recognize | Main purpose | Answer Type | Right (identification) |
| Restate | What is the main topic of the passage? | Answer Type | Somewhat right, but too narrow |
| | | Answer Type | Somewhat right, but too narrow |
| Recall | Racial inequality in America | Answer Type | Flatly false |
| | | Resolve | ●BCD  Confidence ___/5 |

Solutions

## 2

| | | | |
|---|---|---|---|
| Recognize | Function | Answer Type | Tempting words, but not true |
| Restate | What does the phrase "it ought to" do for the author? | Answer Type | Flatly false |
| | | Answer Type | Right (annotations) |
| Recall | Suggest the way things should be (but aren't) | Answer Type | Tempting words, but wrong part (¶8) |
| | | Resolve | Ⓐ Ⓑ ● Ⓓ     Confidence ___/5 |

## 3

| | | | |
|---|---|---|---|
| Recognize | Topic | Answer Type | Right (annotations) |
| Restate | What is the fourth paragraph about? | Answer Type | Tempting words, but not true |
| | | Answer Type | Flatly false |
| Recall | Statistics on race and inequality | Answer Type | Tempting words, but not true |
| | | Resolve | ● Ⓑ Ⓒ Ⓓ     Confidence ___/5 |

## 4

| | | | |
|---|---|---|---|
| Recognize | Vocab | Answer Type | Right (underlining) |
| Restate | What is "the rising tide of discontent?" | Answer Type | Flatly false |
| | | Answer Type | Flatly false |
| Recall | Political unrest | Answer Type | Flatly false |
| | | Resolve | ● Ⓑ Ⓒ Ⓓ     Confidence ___/5 |

## 5

| | | | |
|---|---|---|---|
| Recognize | Inference | Answer Type | Flatly false |
| Restate | What do lines 49-51 suggest? | Answer Type | Tempting words, but not true |
| | | Answer Type | Tempting words, but not true |
| Recall | Race has been an issue for a long time with a clear right and wrong | Answer Type | Right (underlining) |
| | | Resolve | Ⓐ Ⓑ Ⓒ ●     Confidence ___/5 |

## 6

| | | | |
|---|---|---|---|
| Recognize | Function | Answer Type | Tempting words, but not true |
| Restate | Why does Kennedy refer to Lincoln | Answer Type | Tempting words, but wrong part (¶5) |
| | | Answer Type | Right (underlining) |
| Recall | To show how long it's been that America has failed | Answer Type | Flatly false |
| | | Resolve | Ⓐ Ⓑ ● Ⓓ     Confidence ___/5 |

### 7

| | | | |
|---|---|---|---|
| Recognize | Argument | Answer Type | Somewhat right, but too narrow |
| Restate | How do the rhetorical questions help Kennedy's argument? | Answer Type | Tempting words, but not true |
| | | Answer Type | Right (underlining) |
| Recall | Put the white audience in the position of black Americans | Answer Type | Flatly false |
| | | Resolve | Ⓐ Ⓑ ● Ⓓ    Confidence ___/5 |

### 8

| | | | |
|---|---|---|---|
| Recognize | Detail | Answer Type | Tempting words, but not true |
| Restate | Where were problems with desegregation located? | Answer Type | Right (lines 38-48) |
| | | Answer Type | Flatly false |
| Recall | Across the US | Answer Type | Flatly false |
| | | Resolve | Ⓐ ● Ⓒ Ⓓ    Confidence ___/5 |

### 9

| | | | |
|---|---|---|---|
| Recognize | Evidence | Answer Type | Flatly false |
| Restate | What is your evidence? | Answer Type | Right (underlining) |
| | | Answer Type | Tempting words, but wrong part (D) |
| Recall | Lines 38-48 | Answer Type | Flatly false |
| | | Resolve | Ⓐ ● Ⓒ Ⓓ    Confidence ___/5 |

### 10

| | | | |
|---|---|---|---|
| Recognize | Tone | Answer Type | Right (identification) |
| Restate | What is the tone of the passage | Answer Type | Flatly false |
| | | Answer Type | Flatly false |
| Recall | forceful | Answer Type | Flatly false |
| | | Resolve | ● Ⓑ Ⓒ Ⓓ    Confidence ___/5 |

---

#### Online Bonus Content

Want to see what other students how other students classified the correct and incorrect answers to "Civil Rights Addres"?  Submit your questions to tom@professorscompanion.com to add your work and to see other students' creations.

Solutions

### ***MARS ROVER (SOLUTION)***
#### Underline, Annotate, and Identify

This passage is adapted from "NASA Mars Rover's Weather Data Bolster Case for Brine." 2015, NASA. Brines are salt-liquid solutions.

Martian weather and soil conditions that NASA's Curiosity rover has measured, together with a type of salt found in Martian soil, could put liquid brine in the soil at night.

[5] Calcium perchlorate identified in Martian soil by the Curiosity mission, and previously by NASA's Phoenix Mars Lander mission, has properties of absorbing water vapor from the atmosphere and lowering the freezing temperature of water. This has [10] been proposed for years as a mechanism for the possible presence of transient liquid brines at higher latitudes on modern Mars, despite the Red Planet's cold and dry conditions.

New calculations were based on more than a full [15] Mars year of temperature and humidity measurements by Curiosity. They indicate that conditions at the rover's near-equatorial location were favorable for small quantities of brine to form during some nights throughout the year, drying out again after sunrise. [20] Conditions should be even more appropriate at higher latitudes, where colder temperatures and more water vapor can result in higher relative humidity more often.

"Liquid water is a requirement for life as we know [25] it, and a target for Mars exploration missions," said the report's lead author, Javier Martin-Torres of the Spanish Research Council, Spain, and Lulea University of Technology, Sweden. "Conditions near the surface of present-day Mars are hardly favorable for microbial [30] life as we know it, but the possibility for liquid brines on Mars has wider implications for habitability and geological water-related processes."

Curiosity is the first mission to measure relative humidity in the Martian atmosphere close to the [35] surface and ground temperature through all times of day and all seasons of the Martian year. Relative humidity depends on the temperature of the air, as well as the amount of water vapor in it. Curiosity's measurements of relative humidity range from about [40] five percent on summer afternoons to 100 percent on autumn and winter nights.

The air that fills pores in the soil encounters the air just above the ground. When its relative humidity gets above a threshold level, salts can absorb enough water [45] molecules to become dissolved in liquid, a process called deliquescence. Perchlorate salts are especially good at this. Since perchlorate has been identified both at near-polar and near-equatorial sites, it may be present in soils all over the planet.

[50] "Gale Crater is one of the least likely places on Mars to have conditions for brines to form, compared to sites at higher latitudes or with more shading. So if brines can exist there, it strengthens the case they could form and persist even longer at many other [55] locations," said Alfred McEwen of the University of Arizona, who co-authored the new report.

Following its August 2012 landing, Curiosity found evidence for ancient streambeds and a lakebed environment more than three billion years old that [60] offered conditions favorable for microbial life. Now, the rover is examining a layered mountain inside Gale Crater for evidence for how ancient environmental conditions evolved.

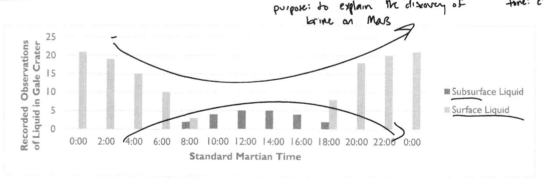

Figure 1 – Observations of liquid in Gale Crater. Adapted from Javier Martin-Torres et al.

## Quick Answer Key

| # | Answer | Question Type | Why My Incorrect Answer Is Wrong | Why the Correct Answer is Right |
|---|---|---|---|---|
| 1 | A | | | |
| 2 | A | | | |
| 3 | D | | | |
| 4 | B | | | |
| 5 | B | | | |
| 6 | B | | | |
| 7 | C | | | |
| 8 | D | | | |
| 9 | A | | | |
| 10 | C | | | |
| 11 | D | | | |
| 12 | A | | | |
| 13 | A | | | |
| 14 | C | | | |
| 15 | B | | | |
| 16 | A | | | |
| 17 | B | | | |
| 18 | C | | | |
| 19 | D | | | |
| 20 | B | | | |
| 21 | D | | | |

## Recognize, Restate, Recall, and Resolve

| Questions | General | Specific | Synthesis | Answers | Reason |
|---|---|---|---|---|---|
| Main Purpose | Purpose | Function | | Wrong | Somewhat right, but too broad |
| Main Idea | Thesis | Topic | | Wrong | Somewhat right, but too narrow |
| Tone | Tone | Attitude | | Wrong | Somewhat right, but too extreme |
| Rhetoric | Structure | Argument | | Wrong | Tempting words, but wrong part |
| Vocabulary | | Vocabulary | | Wrong | Tempting words, but not true |
| Evidence | | Evidence | | Wrong | Tempting words, but irrelevant |
| Detail | | Detail | | Wrong | Flatly false |
| Inference | | Inference | | Right (general): | Give identify evidence |
| Data | | Data Specific | Data Synthesis | Right (specific): | Give line or annotation evidence |
| Paired | | Paired Specific | Paired Synthesis | Right (synthesis): | Give identify evidence |

Solutions

## 1

| | | | |
|---|---|---|---|
| Recognize | Big purpose | Answer Type | Right (identify) |
| Restate | Why did the author write this:? | Answer Type | Somewhat right, but too extreme |
| | | Answer Type | Somewhat right, but too broad. |
| Recall | To explain liquid brines on Mars | Answer Type | Somewhat right, but too broad |
| | | Resolve | ●BCD        Confidence ___/5 |

## 2

| | | | |
|---|---|---|---|
| Recognize | Function | Answer Type | Right (annotations) |
| Restate | What does the final paragraph do? | Answer Type | Somewhat right, but too broad |
| | | Answer Type | Tempting words, but not true |
| Recall | Put discovery into context before and after | Answer Type | Tempting words, but not true |
| | | Resolve | ●BCD        Confidence ___/5 |

## 3

| | | | |
|---|---|---|---|
| Recognize | Thesis | Answer Type | Somewhat right, but too broad |
| Restate | What is the passage about? | Answer Type | Somewhat right, but too extreme |
| | | Answer Type | Tempting words, but not true |
| Recall | Liquid brines on Mars at night | Answer Type | Right (lines 1-5) |
| | | Resolve | ABC●        Confidence ___/5 |

## 4

| | | | |
|---|---|---|---|
| Recognize | Topic | Answer Type | Tempting words, but not true |
| Restate | What is ¶6 about? | Answer Type | Right (annotations) |
| | | Answer Type | Somewhat right, but too broad |
| Recall | How brines form | Answer Type | Flatly false |
| | | Resolve | A●CD        Confidence ___/5 |

## 5

| | | | |
|---|---|---|---|
| Recognize | Topic | Answer Type | Tempting words, but not true |
| Restate | What is ¶2 about? | Answer Type | Right (underlining) |
| | | Answer Type | Tempting words, but not true |
| Recall | Calcium Perchlorate confirmed on Mars | Answer Type | Tempting words, but not true |
| | | Resolve | ●BCD        Confidence ___/5 |

## 6

| | | | |
|---|---|---|---|
| Recognize | Tone | Answer Type | Somewhat right, but too extreme |
| Restate | What is the tone of the passage? | Answer Type | Right (identifications) |
| | | Answer Type | Flatly false |
| Recall | Excited, optimistic | Answer Type | Flatly false |
| | | Resolve | Ⓐ ● Ⓒ Ⓓ     Confidence ___/5 |

## 7

| | | | |
|---|---|---|---|
| Recognize | Attitude | Answer Type | Flatly false |
| Restate | How does McEwen feel? | Answer Type | Somewhat right, but too broad |
| | | Answer Type | Right (underlining) |
| Recall | Hopeful, encouraged | Answer Type | Somewhat right, but too extreme |
| | | Resolve | Ⓐ Ⓑ ● Ⓓ     Confidence ___/5 |

## 8

| | | | |
|---|---|---|---|
| Recognize | Structure | Answer Type | Flatly false |
| Restate | How can you describe the passage generically? | Answer Type | Tempting words, but not true |
| | | Answer Type | Somewhat right, but too extreme |
| Recall | A scientific discovery and its background/implications are discussed | Answer Type | Right (¶2 + ¶8) |
| | | Resolve | Ⓐ Ⓑ Ⓒ ●     Confidence ___/5 |

## 9

| | | | |
|---|---|---|---|
| Recognize | Argument | Answer Type | Right (lines 24-25) |
| Restate | What assumptions are made? | Answer Type | Tempting words, but not true |
| | | Answer Type | Flatly false |
| Recall | Higher latitudes are colder | Answer Type | Tempting words, but not true |
| | | Resolve | ● Ⓑ Ⓒ Ⓓ     Confidence ___/5 |

## 10

| | | | |
|---|---|---|---|
| Recognize | Structure | Answer Type | Tempting words, but not true |
| Restate | How is the passage organized? | Answer Type | Tempting words, but not true |
| | | Answer Type | Right (identify) |
| Recall | Discovery and then its evidence/implications | Answer Type | Flatly false |
| | | Resolve | Ⓐ Ⓑ ● Ⓓ     Confidence ___/5 |

Solutions

## 11

| | | | |
|---|---|---|---|
| Recognize | Vocab | Answer Type | Tempting words, but <u>not true</u> |
| Restate | What does "target" mean? | Answer Type | Tempting words, but <u>not true</u> |
| | | Answer Type | Flatly false |
| Recall | aim | Answer Type | Right (lines 28-32) |
| | | Resolve | Ⓐ Ⓑ Ⓒ ●    Confidence ___/5 |

## 12

| | | | |
|---|---|---|---|
| Recognize | Vocab | Answer Type | Right (line 42) |
| Restate | What does "encounter" mean? | Answer Type | Flatly false |
| | | Answer Type | Tempting words, but <u>not true</u> |
| Recall | Come into contact | Answer Type | Tempting words, but <u>not true</u> |
| | | Resolve | ● Ⓑ Ⓒ Ⓓ    Confidence ___/5 |

## 13

| | | | |
|---|---|---|---|
| Recognize | Detail | Answer Type | Right (lines 43-46) |
| Restate | When does calcium perchlorate absorb water? | Answer Type | Tempting words, but <u>not true</u> |
| | | Answer Type | Tempting words, but <u>wrong part</u> |
| Recall | When the relative humidity gets high enough (lines 43-46) | Answer Type | Flatly false |
| | | Resolve | ● Ⓑ Ⓒ Ⓓ    Confidence ___/5 |

## 14

| | | | |
|---|---|---|---|
| Recognize | Evidence | Answer Type | Tempting words, but <u>wrong part</u> (A) |
| Restate | What is your evidence? | Answer Type | Tempting words, but <u>wrong part</u> (D) |
| | | Answer Type | Right (B) |
| Recall | lines 43-46 | Answer Type | Tempting words, but <u>wrong part</u> (C) |
| | | Resolve | Ⓐ Ⓑ ● Ⓓ    Confidence ___/5 |

## 15

| | | | |
|---|---|---|---|
| Recognize | Detail | Answer Type | Flatly false |
| Restate | What do lines 5-9 say about the Curiosity mission? | Answer Type | Right (underlining) |
| | | Answer Type | Flatly false |
| Recall | Second mission to investigate brines on Mars | Answer Type | Tempting words, but <u>not true</u> |
| | | Resolve | Ⓐ ● Ⓒ Ⓓ    Confidence ___/5 |

### 16

| | | | |
|---|---|---|---|
| Recognize | Inference | Answer Type | Right (lines 20-23 + 51-52) |
| Restate | What does the passage imply about Gale Crater? | Answer Type | Flatly false |
| | | Answer Type | Tempting words, but not true |
| Recall | It is warmer than other places | Answer Type | Flatly false |
| | | Resolve | ●BCD    Confidence ___/5 |

### 17

| | | | |
|---|---|---|---|
| Recognize | Evidence | Answer Type | Tempting words, but wrong part (C) |
| Restate | What is your evidence? | Answer Type | Right (underlining) |
| | | Answer Type | Tempting words, but wrong part (B) |
| Recall | lines 20-23 + 51-52 | Answer Type | Tempting words, but wrong part (D) |
| | | Resolve | A●CD    Confidence ___/5 |

### 18

| | | | |
|---|---|---|---|
| Recognize | inference | Answer Type | Somewhat right, but too extreme |
| Restate | What does the passage imply about JMT? | Answer Type | Flatly false |
| | | Answer Type | Right (lines 30-32) |
| Recall | He thinks we might find microbial life someday | Answer Type | Flatly false |
| | | Resolve | AB●D    Confidence ___/5 |

### 19

| | | | |
|---|---|---|---|
| Recognize | Data synthesis | Answer Type | Flatly false |
| Restate | Where do the data and passage agree? | Answer Type | Flatly false |
| | | Answer Type | Flatly false |
| Recall | Surface liquid at night, subsurface during the day | Answer Type | Right (lines 16-19) |
| | | Resolve | ABC●    Confidence ___/5 |

### 20

| | | | |
|---|---|---|---|
| Recognize | Data synthesis | Answer Type | Flatly false |
| Restate | Where do the data and passage agree? | Answer Type | Right (Figure 1 @ 8:00-18:00) |
| | | Answer Type | Flatly false |
| Recall | Surface liquid at night, subsurface during the day | Answer Type | Flatly false |
| | | Resolve | A●CD    Confidence ___/5 |

Solutions

## 21

| | | | |
|---|---|---|---|
| Recognize | Data specific | Answer Type | Flatly false |
| Restate | When were the surface and subsurface most different? | Answer Type | Flatly false |
| | | Answer Type | Flatly false |
| Recall | In the middle of the night | Answer Type | Right (annotations) |
| | | Resolve | Ⓐ Ⓑ Ⓒ ●    Confidence ___/5 |

---

### Online Bonus Content

Want to see what other students did with "NASA Mars Rover's Weather Data Bolster Case for Brine"? Submit your questions to tom@professorscompanion.com to add your work and to see other students' creations.

# ***REMEMBER THE LADIES (SOLUTION)***

## Underline, Annotate, and Identify

Passage 1 is adapted from Abigail Adams's letter to her husband John Adams, March 31, 1776. Passage 2 is adapted from John Adams's response, April 14, 1776.

### Passage 1

[independency] I long to hear that you have declared an independency. And, by the way, in the new code of laws which I suppose it will be necessary for you to
5 make, I desire you would remember the ladies and be more generous and favorable to them than your ancestors. [limit power] Do not put such unlimited power into the hands of the husbands. Remember, all men would be tyrants if they could. If particular care and attention is
10 [tyrants] not paid to the ladies, we are determined to foment a rebellion, and will not hold ourselves bound by any laws in which we have no voice or representation.
   That your sex are naturally tyrannical is a truth so thoroughly established as to admit of no dispute; but
15 such of you as wish to be happy willingly give up the harsh title of master for the more tender and endearing one of friend. Why, then, not put it out of the power of the vicious and the lawless to use us with cruelty and indignity with impunity? Men of sense in all ages
20 abhor those customs which treat us only as the vassals of your sex; regard us then [protection] as beings placed by Providence under your protection, and in imitation of the Supreme Being make use of that power only for our happiness.

### Passage 2

25  As to Declarations of Independency, be patient …
   As to your extraordinary code of laws, I cannot but laugh. We have been told that our struggle has [unrest] loosened the bands of government everywhere: that children and apprentices were disobedient; that
30 schools and colleges were grown turbulent; that Indians slighted their guardians and Negroes grew insolent to their masters.
   But your letter was the [women's threat] first intimation that another tribe more numerous and powerful than all the rest
35 were grown discontented. This is rather too coarse a compliment but you are so saucy, I wont blot it out.
   Depend upon it, [not really in control] we know better than to repeal our masculine systems. Although they are in full force, you know they are little more than theory. We dare not
40 exert our power in its full latitude. We are obliged to go fair, and softly, and in practice you know we are the subjects. We have only the name of masters, and rather than give up this, [women's despotism] which would completely subject us to the despotism of the petticoat, I hope General
45 Washington, and all our brave heroes would fight. I am sure every good politician would plot, as long as he

would against despotism, empire, monarchy, aristocracy, oligarchy, or ochlocracy[1] — a fine story

[1] Mob Rule

Agree: Despotism and strife are bad
Disagree: who is in control, women or men?
tone 1: principled, matter of fact
tone 2: defensive, sarcastic

## Quick Answer Key

| | | Question Type | Why My Incorrect Answer Is Wrong | Why the Correct Answer is Right |
|---|---|---|---|---|
| 1 | C | | | |
| 2 | B | | | |
| 3 | A | | | |
| 4 | C | | | |

## Recognize, Restate, Recall, and Resolve

| Questions | General | Specific | Synthesis | Answers | Reason |
|---|---|---|---|---|---|
| Main Purpose | Purpose | Function | | Wrong | Somewhat right, but too broad |
| Main Idea | Thesis | Topic | | Wrong | Somewhat right, but too narrow |
| Tone | Tone | Attitude | | Wrong | Somewhat right, but too extreme |
| Rhetoric | Structure | Argument | | Wrong | Tempting words, but wrong part |
| Vocabulary | | Vocabulary | | Wrong | Tempting words, but not true |
| Evidence | | Evidence | | Wrong | Tempting words, but irrelevant |
| Detail | | Detail | | Wrong | Flatly false |
| Inference | | Inference | | Right (general): | Give identify evidence |
| Data | | Data Specific | Data Synthesis | Right (specific): | Give line or annotation evidence |
| Paired | | Paired Specific | Paired Synthesis | Right (synthesis): | Give identify evidence |

### 1

| | | | |
|---|---|---|---|
| Recognize | Paired synthesis | Answer Type | Tempting words, but wrong part |
| Restate | What do the authors agree on? | Answer Type | Tempting words, but irrelevant |
| | | Answer Type | Right (identify) |
| Recall | The British monarchy is bad | Answer Type | Tempting words, but wrong part |
| | | Resolve | Ⓐ Ⓑ ● Ⓓ    Confidence ___/5 |

### 2

| | | | |
|---|---|---|---|
| Recognize | Paired synthesis | Answer Type | Flatly false |
| Restate | What does passage two discuss | Answer Type | Right (lines 26-32) |
| | that passage one does not discuss? | Answer Type | Tempting words, but wrong part |
| Recall | Overall disruption in society | Answer Type | Tempting words, but wrong part |
| | | Resolve | Ⓐ ● Ⓒ Ⓓ    Confidence ___/5 |

### 3

| | | | |
|---|---|---|---|
| Recognize | Paired specific | Answer Type | Right (lines 13-14) |
| Restate | How would Abigail respond to John's claims? | Answer Type | Tempting words, but wrong part |
| | | Answer Type | Flatly false |
| Recall | She would disagree with him | Answer Type | Flatly false |
| | | Resolve | ●BCD     Confidence ___/5 |

### 4

| | | | |
|---|---|---|---|
| Recognize | Evidence | Answer Type | Flatly false |
| Restate | What is your evidence for the previous question? | Answer Type | Tempting words, but wrong part (B) |
| | | Answer Type | Right (underline) |
| Recall | Lines 13-14 | Answer Type | Flatly false |
| | | Resolve | AB●D     Confidence ___/5 |

---

### Online Bonus Content

Want to see what other students did with "Remember the Ladies"? Submit your questions to tom@professorscompanion.com to add your work and to see other students' creations.

Solutions

# ***AUTOMATED VEHICLES (SOLUTION)***
## Underline, Annotate, and Identify

The following passage is adapted from Derek Kan, "Roundtable on Data for Automated Vehicle Safety," published by the U.S. Department of Transportation, 2018.

Increasingly, personal cars and commercial trucks operate with varying degrees of computer assistance, which range from driver assistance to full automation. These Automated Driving Systems (ADS) use visual, positional, and radar data for safety and navigation.

For public transportation officials, vehicle manufacturing companies, and technological experts, they are also a goldmine of data. To mine this motherlode, the United States Department of Transportation (USDOT) established federal guidance for collection and dissemination of the data obtained from automated vehicles.

Industry experts believe that within and across all modes of transportation, data exchanges will be key to accelerating the safe deployment of automated vehicles in the United States. This includes the mutually beneficial exchange of data among private sector entities, infrastructure operators, and policy makers from various levels of government.

Planning and executing such exchanges can be difficult. Data are often siloed, but the USDOT can serve as a convener and facilitator to encourage collaboration in overcoming these challenges. By bringing together thought leaders in their respective areas of expertise, the federal government can collectively consider what voluntary data exchanges should look like and how they can be leveraged to accelerate the safe rollout of automated vehicles.

To act on this vision, the Department hosted the Roundtable on Data for Automated Vehicle Safety in December of 2017. This event brought together over sixty participants from federal, state, and local governments, the private sector (car manufacturers and software companies), transportation-based non-profit organizations, and research institutions to discuss the data exchanges that these participants believe are most critical to the safe deployment of automated vehicles. This roundtable was a key step toward developing a shared understanding of the data to be collected and exchanged, the purpose, and the federal government's unique role in facilitating voluntary data exchanges.

The Roundtable provided the USDOT with many diverse suggestions for next steps in facilitating near-term, voluntary automated vehicle data exchanges. The wide range of roundtable participants provided their initial feedback on core documents that the USDOT plans to refine and use to help organize this work and communicate priorities. Collectively, the various roundtable participants discussed five key areas that can be prioritized for voluntary data exchanges. And, finally, roundtable participants discussed overarching challenges and how the USDOT can help provide solutions.

Much of the day's discussions centered on new initiatives, new technical solutions, and the need for new data. This included not only increasing data collection and management through established channels, but also considering relatively novel approaches. For example, several breakout groups discussed the potential use of crowdsourcing for developing more detailed roadway inventories or real-time incident reporting.

At the same time, some participants noted that there is untapped value in existing data and data exchange models. Many mentioned improving current datasets as an immediate focus to advance emerging automated vehicle technologies. They also suggested studying existing initiatives that can serve as examples for further work by the government and private sector.

| ADS Available Options on Commercial Vehicles | Rank |
|---|---|
| Adaptive Cruise Control | 3.8 |
| Forward Collision Warnings | 2.7 |
| GPS Navigation Systems | 4.2 |
| Tire pressure monitoring systems | 4.5 |
| Vehicle-to-Vehicle Warnings | 1.8 |

Figure 1 – Desirability of five safety features according to a survey of commercial truck drivers (one was most preferred and five was least preferred). Adapted from the National Highway Traffic Safety Administration, 2016.

Figure 2 – "Levels of vehicle automation according to the Society of Automotive Engineers (SAE) International."

## Quick Answer Key

| | Question Type | Why My Incorrect Answer Is Wrong | Why the Correct Answer is Right |
|---|---|---|---|
| 1 | C | | |
| 2 | C | | |
| 3 | D | | |
| 4 | A | | |
| 5 | A | | |
| 6 | A | | |
| 7 | B | | |
| 8 | D | | |
| 9 | A | | |
| 10 | D | | |
| 11 | B | | |

## Recognize, Restate, Recall, and Resolve

| Questions | General | Specific | Synthesis | Answers | Reason |
|---|---|---|---|---|---|
| Main Purpose | Purpose | Function | | Wrong | Somewhat right, but too broad |
| Main Idea | Thesis | Topic | | Wrong | Somewhat right, but too narrow |
| Tone | Tone | Attitude | | Wrong | Somewhat right, but too extreme |
| Rhetoric | Structure | Argument | | Wrong | Tempting words, but wrong part |
| Vocabulary | | Vocabulary | | Wrong | Tempting words, but not true |
| Evidence | | Evidence | | Wrong | Tempting words, but irrelevant |
| Detail | | Detail | | Wrong | Flatly false |
| Inference | | Inference | | Right (general): | Give identify evidence |
| Data | | Data Specific | Data Synthesis | Right (specific): | Give line or annotation evidence |
| Paired | | Paired Specific | Paired Synthesis | Right (synthesis): | Give identify evidence |

### 1

| | | | | |
|---|---|---|---|---|
| Recognize | Thesis | | Answer Type | Somewhat right, but too broad |
| Restate | What is the passage about? | | Answer Type | Tempting words, but not true |
| | | | Answer Type | Right (identify) |
| Recall | Sharing data from automated vehicles | | Answer Type | Tempting words, but wrong part |
| | | | Resolve | Ⓐ Ⓑ ● Ⓓ    Confidence ___/5 |

### 2

| | | | |
|---|---|---|---|
| Recognize | Detail | Answer Type | Tempting words, but <u>wrong part</u> |
| Restate | What could be new sources of data? | Answer Type | Tempting words, but <u>wrong part</u> |
| | | Answer Type | Right (lines 55-63) |
| Recall | Crowdsourcing | Answer Type | Tempting words, but <u>wrong part</u> |
| | | Resolve | Ⓐ Ⓑ ● Ⓓ    Confidence ___/5 |

### 3

| | | | |
|---|---|---|---|
| Recognize | Evidence | Answer Type | Tempting words, but <u>wrong part</u> (A) |
| Restate | What is your evidence? | Answer Type | Tempting words, but <u>wrong part</u> (D) |
| | | Answer Type | Tempting words, but <u>wrong part</u> (C) |
| Recall | lines 55-63 | Answer Type | Right (annotations) |
| | | Resolve | Ⓐ Ⓑ Ⓒ ●    Confidence ___/5 |

### 4

| | | | |
|---|---|---|---|
| Recognize | Rhetoric | Answer Type | Right (underlining) |
| Restate | What do lines 16-19 argue for & what are they arguing against? | Answer Type | Flatly false |
| | | Answer Type | Tempting words, but <u>wrong part</u> |
| Recall | Sharing data is good & sharing is bad | Answer Type | Flatly false |
| | | Resolve | ● Ⓑ Ⓒ Ⓓ    Confidence ___/5 |

### 5

| | | | |
|---|---|---|---|
| Recognize | Vocab | Answer Type | Right (lines 21-22) |
| Restate | What does siloed mean? | Answer Type | Tempting words, but <u>wrong part</u> |
| | | Answer Type | Somewhat right, but <u>too extreme</u> |
| Recall | Not exchanged | Answer Type | Tempting words, but <u>wrong part</u> |
| | | Resolve | ● Ⓑ Ⓒ Ⓓ    Confidence ___/5 |

### 6

| | | | |
|---|---|---|---|
| Recognize | Topic | Answer Type | Right (annotations) |
| Restate | What is ¶4 about? | Answer Type | Somewhat right, but <u>too broad</u> |
| | | Answer Type | Flatly false |
| Recall | How USDOT can help with data | Answer Type | Somewhat right, but <u>too broad</u> |
| | | Resolve | ● Ⓑ Ⓒ Ⓓ    Confidence ___/5 |

Solutions

## 7

| | | | |
|---|---|---|---|
| Recognize | Vocab | Answer Type | Tempting words, but <u>wrong part</u> |
| Restate | What does "novel" mean in context? | Answer Type | Right (annotations) |
| | | Answer Type | Tempting words, but <u>wrong part</u> |
| Recall | Innovative, new | Answer Type | Tempting words, but <u>wrong part</u> |
| | | Resolve | Ⓐ ● Ⓒ Ⓓ     Confidence ___/5 |

## 8

| | | | |
|---|---|---|---|
| Recognize | Function | Answer Type | Tempting words, but <u>wrong part</u> |
| Restate | What is the final ¶ doing? | Answer Type | Flatly false |
| | | Answer Type | Somewhat right, but <u>too broad</u> |
| Recall | Discussing what to do with current data | Answer Type | Right (lines 64-66) |
| | | Resolve | Ⓐ Ⓑ Ⓒ ●     Confidence ___/5 |

## 9

| | | | |
|---|---|---|---|
| Recognize | Data synthesis | Answer Type | Right (annotations) |
| Restate | Where do the passage and the data agree? | Answer Type | Flatly false |
| | | Answer Type | Tempting words, but <u>wrong part</u> |
| Recall | New methods & different types of automated vehicle safety | Answer Type | Flatly false |
| | | Resolve | Ⓐ Ⓑ Ⓒ Ⓓ     Confidence ___/5 |

## 10

| | | | |
|---|---|---|---|
| Recognize | Data detail | Answer Type | Flatly false |
| Restate | What does figure 1 say? | Answer Type | Flatly false |
| | | Answer Type | Tempting words, but <u>wrong part</u> |
| Recall | Lowest number most preferred | Answer Type | Right (annotations) |
| | | Resolve | Ⓐ Ⓑ Ⓒ ●     Confidence ___/5 |

## 11

| | | | |
|---|---|---|---|
| Recognize | Data detail | Answer Type | Flatly false |
| Restate | What does figure 2 say? | Answer Type | Right (annotations) |
| | | Answer Type | Flatly false |
| Recall | Levels of both human and vehicle are in the middle | Answer Type | Flatly false |
| | | Resolve | Ⓐ ● Ⓒ Ⓓ     Confidence ___/5 |

## Online Bonus Content

Want to see what other students how other students classified the correct and incorrect answers to "Automated Vehicles"? Submit your questions to tom@professorscompanion.com to add your work and to see other students' creations.

### ***BENJAMIN BLOOM (SOLUTION)***
#### Underline, Annotate, and Identify

The following passage is adapted from "Meaningful Learning," by Charles Fraatz. Benjamin Bloom (1913-1999) was an educational psychologist.

In 1956, Benjamin Bloom and a team of educational psychologists published *A Taxonomy of Educational Objectives*. This landmark study established the groundwork for how teachers develop
[5] their curricula, from creating learning goals to designing tests to evaluating student work. Bloom's most important innovation was a hierarchical taxonomy to classify learning objectives according to six levels of increasing complexity designed to make
[10] student learning meaningful.

In order to explain Bloom's taxonomy, we can engage in an extended hypothetical situation thousands of English teachers face every year. Imagine that you are an English teacher designing a series of
[15] assignments based on Shakespeare's *Hamlet*, the classic tale of Prince Hamlet's plot to avenge his father's murder. How might you apply Bloom's taxonomy to the creation of assignments for the Bard's great tragedy?

[20] Bloom's first level is knowledge. This level pertains mostly to the retention of facts: "Who wrote *Hamlet*?" "Who are the main characters in *Hamlet*?" As Bloom defines it, knowledge is fundamental to more complex work. If a student cannot identify what soliloquy is (an
[25] extended aside to the audience), they cannot engage in higher-level thinking about Hamlet's monologues.

The second level of Bloom's taxonomy is comprehension. Comprehension requires students to understand the material in greater detail, perhaps
[30] interpreting facts or extrapolating information. For example, a quiz question about how Hamlet plans to reveal his uncle's treachery requires students to not only know who Hamlet is, but also to organize their knowledge about the play.

[35] Bloom's third level is application. When students apply their knowledge to abstract situations, they have to comprehend the material and then make use of that information. If a student were asked "How might Ophelia react to Hamlet's madness if she knew his
[40] motivations?", their response would go beyond what happened to what might happen in a new context.

Bloom describes his fourth level, analysis, with regard to the organization of material and the understanding of the relationship(s) between the
[45] different elements within the material. A test question about how Hamlet's soliloquies disclose the prince's thoughts to the audience, for example, combines students' understanding of the relationship between the play's plot, the protagonist's motivations, and the
[50] meaning of his monologues; each is necessary to analyze how the soliloquies reveal Hamlet's thoughts.

The fifth level, synthesis, has elements of the second, third, and fourth levels, but it is more cohesive, widespread, and ultimately innovative than
[55] comprehension, application, and analysis. As Bloom describes it, an analysis essay may ask a student to describe the effect of Hamlet's madness upon his mother, but a synthesis asks the student to create their own hypothesis about Hamlet's madness; the student
[60] directs their own inquiry. This self-direction generates meaningful payoff for the student's long-term enjoyment of the material.

Bloom's final level, evaluation, should not be seen as the culmination of the five preceding levels, but it
[65] appears last because it is contingent upon the others. An essay on the ethical ramifications of Hamlet's actions, asking students to judge the prince's plot to avenge his father, requires a complexity of thought not found in the other levels. One cannot, according to
[70] Bloom, make judgments about Hamlet's vengeance without the cognitive ability to know its contents, comprehend the plot and characters, apply this comprehension to new or abstract situations, analyze its constituent parts, and finally synthesize one's
[75] thoughts cohesively. Similarly, students' evaluations of a scholar's interpretation require them to employ all the levels in the taxonomy.

Bloom's taxonomy was widely influential in both the US and abroad, having been translated into twenty
[80] languages. At the turn of the century, Bloom's student and co-author David Krathwohl and a new generation of educational psychologists revised Bloom's taxonomy. One change was to change the nouns to verbs to indicate the activity of education: students
[85] don't *have comprehension*, they *comprehend*; and they don't *make analysis*, they *analyze*. Krathwohl and his co-editors also condensed the fifth and sixth levels and added a new creative level. Creative learning, they argued, especially the acts of generating hypotheses,
[90] planning the tasks and subtasks necessary to test their hypotheses, and ultimately producing something, is the most complex learning objective. Fittingly, Bloom's heirs learned from their teacher and created something new of their own.

## Recognize, Restate, Recall, and Resolve

| Questions | General | Specific | Synthesis | Answers | Reason |
|---|---|---|---|---|---|
| Main Purpose | Purpose | Function | | Wrong | Somewhat right, but too broad |
| Main Idea | Thesis | Topic | | Wrong | Somewhat right, but too narrow |
| Tone | Tone | Attitude | | Wrong | Somewhat right, but too extreme |
| Rhetoric | Structure | Argument | | Wrong | Tempting words, but wrong part |
| Vocabulary | | Vocabulary | | Wrong | Tempting words, but not true |
| Evidence | | Evidence | | Wrong | Tempting words, but irrelevant |
| Detail | | Detail | | Wrong | Flatly false |
| Inference | | Inference | | Right (general): | Give identify evidence |
| Data | | Data Specific | Data Synthesis | Right (specific): | Give line or annotation evidence |
| Paired | | Paired Specific | Paired Synthesis | Right (synthesis): | Give identify evidence |

Since you wrote the answer choices, you'll find solutions for **Restate** and **Recall** for this passage, but not **Resolve**. Submit your answers to tom@professorscompanion.com to see other students' creations and share yours!

### 1

| | | | |
|---|---|---|---|
| Recognize | Purpose | Answer Type | |
| Restate | What is the author's purpose? | Answer Type | |
| | | Answer Type | |
| Recall | To explain Bloom's taxonomy | Answer Type | |
| | | Resolve  Ⓐ Ⓑ Ⓒ Ⓓ | Confidence ___/5 |

### 2

| | | | |
|---|---|---|---|
| Recognize | Detail | Answer Type | |
| Restate | What does the author think about | Answer Type | |
| | Bloom's work? | Answer Type | |
| Recall | They like it | Answer Type | |
| | | Resolve  Ⓐ Ⓑ Ⓒ Ⓓ | Confidence ___/5 |

### 3

| | | | |
|---|---|---|---|
| Recognize | Evidence | Answer Type | |
| Restate | What is your evidence? | Answer Type | |
| | | Answer Type | |
| Recall | Lines 3-10 | Answer Type | |
| | | Resolve  Ⓐ Ⓑ Ⓒ Ⓓ | Confidence ___/5 |

Solutions

## 4

| | | | |
|---|---|---|---|
| Recognize | Vocabulary | Answer Type | |
| Restate | What does "designing" mean? | Answer Type | |
| | | Answer Type | |
| Recall | Creating | Answer Type | |
| | | Resolve Ⓐ Ⓑ Ⓒ Ⓓ | Confidence ___/5 |

## 5

| | | | |
|---|---|---|---|
| Recognize | Rhetoric | Answer Type | |
| Restate | How does the hypothetical scenario support the author's argument? | Answer Type | |
| | | Answer Type | |
| Recall | It puts the reader into the discussion | Answer Type | |
| | | Resolve Ⓐ Ⓑ Ⓒ Ⓓ | Confidence ___/5 |

## 6

| | | | |
|---|---|---|---|
| Recognize | Function | Answer Type | |
| Restate | What does ¶7 do? | Answer Type | |
| | | Answer Type | |
| Recall | Explains the fifth level | Answer Type | |
| | | Resolve Ⓐ Ⓑ Ⓒ Ⓓ | Confidence ___/5 |

## 7

| | | | |
|---|---|---|---|
| Recognize | Vocabulary | Answer Type | |
| Restate | What does "employ" mean? | Answer Type | |
| | | Answer Type | |
| Recall | Use | Answer Type | |
| | | Resolve Ⓐ Ⓑ Ⓒ Ⓓ | Confidence ___/5 |

## 8

| | | | |
|---|---|---|---|
| Recognize | Inference | Answer Type | |
| Restate | What does the passage imply about Krathwohl and Bloom? | Answer Type | |
| | | Answer Type | |
| Recall | He valued Bloom's taxonomy and worked to improve it | Answer Type | |
| | | Resolve Ⓐ Ⓑ Ⓒ Ⓓ | Confidence ___/5 |

### 9

| | | | |
|---|---|---|---|
| Recognize | Evidence | Answer Type | |
| Restate | What is your evidence? | Answer Type | |
| | | Answer Type | |
| Recall | Last paragraph | Answer Type | |
| | | Resolve | Ⓐ Ⓑ Ⓒ Ⓓ    Confidence ___/5 |

### 10

| | | | |
|---|---|---|---|
| Recognize | Attitude | Answer Type | |
| Restate | How does the author feel about Bloom? | Answer Type | |
| | | Answer Type | |
| Recall | They like him. | Answer Type | |
| | | Resolve | Ⓐ Ⓑ Ⓒ Ⓓ    Confidence ___/5 |

---

#### Online Bonus Content

Want to see other students' answers for "Benjamin Bloom"? Submit your questions to tom@professorscompanion.com to add your work and to see other students' creations.

Solutions

### ***THE BLACK POODLE (SOLUTION)***
#### Underline, Annotate, and Identify

The following passage is from the short story "The Black Poodle" by F. Anstey. The setting is late 19th century Britain.

I have set myself the task of relating in the course of this story, without suppressing or altering a single detail, the most painful and humiliating episode in my life. I do this, not because it will give me the least
5   pleasure, but simply because it affords me an opportunity of extenuating myself which has hitherto been wholly denied to me.

As a general rule I am quite aware that to publish a lengthy explanation of one's conduct in any
10  questionable transaction is not the best means of recovering a lost reputation; but in my own case there is one to whom I shall never more be permitted to justify myself by word of mouth — even if I found myself able to attempt it. And as she could not possibly
15  think worse of me than she does at present, I write this, knowing it can do me no harm, and faintly hoping that it may come to her notice and suggest a doubt whether I am quite so unscrupulous a villain, so consummate a hypocrite, as I have been forced to appear in her eyes.
20  The bare chance of such a result makes me perfectly indifferent to all else: I cheerfully expose to the derision of the whole reading world the story of my weakness and my shame, since by doing so I may possibly rehabilitate myself somewhat in the good
25  opinion of one person. Having said so much, I will begin my confession without further delay:

My name is Algernon Weatherhead and I may add that I am in one of the Government departments; that I am an only son, and live at home with my mother.
30  We had had a house at Hammersmith until just before the period covered by this history, when, our lease expiring, my mother decided that my health required country air at the close of the day, and so we took a 'desirable villa residence' on one of the many
35  new building estates which have lately sprung up in such profusion in the home counties. We have called it 'Wistaria Villa.' It is a pretty little place, the last of a row of detached villas, each with its tiny rustic carriage gate and gravel sweep in front, and lawn enough for a
40  tennis court behind, which lines the road leading over the hill to the railway station. It is a pleasant house, and I can now almost forgive the landlord for what I shall always consider an act of gross selfishness on his part.
45  In the country, even so near town, a next-door neighbor is something more than a mere numeral; he is a possible acquaintance, who will at least consider a new-comer as worth the experiment of a call. I soon knew that 'Shuturgarden,' the next house to our own,
50  was occupied by a Colonel Currie, a retired Indian officer; and often, as across the low boundary wall I caught a glimpse of a graceful girlish figure flitting about amongst the rose-bushes in the neighboring garden, I would lose myself in pleasant anticipations of
55  a time not far distant when the wall which separated us would be (metaphorically) levelled.

I remember — ah, how vividly! — the thrill of excitement with which I heard from my mother on returning from town one evening that the Curries had
60  called, and seemed disposed to be all that was neighborly and kind. I remember, too, the Sunday afternoon on which I returned their call — alone, as my mother had already done so during the week. I was standing on the steps of the Colonel's villa waiting for
65  the door to open when I was startled by a furious snarling and yapping behind, and, looking round, discovered a large poodle in the act of making for my legs.

He was a coal-black poodle, with half of his right
70  ear gone, and absurd little thick moustaches at the end of his nose; he was shaved in the sham-lion fashion, which is considered, for some mysterious reason, to improve a poodle, but the barber had left sundry little tufts of hair which studded his haunches capriciously.
75  He made me intensely uncomfortable, for I am of a slightly nervous temperament, with a constitutional horror of dogs and a liability to attacks of diffidence on performing the ordinary social rites under the most favorable conditions, and certainly the consciousness
80  that a strange and apparently savage dog was engaged in worrying the heels of my boots was the reverse of reassuring.

purpose: to describe Algernon's shame/apology
tone: pleading/remorseful, self-aware
topic: a man explaining unfortunate events

| 4 | C |
| 5 | D |
| 6 | A |
| 7 | B |
| 8 | B |
| 9 | B |
| 10 | C |

## Recognize, Restate, Recall, and Resolve

| Questions | General | Specific | Synthesis | Answers | Reason |
|---|---|---|---|---|---|
| Main Purpose | Purpose | Function | | Wrong | Somewhat right, but too broad |
| Main Idea | Thesis | Topic | | Wrong | Somewhat right, but too narrow |
| Tone | Tone | Attitude | | Wrong | Somewhat right, but too extreme |
| Rhetoric | Structure | Argument | | Wrong | Tempting words, but wrong part |
| Vocabulary | | Vocabulary | | Wrong | Tempting words, but not true |
| Evidence | | Evidence | | Wrong | Tempting words, but irrelevant |
| Detail | | Detail | | Wrong | Flatly false |
| Inference | | Inference | | Right (general): | Give identify evidence |
| Data | | Data Specific | Data Synthesis | Right (specific): | Give line or annotation evidence |
| Paired | | Paired Specific | Paired Synthesis | Right (synthesis): | Give identify evidence |

### 1

| | | | |
|---|---|---|---|
| Recognize | Function | Answer Type | Right (annotations) |
| Restate | What does the first ¶ do? | Answer Type | Tempting words, but not true |
| | | Answer Type | Somewhat right, but too narrow |
| Recall | To set up the rest of the passage | Answer Type | Flatly false |
| | | Resolve | ●BCD   Confidence ___/5 |

Solutions

## 2

| | | | |
|---|---|---|---|
| Recognize | Structure | Answer Type | Tempting words, but not true |
| Restate | How is the passage organized? | Answer Type | Flatly false |
| | | Answer Type | Flatly false |
| Recall | The background is given for a fateful encounter between a man and a dog | Answer Type | Right (identify) |
| | | Resolve | Ⓐ Ⓑ Ⓒ ●     Confidence ___/5 |

## 3

| | | | |
|---|---|---|---|
| Recognize | Vocabulary | Answer Type | Tempting words, but not true |
| Restate | What does "bare" mean? | Answer Type | Right (underlining) |
| | | Answer Type | Tempting words, but not true |
| Recall | small | Answer Type | Flatly false |
| | | Resolve | Ⓐ ● Ⓒ Ⓓ     Confidence ___/5 |

## 4

| | | | |
|---|---|---|---|
| Recognize | Inference | Answer Type | Tempting words, but not true |
| Restate | What do lines 30-36 imply? | Answer Type | Flatly false |
| | | Answer Type | Right (annotations) |
| Recall | They recently moved to the country | Answer Type | Flatly false |
| | | Resolve | Ⓐ Ⓑ ● Ⓓ     Confidence ___/5 |

## 5

| | | | |
|---|---|---|---|
| Recognize | Function | Answer Type | Flatly false |
| Restate | What's the function of ¶5? | Answer Type | Flatly false |
| | | Answer Type | Flatly false |
| Recall | Describe the setting of the events that follow | Answer Type | Right (annotations) |
| | | Resolve | Ⓐ Ⓑ Ⓒ ●     Confidence ___/5 |

## 6

| | | | |
|---|---|---|---|
| Recognize | Attitude | Answer Type | Right (lines 75-82) |
| Restate | How does Algernon respond to the dog? | Answer Type | Flatly false |
| | | Answer Type | Flatly false |
| Recall | It scares him | Answer Type | Tempting words, but not true |
| | | Resolve | ● Ⓑ Ⓒ Ⓓ     Confidence ___/5 |

### 7

| | | | |
|---|---|---|---|
| Recognize | Vocabulary | Answer Type | Tempting words, but not true |
| Restate | What does "constitutional" mean? | Answer Type | Right (annotations) |
| | | Answer Type | Flatly false |
| Recall | Natural | Answer Type | Flatly false |
| | | Resolve | Ⓐ ● Ⓒ Ⓓ    Confidence ___/5 |

### 8

| | | | |
|---|---|---|---|
| Recognize | Attitude | Answer Type | Tempting words, but not true |
| Restate | What does Algernon think the girl's attitude toward him is? | Answer Type | Right (lines 16-18) |
| | | Answer Type | Tempting words, but not true |
| Recall | She hates him | Answer Type | Flatly false |
| | | Resolve | Ⓐ ● Ⓒ Ⓓ    Confidence ___/5 |

### 9

| | | | |
|---|---|---|---|
| Recognize | Evidence | Answer Type | Flatly false |
| Restate | What is your evidence | Answer Type | Right (annotations) |
| | | Answer Type | Tempting words, but not true (A) |
| Recall | Lines 16-18 | Answer Type | Tempting words, but not true (C) |
| | | Resolve | Ⓐ ● Ⓒ Ⓓ    Confidence ___/5 |

### 10

| | | | |
|---|---|---|---|
| Recognize | Tone | Answer Type | Flatly false |
| Restate | What is the tone of the passage? | Answer Type | Flatly false |
| | | Answer Type | Right (identify) |
| Recall | apologetic | Answer Type | Tempting words, but not true |
| | | Resolve | Ⓐ Ⓑ ● Ⓓ    Confidence ___/5 |

---

#### Online Bonus Content

Want to see what other students how other students classified the correct and incorrect answers to "The Black Poodle"? Submit your questions to tom@professorscompanion.com to add your work and to see other students' creations.

Solutions

# AT-A-GLANCE ANSWER KEY

## Let Us Calculate!

Purpose: To explain Leibniz's machine and its legacy for computing

Tone: appreciative, retrospective

Topic: Leibniz's calculator

1. C
2. A
3. B
4. A
5. D
6. C
7. B
8. D
9. C
10. C

## Civil Rights Address

Purpose: To argue that American needs to fulfill its promises of equality

Tone: forceful, ardent

Topic: Civil Rights in America

1. A
2. C
3. A
4. A
5. D
6. C
7. C
8. B
9. B
10. A

## A Jury of Her Peers

Purpose: To describe Mrs. Hale's uneasy journey to Minnie Foster's House

Tone: tense/eerie

Topic: A woman joins a police investigation

1. B
2. D
3. C
4. A
5. D
6. A
7. B
8. D
9. A
10. C

## Mars Rover

Purpose: To explain the discovery of brine on Mars

Tone: optimistic, excited

Topic: Mars + liquid brines

Data: Subsurface in the day, surface at night

1. A
2. A
3. D
4. B
5. B
6. B
7. C
8. D
9. A
10. C
11. D
12. A
13. A
14. C
15. B
16. A
17. B
18. C
19. D
20. B
21. D

## Remember the Ladies

Agree: Despotism and strife are bad

Disagree: Who is in control, men or women?

Tone 1: principled, matter of fact

Tone 2: defensive, sarcastic

1. C
2. B
3. A
4. C

## Automated Vehicles

Purpose: To explain data exchanges and their benefits

Tone: technical, detailed

Topic: Benefits of data exchanges

Data 1: Most desire = low

Data 2: Increasing Automation

1. C
2. C
3. D
4. A
5. A
6. A
7. B
8. D
9. A
10. D
11. B

## Benjamin Bloom

Purpose: To explain Bloom's taxonomy and its importance

Tone: analytical, approving

## The Black Poodle

Purpose: To describe an embarrassing encounter

Tone: pleading, self-reflective

Topic: A man apologizes/explains unfortunate events

1. A
2. D
3. B
4. C
5. D
6. A
7. B
8. B
9. B
10. C

# MORE FROM THE PROFESSOR'S COMPANION

Looking for more prep? Check out more titles from The Professor's Companion to Test Prep at Amazon and www.professorscompanion.com!

"**What was the last book you read for fun?**" I ask this question when I start working with new students. They typically laugh, then pause, and finally admit to me (and to themselves) that they can't remember the last time they read something for fun. The best way to improve your reading score is to read, but it can be hard to pick up reading again when it's been years since you've done it for pleasure. The Professor's Companion's *SAT® + ACT® Reading Workbook* will help you remember what it was like to enjoy reading. With 50 Passages for you to read, enjoy, and prep for your tests, this book will help you prepare for the test in three ways. First, you will **(re)-learn to read for fun**. You'll get more out of reading when you read something you want to read. Second, **you'll know what to expect on the test**. The passages here, more or less, conform to the types of passages you'll see on test day. Third, **you'll learn to focus, relax, and pace yourself**. These tests are stressful enough as it is. Preparing will remove some anxiety and give you the confidence to succeed.

The grammar section on the ACT® and SAT® can intimidate even the best of students, and for good reason. Most of us haven't been over the rules of grammar since we were in elementary school. If you don't know your semicolons from your commas and your whos from your whoms, *A Strategy Guide to SAT® & ACT® Grammar* is here to help! This workbook will work with the official test materials to help you **master the grammar of both the SAT® and ACT®**. Whatever your ability level, by pushing yourself to do your best, you'll maximize your test taking abilities and improve your written work in high school and beyond. This book includes **a strategy guide** to taking the grammar tests, **practice solutions to the official tests** from the makers of the test, and **twenty-four worksheets and solution-sets** to take advantage of Khan Academy's free materials. Studying for the grammar can be hard, but whether you're taking the SAT®, ACT®, or both, *A Strategy Guide to SAT® & ACT® Grammar* will improve your abilities, your confidence, and your score.

Mark Twain's *Adventures of Tom Sawyer* will help you get the score you want while having fun with a classic novel of American humor. As you read, you'll find **888 words** highlighted for you to identify their synonyms or contextual meanings. In the back of the book are **dictionary and thesaurus entries** for each of these words, so you don't have to go too far if you get stumped. You'll also find **77 questions** stimulate your brain and encourage you to read as the tests demand. These questions run from basic comprehension to more complex questions of Twain's intent, biases, and humor. By reading to answer the kinds of questions you'll find on the test, you'll train yourself now to *succeed on test day*. You'll also find **33 games and puzzles with full solutions** to reinforce your learning. You can also check out these puzzles online along with exclusive bonus content for students and teachers. The Professor's Companion to Test Prep's *Adventures of Tom Sawyer* is a great resource for SAT®, ACT®, GRE® and advanced SSAT® students.

Made in the USA
Middletown, DE
19 January 2020